INTERGROUP RELATIONS

MAPPING SOCIAL PSYCHOLOGY

Series Editor: Tony Manstead

Current titles:

Icek Ajzen: *Attitudes, Personality and Behaviour*
Robert S. Baron and Norbert L. Kerr: *Group Process, Group Decision, Group Action (Second Edition)*
Marilynn B. Brewer: *Intergroup Relations (Second Edition)*
Steve Duck: *Relating to Others (Second Edition)*
J. Richard Eiser: *Social Judgement*
Russell G. Geen: *Human Aggression (Second Edition)*
Howard Giles and Nikolas Coupland: *Language: Contexts and Consequences*
Dean G. Pruitt and Peter J. Carnevale: *Negotiation in Social Conflict*
Wolfgang Stroebe: *Social Psychology and Health (Second Edition)*
John Turner: *Social Influence*
Leslie A. Zebrowitz: *Social Perception*

Forthcoming titles include:

Agneta Fischer and Bertjan Doosje: *Cultural Social Psychology*
Richard Petty et al.: *Attitude Change*
Miles Hewstane et al.: *Stereotyping and Social Cognition*

INTERGROUP RELATIONS

SECOND EDITION

Marilynn B. Brewer

OPEN UNIVERSITY PRESS
Buckingham · Philadelphia

Open University Press
Celtic Court
22 Ballmoor
Buckingham
MK18 1XW

email: enquiries@openup.co.uk
world wide web: www.openup.co.uk

and
325 Chestnut Street
Philadelphia, PA 19106, USA

First published 1996
First published in this second edition 2003

A catalogue record of this book is available from the British Library

ISBN 0335 20989 0 (pb)   0335 20990 4 (hb)

Library of Congress Cataloging-in-Publication Data
Brewer, Marilynn B., 1942–
    Intergroup relations / Marilynn B. Brewer. — 2nd ed.
       p. cm. — (Mapping social psychology series)
    Includes bibliographical references and index.
    ISBN 0-335-20990-4 — ISBN 0-335-20989-0 (pbk.)
    1. Intergroup relations.   2. Social psychology.   I. Title.   II. Series.
    HM1111 .B74 2003
    302.3—dc21   2002030419

Typeset by Graphicraft Limited, Hong Kong
Printed in Great Britain by Biddles Limited, Guildford and Kings Lynn

CONTENTS

Preface   viii

ONE   **From basic psychological processes to intergroup**
        behaviour   1
        What are intergroup relations?   2
        Defining intergroup settings   2
        What behaviour is studied in intergroup research?   3
        Building blocks for the study of intergroup relations   4
        Social cognition: categorization   4
        Social cognition: attribution   9
        Social emotions: affect and cognition   12
        Social comparison: evaluating self and others   13
        Social motives: cooperation or competition   16
        Perspectives on individuals and social groups   18
        Further readings   19

TWO   **Ethnocentrism and ingroup identity: the need for**
        'we-ness'   20
        Ethnocentrism: the ingroup and the self   20
        Behavioural consequences of group identity   23
        Speech style   23
        Polarization of beliefs and attitudes   24
        Bases of attraction   25
        Deprivation and social justice   26
        Cooperation and competition   29
        Summary   32
        Theories of group identification   32
        Human sociobiology   32
        Psychodynamic theories   33
        Social comparison theory   34
        Social identity and self-categorization theory   35
        Motivational theories of social identification   36

Do ingroups require outgroups?   41
Further readings   41

THREE   Intergroup discrimination: what is just to us is
         unfair to them   43
         Discrimination in the minimal intergroup situation   45
           Discrimination and the rules of fairness   45
           Implications for affirmative action   47
           The positive–negative asymmetry   47
         Some possible mechanisms: reasons for ingroup bias   48
           Ethnocentric attributions   48
           The intergroup schema   50
           Positive distinctiveness and self-esteem   52
           Threats to intergroup distinctiveness   54
           Intergroup status and power differentials   55
           Reverse discrimination and outgroup bias   58
           Summary   61
         Social identity and collective movements   61
         Conclusions   65
         Further readings   67

FOUR   Outgroup prejudice: negative affect and hostility   68
         Intergroup affect and prejudice   69
           The effects of arousal and mood on responses toward
           the outgroup   69
           Incidental affect and affective priming   72
           Integral affect   73
         Affect and aggression   78
           Factors that moderate the expression of direct and
           indirect aggression   79
           Displaced aggression   82
         Intergroup emotions   83
           Differentiating negative emotions   84
           Threat and social change   85
         Conclusion   86
         Further readings   87

FIVE   Intergroup contact, cooperation and competition:
         does togetherness make friends?   88
         Intergroup contact: the social psychology of
         desegregation   88
           Some qualifying conditions   89
           Robbers Cave: a classic experiment in intergroup relations 90
           School desegregation: the record   92
         Contact experiments: defining the limits   93
           Amount of contact   93
           Intergroup anxiety   94
           Cooperation   94
           Status equality   95

Theoretical perspectives on contact and cooperation   96
Realistic group conflict and intergroup relations   97
Social categorization and intergroup contact   98
Integrating theoretical perspectives   102
Assimilation versus cultural pluralism: is multiculturalism
possible?   106
Some important caveats   107
Conclusion   108
Further readings   108

SIX   **International conflict: what makes war possible?**   110
Theories of human nature: the biological perspective   111
'Macho pride': a motivational basis for war   111
The genetic imperative   111
Perception and misperception: the cognitive perspective   112
The image of the enemy   113
Attributional biases   114
The arms race and the psychology of escalating conflict   114
Beyond rational cognition: images and emotions   118
Faulty decision making: the group dynamics perspective   123
The psychology of groupthink   123
Concluding perspectives: putting the building
blocks together   126
Further readings   127

Glossary   128
References   134
Index   160

PREFACE

When Norman Miller and I wrote the first edition of this volume, the social psychology of intergroup relations had just emerged from a period of relative neglect in the social sciences and in society at large. The era of the 'Cold War' during the 1960s and 1970s focused attention on relations between the two political superpowers in the world, and other forms of regional, religious and ethnic intergroup conflict were either ignored or believed to be largely resolved. By 1990 this complacency had been shattered. The demise of the Soviet Union and the apparent resurgence of ethnic conflicts throughout the world gave rise to the idea that local group loyalties and intergroup hostilities were never far below the surface. The media began talking about the 'new tribalism' that seemed to be emerging everywhere. As public interest in these issues grew, so did the resurgence of interest in theory and research on intergroup relations within social psychology, in Europe and in the USA.

The first edition attempted to capture much of this explosion of new work in the field. Even when the focus of theory and research has not been on the study of intergroup relations directly, social psychology's goal of understanding the links between individuals and social groups has produced a wealth of knowledge about the cognitive and motivational underpinnings of perceptions, attitudes and behaviours towards one's own and other groups. The purpose of the book was to review and highlight those contributions from social psychological research.

At the turn of the millennium, concern about issues of intergroup relations has become even more intense for social scientists and lay persons alike. In addition to organized conflict carried on by nations against nations, states against subgroups within their own populations, and ethnic and religious conflicts within nations, acts of international terrorism by small groups of extremists have riveted attention and concern across the globe. It is more clear than ever that group identities play a major role in human behaviour – impelling heroic action on behalf of **ingroups**, as well as horrific atrocities against designated **outgroups**. Social psychological understanding of these processes has also grown as the study of intergroup relations took centre stage within the discipline. Hence an update of this book seemed both needed and timely. Much of the structure and basic principles have remained the same, but new research and ideas have added substantively to what social psychology has to offer.

The essence of the social psychological approach to the study of intergroup relations is to understand the causes and consequences of the distinction between ingroups (those groups to which an individual belongs) and outgroups (social groups that do not include the individual as a member) – the apparently universal propensity to differentiate the social world into 'us' and 'them'. As in the first edition, I have deconstructed ingroup–outgroup relations into three related but conceptually independent constituent elements. Following an initial introductory chapter on basic psychological concepts, the second chapter discusses the psychological needs and motives associated with individuals' attachment and loyalty to ingroups. Chapter 3 then reviews research on comparisons between ingroups and outgroups that lead to ingroup bias and **intergroup discrimination**, followed by a chapter on attitudes and emotions directed toward outgroups. In the final two chapters, the basic research and theories on intergroup differentiation are then applied to issues of reducing intergroup **prejudice** (Chapter 5) and understanding intergroup conflict and war (Chapter 6).

Ultimately, of course, it is our hope that these perspectives on the causes and consequences of ingroup–outgroup differentiation will not only help us understand why intergroup relations can become so volatile but also provide insights on how to reduce and prevent the negative manifestations of intergroup distinctions while preserving the values of group loyalty and community.

ONE

FROM BASIC PSYCHOLOGICAL PROCESSES TO INTERGROUP BEHAVIOUR

Key concepts: social categorization, attribution, affect, social comparison, social motives

It is a basic fact of human existence that people are organized into social groups. We are all members of many different types of groups, ranging from small, face-to-face groupings of family and friends, to large social categories such as gender, religion and nationality. As a consequence, a great deal of our interactions with others take place in a group setting, where we are not only individual persons but also representatives of our respective social groups. The purpose of this book is to review our knowledge about how social interactions are affected by this group context.

Social psychology is unique among the subdisciplines of psychology in dealing with three different levels of analysis – the individual, the interpersonal and the group. Many of the concepts and ideas that are fundamental in social psychological theory appear at all three levels. *Social cognition* is the study of how individuals process information about themselves and other individual persons, but it is also about the perceptions that guide interpersonal exchanges, and about cognitive representations of social groups. *Social motivations* include not only personal achievement and enhancing individual self-esteem, but also interpersonal attraction and cooperation, and group loyalty and status. My goal in this book is to describe how cognition and motivation at the individual, interpersonal and group levels interact and combine to determine intergroup behaviour. In this first chapter I set the stage by presenting essential conceptual ingredients for later chapters and by giving my general perspective on what it means to talk about the 'social psychology' of intergroup relations.

WHAT ARE INTERGROUP RELATIONS?

The study of intergroup relations is part of the broader field of social relations. It is concerned with what goes on between humans when social category distinctions exist or are salient. Within the general domain of social psychology, it is a much broader and more complex topic than many others. Understanding intergroup relations invokes virtually every area of social psychological inquiry – from the study of person perception, social attitudes, aggression, self-esteem, **social comparison**, **equity**, cooperation and competition, to conformity and compliance. From research in all of these areas we have a wealth of information about the cognitive and motivational underpinnings of intergroup perception and behaviour.

In a sense, then, the study of intergroup relations is applied social psychology. It concerns the bearing of specific and more fundamental domains of social psychological knowledge on a particular context – a situation in which there is more than one group. Consequently, the knowledge and principles that have developed within each of these more basic areas need to be considered and applied in terms of their relevance to intergroup relations. At the same time, science seeks to be analytical, which means that complex behaviours must be broken down into their distinct conceptual components. Therefore, as indicated, this chapter will identify basic distinctions and key processes. Later, in subsequent chapters, we shall discuss each of them in more detail, examining, in particular, their application to group settings.

Defining intergroup settings

First, however, we discuss some preliminary issues. What do we mean by an intergroup setting? For social psychologists, the classic definition of intergroup situations is that provided by Sherif (1966a: 12): 'Whenever individuals belonging to one group interact, collectively or individually, with another group or its members in terms of their group identification, we have an instance of intergroup behavior.'

What this definition implies is that intergroup relations can occur at the level of two persons interacting (the dyadic level) as well as the level of exchanges between groups as a whole (the intergroup level). When Jones, a white male in the personnel department of a company, interviews Smith, a black male who is applying for a job, the interaction is dyadic and at an interpersonal level. Nevertheless, intergroup relations come into play because the social categories of the two actors are manifestly different and likely to affect their interaction. In cross-racial interactions majority members are more uncomfortable and awkward (Henley 1977; Ickes 1984). They exhibit more avoidant nonverbal behaviours, such as less eye contact, and other symptoms of anxiety such as speech errors (Crosby et al. 1980). At the same time, the minority group member is likely to be suspicious and distrustful of the majority member (Crocker and Major 1989; Feagin 1992), see him as prejudiced (Crocker et al. 1991), and be less communicative (Berg and Wright-Buckley 1988).

When personnel officer Jones examined Mr Smith's application file prior to inviting him in for an interview, intergroup relations were represented symbolically rather than behaviourally. At that stage there was no actual exchange between Jones and Smith, but nevertheless, the fact that Smith's social category differed from that of Jones was likely to affect Jones's thoughts and evaluations, again making the situation a part of the more general arena covered by intergroup relations. Jones's beliefs (stereotypes) about and affect (attitude) towards the social category, African American, will distort his evaluation of Smith's attributes or job qualifications (Jussim et al. 1987), his inferences or explanations (attributions) for why Smith has the positive and the negative qualities evident in the file (Hewstone 1990), and his predictions for Smith's future behaviour (Jackson et al. 1993).

This same distinction between face-to-face interaction and symbolic representation applies to intergroup settings in which multiple persons of each social category are present. Members of a sixteen-person school board of governors may organize themselves into competing factions when discussing how to distribute monies throughout the district. The racial/ethnic identities of the various board members may cause them to act as distinct groups, each representing their own ethnic constituency in their face-to-face bargaining. On the other hand, when the three males who comprise the executive committee of the personnel department meet to discuss company policy for leaves of absence, members of the social category female are not present. Nevertheless, females may be a symbolically represented category, made salient because of recent media attention to the potential need of female workers for maternity leaves. Finally, some groups contain so many members that the possibility of simultaneous face-to-face interaction between their respective members is impossible. In such instances, a representative of each may interact, as when the leaders of two nation-states that are in conflict meet to discuss an issue of contention. Though the interaction is dyadic, each category is symbolically present as a whole.

Intergroup settings, then, can include dyadic interactions or group interactions where group members are actually physically present or symbolically present.

What behaviour is studied in intergroup research?

In the most general sense, two kinds of responses toward a group or one of its members are potentially available: prosocial behaviour and antisocial behaviour. Although both positive and negative interactions are studied in the realm of interpersonal relationships, intergroup relations are most often seen as fraught with tension, conflict and antagonism. Indeed, the study of intergroup relations has become synonymous with the study of intergroup conflict.

The most salient cases of intergroup behaviour in the real world often consist of violent acts, such as the shooting of a rival gang member, or the deaths incurred by war. Statistically, most instances of assault, violence and aggression occur within, not between, groups. Nevertheless, acts of intergroup aggression are more newsworthy, perhaps in part because they have the potential to escalate into more widespread violence. In fact, there is evidence that intergroup aggression is perceived as more violent and severe than acts of interpersonal aggression (Otten et al. 1995).

Although escalation of conflict and hostility between groups is the form of intergroup relationships of most concern in the real world, social psychological research on intergroup behaviour starts with other, more subtle, forms of responding which reflect differences in disposition toward others as a function of their group membership. In general, feelings, beliefs and interpersonal behaviours tend to be more positive when they involve members of the same group than when they occur between groups. As we shall see in later chapters, it is not just that individuals are more negative in their attitudes and behaviours toward outgroup members, but also that prosocial behaviours such as helping and cooperation are more likely to be extended to members of the ingroup and withheld from the outgroup. Understanding how basic perceptions, affect and motives are influenced or transformed by an intergroup setting is the essence of the social psychological approach to the study of intergroup relations.

BUILDING BLOCKS FOR THE STUDY OF INTERGROUP RELATIONS

We turn now to the separate ingredients or building blocks that need to be considered in understanding intergroup relations from a social psychological perspective. These basic processes come from research on social cognition, social emotions, social comparison and social motives, and we provide a brief overview of each of these in the following sections.

Social cognition: categorization

Perhaps the most basic process of human judgement and cognition is that of categorization – the lumping together of objects and events into meaningful groupings that enables a person to deal with incoming information quickly and automatically. Categorization is a natural product of how the human mind operates and is fundamental to the study of intergroup relations in that it is the basis upon which groups are identified in the first place.

In his now classic analysis of the nature of prejudice, Allport (1954) notes five important characteristics of categorization:

- it forms large classes and clusters for guiding our daily adjustments
- categorization assimilates as much as it can to the cluster
- the category enables us to quickly identify a related object
- the category saturates all that it contains with the same ideational and emotional flavour; that is, the same affect is elicited by all instances of the category
- categories are rational in that they are based on existing differences between characteristics of objects classified into separate categories.

These features identified by Allport hold for both **social categorization** and nonsocial categorization. Social categories, however, have a special feature that is not associated with categorizations of objects or events outside of the social domain. Individuals themselves are members of social categories. Thus, the act of categorizing a person into a social grouping automatically classifies that individual as a member of an ingroup (a category to which the perceiver belongs) or an outgroup (a category to which the perceiver does not belong). It is perhaps for this reason that Allport felt that social categories tend to be less rational than other categorizations in that the beliefs we hold about social groupings often do not rest on firm evidence of actual intergroup differences.

Researchers in cognitive psychology have distinguished between natural categories (for example animals, plants) and social categories (for example political parties, ethnic groups). Natural categories are thought to have essential characteristics that account for why one sees specific instances of the category as similar – as sharing the 'essence' of the category (Medin 1989). Some social categories, such as ethnicity, eventually come to be seen as 'naturalized', as sharing an essence as do natural categories (Rothbart and Taylor 1992; Haslam and Rothschild 2000).

Most researchers assume that this tendency to see some social categories as equivalent to natural categories is culturally learned. Others, however, point to evidence that the human has distinct cognitive competences (for example Cheng and Holyoak 1985) and that the infant and young child have predispositions for certain types of information and tasks (Gelman 1988; Gelman and Wellman 1991). Building on these domain-specific predispositions and cognitive capacities, they argue that such domain-specificity extends to social categories. By contrast to other social categories such as political parties, race/ethnicity does not become similar to natural categories as a result of cultural learning, but instead is a domain for which infants have a predisposition for categorization (Hirchfield 1988). Regardless of which explanation is correct, social categories that have some biological basis, such as those based on gender or ethnic inheritance, have acquired a special status in the study of intergroup relations.

Category accentuation

One feature of categorization processes that was not discussed by Allport is especially important to an understanding of intergroup perceptions. Although categories may be based initially on actual differences among objects, once categories have been formed there is a tendency for perceivers to exaggerate the extent of differences between members of one category and another. This **category accentuation** is a consequence of processes of assimilation and contrast whereby we judge items within the same category as more similar (assimilation) and items from different categories as more dissimilar (contrast) than they actually are (Campbell 1956; Tajfel 1969). The result is an increase in perceived homogeneity within categories and distinctiveness between categories.

A concrete demonstration of category accentuation was provided in a judgement experiment by Tajfel and Wilkes (1963). The stimuli in that experiment were eight lines, varying in length from 16.2 cm to 22.9 cm.

For some judges, the lines were presented without labels. For others, the four shorter lines were labelled with the letter 'A' and the four longer lines were labelled 'B'. Judges were shown the lines, one at a time in random order, and asked to estimate the length of each. The average estimates produced by judges in the categorization (label) condition, compared to those in the no label condition, exaggerated the difference in length between lines labelled 'A' and lines labelled 'B'. This effect was particularly marked for the two lines at the boundary of the categories. The difference between the perceived length of the longest line in category A and the shortest line in category B was much greater than the actual difference between the two lines. As a result, the perceived distinctiveness of the two categories was accentuated. Similar effects are obtained when people judge heights of men and women (Biernat et al. 1991). On average, men are taller than women but this difference is exaggerated when judges make estimates of the heights of individual males and females.

By the same process, members of a social group are perceived to have similar attitudes and to be different from members of other groups, even when the group assignments have been arbitrary (Wilder 1981). In general, the more salient category distinctions are, the less we notice individual differences within categories and the more we see each group as a single, homogeneous unit. Once categories have been formed, we are biased toward information that enhances the differences between categories and less attentive to information about similarities between members of different categories (Krueger et al. 1989). These effects of categorization are now widely recognized as the psychological foundation for social stereotyping and intergroup prejudice (Tajfel 1969; Hamilton and Trolier 1986; Wilder 1986a; Hewstone et al. 1991).

Category salience

Within the social domain, the most fundamental category distinctions are those that differentiate ingroups from outgroups. As we shall see in subsequent chapters, this ingroup–outgroup distinction – and the consequent accentuation of differences between ingroup categories and others – is the fundamental component of social psychological theories of intergroup relations. Thus, in order to understand the dynamics of intergroup behaviour, we must first understand what bases of social categorization are used to draw these important ingroup–outgroup differentiations.

As was mentioned above, the relevance and salience of any particular social categorization may be context specific. Some category memberships may be highly meaningful in one social situation (for example the difference between psychologists and sociologists at an academic conference) and irrelevant in others (for example a social reception for foreign dignitaries). Bruner (1957) hypothesized that the likelihood of using a particular categorization was determined in part by what the perceiver expected to see and in part by the nature of the stimulus objects or events in the environment. More specifically, Bruner stated that the salience of any particular category distinction would be determined by the interaction between **category accessibility** (the frequency or importance of that categorization to the perceiver) and fit (the match between category speci-fications and the current stimuli).

Applying Bruner's model to the categorization of people in social groups, Oakes and colleagues (1991, 1994) have suggested that the perceived 'fit' for social categories has two aspects. The first is **comparative fit** – the extent to which differences within categories are less than differences between categories among the persons in a particular context. The second is **normative fit** – the extent to which the specific persons match expectations about category differences. For instance, in a group of six persons containing three females and three males, gender is likely to be an access-ible and salient categorization. In most cases, physical features, appear-ance and dress will be more similar within gender than between. How-ever, if all members of our six-person group have short hair, are wearing jeans and flannel shirts, and talking about football, gender will not be a salient categorization because neither the comparative fit (differentiation between categories) nor normative fit (match to expected gender differ-ences) are high.

An experimental study by van Knippenberg et al. (1994) confirmed the importance of normative fit in determining whether a particular category distinction becomes salient. Participants viewed a videotape of a discus-sion group among male and female students and teachers. Results of a later test of participants' memory for material on the videotape indicated that categorization by gender was greater when the topic of the discussion was gender related (that is, the merits of positive discrimination in favour of women) rather than unrelated (for example preventing welfare fraud), particularly when the positions taken by the males and females on the tape were consistent with gender expectations.

Automatic categorization

Although contextual salience often determines what category distinctions are activated and applied in a particular social interaction, some category distinctions are so familiar and frequently utilized that they are automat-ically activated whenever relevant cues are present (Bargh 1989; Devine 1989). Research using computer-aided reaction time measures reveals that social categorization on the basis of sex, age or race occurs within milliseconds of the initial presentation of a photo or video of an indi-vidual person (for example Zarate and Smith 1990; Hewstone et al. 1991; Kawakami and Dovidio 2001). Further, this initial classification is accom-panied by automatic arousal of affect or evaluations associated with the category, often without conscious awareness. Because of this, techniques for assessing **automatic categorization** are used to detect implicit attitudes – positive or negative reactions to members of particular social groups that perceivers are often unaware of or deny when asked about their explicit conscious attitudes (Dovidio et al. 2001). Numerous experiments using these methods have demonstrated that words or visual cues that represent ingroup categories automatically activate positive affect, by com-parison to cues for outgroup categories which activate less positive or more negative **automatic evaluations** (for example Perdue et al. 1990; Fazio et al. 1995; Greenwald et al. 1998).

Highly accessible categories also influence how we resolve ambiguous situations. In 1957, J.W. Bagby asked artists, students and school teachers from the United States and from Mexico to look into a stereoscope, a device that simultaneously shows a different picture to each eye. Photos were presented so that one eye saw a picture of a baseball player, the other a picture of a bullfighter. When asked to describe what they saw, the overwhelming proportion of Americans described the baseball player, while the overwhelming proportion of Mexicans described the bullfighter. How is it that people who receive the same visual stimuli 'see' something different? Bagby explained his results as follows:

> Differences in ways of perceiving come about as a consequence of differences in past experiences and purposes. These in turn emerge from influences in the home, in the school, and in the various groups with which the individual identifies.

(Bagby 1957: 334)

This and other studies provide evidence that who we are influences how we perceive that which is around us. Memory structures, the sum of our experiences, create a kind of filter through which new experiences are classified and interpreted. In this experiment, participants 'saw' the image that represented the stereotypical national sport of their respective cultures/ countries. A person born and raised in Mexico is likely to have many more specific instances of 'bullfighter' or 'bullfighting' stored in his or her memory (in the form of bullfights attended, observed on television, read about in the fiction or non-fiction stories, represented in paintings, sculptures or other forms of art) than one born and raised in the United States. Thus, when confronted with competing or confusing stimuli, this relatively larger amount of information stored in memory biases the probability that ambiguous information will be interpreted in the direction of that which is familiar. That is, we are likely to 'see' what we have seen before.

Cross-categorization

Much of the social psychological research on intergroup relations has been conducted in settings in which one, and only one, ingroup–outgroup category distinction is highly salient or dominant. But in a pluralistic society, individuals simultaneously hold memberships in multiple social categories. Within the same setting, a particular person might be identified in terms of gender, ethnicity, political party affiliation, religion or occupation. Any two persons in that situation may share membership in some of those categories, but belong to different categories in others. When two or more category distinctions are available, the implications for how ingroup–outgroup differentiations are drawn are not always clear.

Circumstances in which more than one social categorization may be salient, and where persons share category membership on one dimension but not another, have been defined as instances of **crossed categorization** (Deschamps and Doise 1978; Hewstone et al. 1993). The interesting question in situations of cross-categorization is what happens to ingroup–outgroup distinctions when more than one categorization is available?

One possible effect of crossed category distinctions would be to dilute the meaningfulness of any ingroup–outgroup differentiation and eliminate category accentuation effects. In this case, ingroup–outgroup differences would be reduced or eliminated and perceptions of others would be equivalent, regardless of category membership. Such cancelling effects have been demonstrated in experiments by Deschamps and Doise (1978) and Vanbeselaere (1987).

A second possibility is that the two category distinctions are additive in their effects, so that shared membership on either dimension provides some basis for ingroup differentiation. Alternatively, the two dimensions may be additive, but one is more important or dominant. Such additive patterns have been observed in a number of studies involving combinations of gender, ethnicity and religious categories (Brewer et al. 1987; Hagendoorn and Henke 1991; Hewstone et al. 1993).

Finally, individuals might be especially sensitive to any form of ingroup or outgroup differentiation, regardless of the dimension of categorization. Sometimes we are attentive to any information that indicates similarity between ourselves and others; at other times we are tuned to information about dissimilarity. If individuals are looking for similarity, shared ingroup membership will be what matters. In that case, only a 'double outgroup' will be perceived as an outgroup (Brown and Turner 1979). On the other hand, if cues to dissimilarity are salient, the individual will be more sensitive to nonshared categories. In this case, outgroup distinctions of any kind may dominate, only the 'double ingroup' will be perceived as an ingroup, all others categorized as an outgroup (Schofield and Sagar 1977; Eurich-Fulcer and Schofield 1995). In later chapters we shall consider the conditions under which individuals might be especially sensitive to ingroup versus outgroup classifications in defining any intergroup situation.

Social cognition: attribution

It is a basic tenet of social cognition research that people find it unpleasant to be in a state of uncertainty. They actively seek to explain and interpret the causes of events and experiences. Further, the explanations that they come up with have a major impact on how they react – both emotionally and behaviourally – to events. **Attribution theory** is that branch of social cognition research that deals with how people perceive the causes of social events and of their own and others' behaviour.

Theory and research on causal attribution owes a major debt to Fritz Heider, who attempted to account for how the untrained observer or naive psychologist makes sense out of, or accounts for, why another person behaved as she did (Heider 1944, 1958). Heider provided several key ideas that were important to subsequent research and theorizing about attributional processes.

First, Heider emphasized that the naive perceiver does not assimilate information objectively. In developing an account for another person's action, it is not just the action itself that is important, but how that action is understood by the observer. Thus, the observer's emotional reaction to the behaviour, as well as the beliefs that the observer holds about the other person, will affect how the action is interpreted and how the observer explains the behaviour.

Heider's second important contribution was the distinction between the person versus the situation, as potential causes of a particular behaviour. When trying to account for the reasons a behaviour occurred, we can look either to factors internal to the person or to factors in the external environment. Heider noted that we tend to ignore or underestimate the importance of situational determinants of behaviour and emphasize instead internal attributes of the behaving person.

In discussing this bias, Heider used the phrase, 'behaviour engulfs the field'. What he meant was that the array of situational influences in the environment in which the actor is located (the 'field') is obscured or masked by the salience of the behaviour being observed and its natural link to the person generating that behaviour. In the eye of the observer, a behaviour is not seen as separate from the actor. Thus, it is easy or automatic to see behaviour as a product of some characteristic or trait of the person. This tendency to interpret or explain an action in terms of the actor's character, personality or traits, and to underestimate the influence of situational factors in prompting that action has been termed the 'fundamental attribution error' (Ross 1977).

Causal explanations for events and behaviours can differ in other ways besides whether they are internal or external to the person. For instance, both ability and effort are internal factors, but ability is typically thought to be a stable characteristic of the individual whereas the amount of effort an individual makes can change from one situation to another. The locus of a cause refers to the person versus situation distinction whereas stability refers to the temporal nature of a cause. A stable cause is one that involves a persistent characteristic, invariably present over time, as opposed to a factor that is variable, sometimes present and other times not.

A third important distinction among causal attributions is that of controllability, the degree to which the cause is something that can be determined by volition or intent. Ability as an explanation of good performance is an internal, stable attribution, but to the extent that it is based on heritable characteristics, it is one that is uncontrollable. Effort, in contrast, is unstable but under control of the actor, and is thus, both unstable and controllable. Controllability is related to perceived responsibility for actions, and underlies the distinction between excuses and justification for negative behaviours (Weiner et al. 1987). A justification does not deny that one is responsible for the behaviour, but it does undermine the negative evaluation of that behaviour. In contrast, an excuse acknowledges that the behaviour may have been bad or morally wrong, but diminishes or denies one's responsibility for having engaged in it.

These three general dimensions of causal attributions – locus, stability and controllability – constitute a basic taxonomy of social attributions (Weiner 1985, 1986). More importantly, they influence how we respond to another person's actions. When we perceive a behaviour as caused by internal, stable attributes of the person being observed, we react differently than if the behaviour is seen as externally caused or unstable. For instance, if the individual ahead of you in a queue steps on your foot, you will feel angry (and perhaps retaliate) if you believe it was a controllable act of hostility, but if you interpret it as an uncontrollable accident caused by crowding, you are likely to respond quite differently. In the case of violent behaviours, excuses may produce less escalation of conflict than might justifications.

Since attributions have implications for how we treat another person, and since attributions are subjective judgements, understanding attributional processes is one key to understanding intergroup behaviour. This is particularly true if the attributions we make about another individual's actions are influenced by group membership, as indicated by results of research on attributional biases.

Biases in attribution

We have previously discussed the internal/external dimension and the fundamental attribution error. Research has revealed another type of attributional bias that operates within the context of the fundamental attribution error. Even though there is an overall tendency toward explaining events in terms of person attributes, this tendency is stronger when we are making attributions about the causes of other people's behaviour than when we explain our own actions. We are more likely to see our own behaviour as being responsive to the situation, that is, as having external causes. This is particularly true for negative behaviours or outcomes. When individuals take internal responsibility for good actions but attribute bad outcomes to unstable or external causes, this is known as a self-serving attributional bias.

Self-serving biases appear to extend to intergroup attributions as well. Good outcomes for the ingroup are explained by stable, internal attributions. Bad outcomes for the ingroup are explained by situational factors, or unstable internal attributes. By contrast, good outcomes for the outgroup are explained by situational factors, or by unstable internal factors (such as effort or luck). Bad outcomes for the outgroup are explained by stable, internal factors. Pettigrew (1979) termed this pattern of intergroup attributions the **ultimate attribution error**. This particular bias serves both to enhance a positive image of the ingroup, compared to outgroups, and to protect the ingroup from the negative implications of bad actions (Hewstone 1990; Weber 1994).

Ingroup-enhancing attributional biases play an important role in maintaining ingroup harmony and loyalty (see Chapter 2). The ingroup protective biases also have important implications for initiation and maintenance of intergroup hostilities, as discussed in Chapter 6. If we attribute a negative action to evil intent or aggression dispositions, we are much more likely to respond with retaliatory violence than if we attribute that same act to a temporary situation (Betancourt and Blair 1992). Actions by ingroup members that are hostile or violent are more likely to be perceived as justified by the situation than are similar actions by outgroup members (Hewstone 1990; Weber 1994). Among the external factors in the situation that account for our behaviour is the behaviour of the other group. *We* see ourselves as responding to *their* provocation. By contrast, in our view of the outgroup, we account for their actions in terms of their internal attributes, their natural characteristics – not the situation that we may in part have actually created for them. Whereas we see ourselves as responding to the situation and to them, their behaviour is perceived as due to their characteristics and aggressive intent. Thus, intergroup attributional biases help to perpetuate conflict because both sides in a conflict can feel justified in continuing aggression.

Social emotions: affect and cognition

The role of causal attributions in determining how we respond to a social situation or event makes clear the close connection between the way in which we perceive and interpret experiences cognitively and the way in which we react emotionally. An emotion is defined as a specific affect that has an identifiable source and target (Wilder and Simon 2001). As compared to moods, which are diffuse positive or negative affective states, emotions (such as joy, sympathy, anger, disgust) are highly differentiated and more focused. From this definition it is clear that emotions have both a cognitive and an affective arousal component. The cognitive element comes in the form of an **appraisal** that an object or event has some significant positive or negative implications for the person's goals or values (Smith and Lazarus 1990). The classic experiments demonstrating the importance of appraisals in emotions were conducted by Richard Lazarus (1966), who demonstrated that emotional reactions (including physiological responses) to viewing unpleasant films could be moderated by the cognitive 'set' that viewers adopted during the presentation.

Since these early experiments, appraisal theories of emotions have been further developed to provide models for how particular patterns of cognitive appraisal map onto specific emotions (for example Roseman 1984; Smith and Ellsworth 1985; Scherer 1988). More specifically, these models postulate that individuals assess situations in terms of

- *goal significance*: how will this object or event affect me in a positive or negative way?
- *coping potential*: how much power or control do I have over the situation?
- *legitimacy*: does this situation violate norms or expectations?

Specific emotions arise from specific configurations of these three components of appraisal. Anger, for instance, is activated by appraisals that the situation constitutes a threat to one's well-being or goals, particularly if this threat is seen as illegitimate, and that the perceiver has the power or resources to cope with the threat. Fear, on the other hand, arises from an appraisal of threat combined with an assessment of low power or control.

Emotions and behaviour

Emotions serve to regulate behaviour, and appraisal theorists generally argue that specific emotions have corresponding behavioural orientations that function to prepare the individual for actions that are adaptive to the situation as appraised (Smith and Lazarus 1990). Fear, for instance, instigates a 'flight or fight' response whereas anger is associated with a propensity to attack or harm the source of threat. The expression of emotions also serves a communicative function (Darwin 1872; Fridlund 1994), reflecting both how the individual has interpreted a situation and how they intend to respond. For this reason, many theorists believe that all emotions are social in nature, but social emotions more specifically are emotional reactions elicited by and directed toward other persons.

Intergroup emotions

Although the role of cognitive biases in intergroup relations has been the focus of study for a long time in social psychology, the influence of emotions in intergroup behaviour is just recently receiving more extensive attention (E.R. Smith 1993; Wilder and Simon 2001; Mackie and Smith 2002). Just as individuals react emotionally to events that affect them personally, people can experience emotions on behalf of the groups to which they belong and feel identified. An appraisal that the ingroup is threatened can engender fear or anger, even if the individual's own personal safety is not at issue (Mackie et al. 2000). Response to the terrorist attack on the World Trade Center in New York City on 11 September 2001 provided a vivid example of how a whole nation could react emotionally to an event that directly affected only a small portion of the group membership. Consistent with appraisal theories of emotion, group-based anger and fear were activated immediately with the perception that the security and well-being of the ingroup had been threatened. Further, since the ingroup in this case was appraised as being relatively strong (that is, high in resources), the dominant emotion was that of anger and associated fight/attack behaviour orientation. Also consistent with emotion theory, the group quickly focused on a specific outgroup target as both the source of the anger and the object of retaliation. The role of such **intergroup emotions** in eliciting and maintaining hostility toward outgroups will be discussed more extensively in Chapter 4.

Social comparison: evaluating self and others

In addition to their need to interpret and explain others' behaviour, individuals have a strong need to evaluate their own abilities and characteristics – to know where they stand on various dimensions of behaviour or performance (Festinger 1954). Such evaluations are often comparative by nature. Some comparisons are based on changes in the self over time (Albert 1977; Brown and Middendorf 1996). Children, for instance, often take pride in their growth, marking their height on the back of a door and noting with glee the difference between last year's mark and that achieved this year. The comparison of marks provides a basis for judgement about how much better one is now than before. Similarly, one can mark improvement in skills or in performance in games such as golf by comparison with one's own past performance.

Self-evaluations are more difficult with respect to attributes for which there is no physical or absolute standard. In such instances, judgements about good and bad are based on comparison with others. If one gets a C+ in a class in which most others obtain As and Bs, one may not take much pride from that outcome. Yet, in a class in which the instructor imposes very stringent and perhaps indefensible standards, knowing that one got a C+, and that there were only a few Bs and no As, may be a legitimate source of pride.

There are two important points here. The first is that most judgements are relative rather than absolute, as shown by adaptation level theory (Helson 1964). Any one stimulus is judged against the background of prior stimuli within that domain. A two-gram weight will appear light to the weight-lifter, but heavy to someone who repairs watches. Bench-pressing a hundred pounds will be easy (light) for the weight-lifter, but heavy for the novice. The second is that for many dimensions of judgement, there is no physical standard against which one can base one's evaluation. In such cases, one must rely on social comparison to other persons or groups. Because judgements about the goodness of one's performance or one's outcomes are often necessarily comparative, there is a sense in which such comparisons are intrinsically competitive. In order to validate a posit-ive perception of myself, it is not enough to be 'good' in an absolute sense but to be 'better' than others (Wills 1981).

The basic motives of self-evaluation and self-enhancement can be met by actual comparisons between oneself and other persons or groups, or by making certain assumptions about others' attributes. For instance, people often assume that others are similar to themselves in attitudes and beliefs, thereby providing social support for their own view (Gerard and Orive 1987; Spears and Manstead 1990). Such perceived consensus can fulfil self-enhancement motives. For attitudes and many behaviours, what is good and correct is defined by social consensus. Thus, the tendency to overestimate consensus with respect to one's own beliefs and actions can contribute to self-worth and self-consistency.

Self-enhancement motivation, however, can also motivate imagined difference rather than consensus. Ordinarily, people are inclined to see themselves as similar to others in their attitudes, but for abilities, unique-ness may be more positive (Marks 1984). A distinctively good ability sets one apart from the pack, and bolsters self-esteem. This may also be the case for attitudinal dimensions that have moral implication, where the good and bad ends of the dimension are clearly discernible. For these types of issues, individuals are more likely to see their own position as unique and dissimilar to others rather than as similar to them.

Social comparison also operates at the intergroup level. The distinctive-ness and value of one's own group is derived, at least in part, from com-parison to other groups. Comparisons that favour the ingroup enhance group esteem, and group members are likely to prefer intergroup situ-ations in which their own group maintains **positive distinctiveness** and to minimize or resist intergroup comparisons that are not so favourable to the ingroup (Turner and Brown 1978; Brewer 1979). The consequences of such biased intergroup comparison provide much of the foundation for intergroup discrimination discussed in Chapter 3.

Relative deprivation and perceived justice

Just as abilities and attributes are evaluated by comparison with others, the value attached to outcomes such as economic or social rewards may also be determined by social comparison. The same salary could be a source of satisfaction or dissatisfaction, depending on whether other people are earning more than I am. A great deal of research on social justice supports the idea that individuals' feelings of being deprived or disadvantaged are based on the comparisons they make rather than the absolute value of their own condition. Feelings of resentment and the sense of injustice that arises from perceiving that one has less than is deserved (compared to others) is called **relative deprivation**.

The concept of relative deprivation was developed by social scientists during the Second World War to explain some paradoxical findings that emerged in the study of morale among American soldiers (Stouffer et al. 1949). Researchers found, for instance, that soldiers in air force units, where rates of promotion were quite high, had more complaints about the promotion system than did soldiers in the military police, where promotions were few and far between. Equally surprising, they found that black soldiers who were stationed in southern states in the USA (where overt discrimination based on race was very visible) had higher morale than black soldiers stationed in the less racist northern states. Stouffer and his colleagues explained these anomalous results in terms of different standards of comparison being used by soldiers in different units. Compared to peers who were advancing at a rapid rate, air force soldiers who had not yet been promoted felt deprived, even though their objective chances of promotion were higher than those of soldiers in other units. Similarly, the high morale of black soldiers stationed in the south may have derived from comparisons with black civilians who fared very poorly; black soldiers in the north, on the other hand, may have felt deprived relative to civilian blacks in that region who were earning higher wages in war-related factory jobs.

Relative deprivation may be experienced even by those who are objectively advantaged but feel they are losing by comparison to previous expectations. This principle was dramatically illustrated by behaviour of young members of the upper castes of India in a series of incidents in 1990. During one period that year, scores of middle-class youths (members of the Brahmin, Kshatriya and Vaishya castes) committed suicide in protest against government policies opening more jobs to the poor. By any objective standards, the upper castes were doing quite well, even in the face of government economic reforms designed to benefit the disadvantaged castes. Yet the perception that their own caste was losing position relative to the lower castes created a sense of comparative disadvantage that was sufficient to motivate dramatic protest against the reforms.

Just as experiences of relative deprivation can occur even among the advantaged, members of disadvantaged groups in general may not feel deprived or aggrieved if they compare themselves to similarly disadvantaged others. Women professionals, for instance, tend to feel satisfied with their jobs, despite lower pay and status, as long as they compare their outcomes with those of other female colleagues and not with male colleagues (Zanna et al. 1987).

Since individuals do tend to limit their interpersonal social comparisons to members of their own ingroups, does this mean that women and other economically and politically disadvantaged groups never resent their position relative to men or higher status groups? The answer to that question rests on an important distinction between the experience of relative deprivation at the personal level and what Runciman (1966) called **fraternal deprivation**. Fraternal deprivation arises from comparisons between the outcomes of one's ingroup as a whole and those of more advantaged groups. While personal deprivation depends on interpersonal comparisons with similar others, fraternal deprivation involves intergroup comparisons between dissimilar groups. Feelings of personal deprivation and fraternal deprivation are not necessarily closely connected. Indeed, it is frequently found that members of disadvantaged groups perceive that their group is discriminated against but report that they, personally, have not experienced any discrimination (Crosby 1982; Taylor et al. 1990). As we shall discuss in more detail in Chapter 3, feelings of injustice arising from relative deprivation have very different consequences depending on whether the comparison involves personal or fraternal deprivation (Vanneman and Pettigrew 1972; Walker and Pettigrew 1984).

Social motives: cooperation or competition

Responses to relative deprivation reflect the influence of social motivation. Social motives refer to the value an individual places on outcomes received by the self and others. If a person is interested strictly in the absolute value of outcomes to themselves, this form of self-interest represents an asocial motive, in the sense that others' outcomes are not taken into account, only one's own. In most situations, however, people do not seem to evaluate their costs and benefits in this absolute sense, but instead value their own outcomes in relation to those obtained by others.

The theory of social motives (McClintock 1972; MacCrimmon and Messick 1976; McClintock and Liebrand 1988) designates five forms of social motivation that are particularly important in the conduct of human affairs. These motives represent different orientations that an individual can bring to a social interaction and determine what that individual is seeking to achieve in the interaction and how satisfied they will be with the outcomes. The five basic social motives are **relative gain** orientation, **joint gain** orientation, **equality**, other's gain orientation and other's loss orientation.

- *Relative gain orientation*: seeking to maximize the difference between outcomes to oneself compared to others. This is the motivational orientation associated with pure competition, where the value associated with one's own outcomes is determined by how much they exceed another's outcomes. In a competitive game such as soccer, for instance, it is not the absolute number of points that a team scores that counts, only the number more than that scored by the other team.
- *Joint gain orientation*: seeking to maximize the total outcomes for self and others combined. This is the motivational orientation of pure cooperation. This motivation would be characteristic of members of a team whose goal is to score as many points as possible for the group as a whole; it is also the motivation associated with cooperative partnerships

and other ventures in which the goal is to maximize profits for every-one in the group.

- *Equality*: seeking to minimize the difference between one's own and others' outcomes. This is the social motive that is opposite to that asso-ciated with competition. With this orientation, goals of fairness and equal distribution of outcomes are primary.
- *Other's gain orientation*: seeking to maximize the value of outcomes to another person, regardless of one's own outcomes. This is the orienta-tion associated with pure altruism. Altruism does not necessarily imply that the individual sacrifice in order to benefit another, but that his or her primary concern is the welfare of the other person rather than the self. This is the motivational orientation associated with parental care or other caregiving relationships.
- *Other's loss orientation*: seeking to minimize the outcomes of another person. In contrast to altruism, this is the social motive associated with pure aggression, where the individual's primary goal is to harm the other, regardless of outcomes to the self.

Pairings of outcomes for self and other

	A	B	C	D	E	F
Self	50	40	40	40	20	20
Other	40	20	40	60	70	10

Figure 1.1   Assessing social motives

The differences among the five motivational orientations can be illus-trated by considering the array of alternative pairs of outcomes displayed in Figure 1.1. Imagine that the numbers in these arrays represent the absolute value of psychological and materials outcomes that are achieved by one person (self) and another. The different pairings of outcomes represent different possible relationships between those achieved by the self compared to the other. An individual who was purely self-interested would prefer option A to all of the others because that is the one in which self-gain is highest, ignoring what the outcomes to the other are. An individual with a relative gain orientation, however, would prefer option B. Even though this alternative gives lower outcomes to the self than does option A, it is the one in which the relative difference between self and other is greater in one's own favour. Similarly, someone with an equality orientation would prefer C over A, because equal outcomes are more important than absolute gain.

From the array in Figure 1.1, an individual with a joint-gain (cooperat-ive) social orientation would prefer option D over all others because that is the pairing in which the total outcomes to both parties is maximized. An individual with an altruistic orientation would prefer option E, whereas someone who was motivated by aggression would choose option F. These latter preferences are dictated by the value of the outcomes to the other person, ignoring one's own outcomes.

The five social motives defined above represent pure motivational states, where the individual has a single goal that drives preferences within a social interaction. In many situations, of course, an individual will have mixed orientations. For instance, relative gain may be moderated by some concern for equality, so that the individual seeks to be better off than others but not by too wide a margin. Altruism and aggression may be moderated by concern for one's own outcomes, and so forth. To some extent, the social motives that an individual brings to a situation are determined by individual differences in socialization and values – some people are dispositionally competitive across a wide range of social situations; others are dispositionally cooperative (McClintock and Liebrand 1988). But motives can also be influenced by the situation itself. Many games and competitions, for instance, require a relative gain orientation, while other situations of social interdependence require mutual cooperation. Of particular concern to intergroup relations is the distinction between cooperative and competitive social motives. In later chapters we shall discuss evidence that individuals are more likely to adopt a cooperative orientation in interactions within their ingroup, but switch to a competitive orientation when the interaction involves outgroup members.

PERSPECTIVES ON INDIVIDUALS AND SOCIAL GROUPS

Social categorization, causal attribution, social emotions, social comparison, cooperation and competition are the cognitive and motivational processes on which current social psychological theories of intergroup relations are built. These processes are significantly influenced by the group context in which the individual is operating. In the research reviewed in this chapter we have seen many examples of how cognition, affect and motivations are influenced by the social structure of the situation – by what social categories are salient and meaningful. But these psychological responses, in turn, shape the behaviours that lead to collective consequences; the social structure of the situation is influenced by the cognitions, affect and motivations of the individual participants. From the social psychological perspective, the individual and the social group constitute a reciprocal causal system in which cognitions and motivation are the associative links, as represented in Figure 1.2.

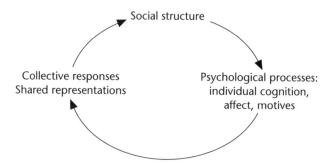

Figure 1.2 The interrelationship of individual and group processes

In the chapters that follow we shall demonstrate how social psychological research and theory have forged these associative links between individual and group processes. We begin with a focus on the cognitive and motivational origins of attachment to one's own social groups – the formation of ingroups. Next, we focus on the social psychology of differentiation between the ingroup and outgroups, and its consequences for intergroup discrimination and conflict. We then move to the psychology of prejudice against outgroups – attitudes and emotions directed toward those who are distinguished from 'us'. Finally, the last two chapters deal with applications of the social psychological approach toward reducing prejudice and discrimination and understanding the origins of war. Running throughout these chapters is the general theme that individual psychology and group psychology are inextricably intertwined.

FURTHER READINGS

Allport, G.W. (1954) *The Nature of Prejudice*. Cambridge, MA: Addison-Wesley. The classic book on social psychological underpinnings of intergroup relations.

Mackie, D.M. and Smith, E.R. (1998) intergroup relations: insights from a theoretically integrative approach, *Psychological Review*, 105: 499–529. An integration of research and theory on social cognition and intergroup behaviour.

McClintock, C.G. (1972) Social motivation: a set of propositions, *Behavioral Science*, 17: 438–54. A taxonomy of different social motives or orientations to interpersonal exchanges.

Tajfel, H. (1969) Cognitive aspects of prejudice, *Journal of Social Issues*, 25: 79–97. The initial paper on social categorization theory.

TWO

ETHNOCENTRISM AND INGROUP IDENTITY: THE NEED FOR 'WE-NESS'

> **Key concepts**: ethnocentrism, ingroup, outgroup, social identity, group polarization, optimal distinctiveness

On 18 November 1978, more than 900 men, women and children committed suicide at Jonestown in Guyana. Told that their group was under siege, members of the Reverend Jim Jones's People's Temple lined up to receive glasses of red KoolAid laced with cyanide. All drank the liquid as they were told, and almost all died within 30 minutes.

The dramatic suicides of members of the Jonestown cult illustrate the extremes to which individuals will go on behalf of the groups to which they belong. Warfare brings out acts of extreme cruelty and of extreme heroism, both in the name of group loyalty. At a more mundane level, many of the things we do make sense only if they are understood as expressions of our identification with a group. Many of our day-to-day choices about what to wear, how to spend leisure time, and what political positions to espouse are influenced by a desire to symbolize or represent our important group memberships. In this chapter we shall review research on the formation of group identities and the evidence for the powerful effects of group identification on individual behaviour. This will be followed by a discussion of theories about why individuals become attached to social groups and what role this plays in intergroup relations.

ETHNOCENTRISM: THE INGROUP AND THE SELF

The apparently universal tendency for human beings to differentiate themselves according to group membership was documented in rich anthropological observations compiled by Sumner (1906). Sumner adopted the terms 'in-group' and 'out-group' to refer to social groupings to which a particular individual belongs or does not belong, respectively. Ingroups could be of many different types, ranging from small, face-to-face group-ings of family and friends, to large social categories such as gender, reli-gion and nationality. The psychological meaning of group membership does not seem to be restricted by group size or direct interaction with fellow group members. For some people, national citizenship or social class has as much influence on their behaviour as their own immediate family.

Ingroup membership is more than mere cognitive classification – it car-ries emotional significance as well. Attachment to ingroups and preference of ingroups over outgroups may be a universal characteristic of human social life. Sumner (1906) coined the term **ethnocentrism** to refer to this social psychological phenomenon:

> a differentiation arises between ourselves, the we-group, or in-group, and everybody else, or the others-groups, out-groups. The insiders in a we-group are in a relation of peace, order, law, government, and industry, to each other . . . Ethnocentrism is the technical name for this view of things in which one's own group is the center of every-thing, and all others are scaled and rated with reference to it . . . Each group nourishes its own pride and vanity, boasts itself superior, exalts its own divinities, and looks with contempt on outsiders.
>
> (Sumner 1906: 12–13)

Such group loyalties are apparently acquired early in life. By age 6 or 7, for instance, children exhibit strong preference for their own nationality, even before the concept of 'nation' has been fully understood (Tajfel et al. 1970). Evidence for the pervasiveness of ingroup preference extends be-yond the literature on ethnic and national identity. Experimental social psychologists have demonstrated that even classifying individuals into arbitrary categories in the laboratory can elicit ingroup–outgroup feelings (Tajfel et al. 1971; Turner 1978; Brewer 1979). And there is experimental evidence that the concepts 'we' and 'us' carry positive emotional signific-ance that is activated automatically and unconsciously (Perdue et al. 1990).

According to Sumner's analysis, the essential characteristics of an indi-vidual's relationship to ingroups are loyalty and preference. Loyalty is rep-resented in adherence to ingroup norms and trustworthiness in dealings with fellow ingroup members. Preference is represented in differential acceptance of ingroup members over members of outgroups and positive evaluation of ingroup characteristics that differ from those of outgroups. Ethnocentric loyalty and preference are analogous to self-integrity and self-esteem. Ethnocentrism at the group level parallels egocentrism at the individual level (Messick and Mackie 1989). There is now considerable experimental evidence that once the self has become attached to a social group or category, positive affect and evaluations associated with the self-concept are automatically transferred to the group as a whole (Farnham et al. 1999; Otten and Wentura 1999; Otten and Moskowitz 2000).

The comparison between egocentrism and ethnocentrism has been re-formulated by social psychologists Henri Tajfel and John Turner in terms of a distinction between personal identity and **social identity** (Turner

1982; Hogg and Abrams 1988). Personal identity refers to self conceptualizations that define the individual in relation to (or in comparison to) other individuals. Social identities refer to conceptualizations of the self that derive from membership in emotionally significant social categories or groups (Turner 1985). Tajfel and Turner's distinction between personal and social identity is similar to Harry Triandis's distinction between the private self and the collective self in cross-cultural contexts (Triandis 1989; Trafimow et al. 1991). It is also represented in the distinction between individual and **collective self-esteem** as bases of self-worth (Crocker and Luhtanen 1990; Luhtanen and Crocker 1992).

Although both are aspects of the individual self, personal identity and social identity are different levels of self-definition. Classification of oneself as a group member entails 'a shift towards the perception of the self as an interchangeable exemplar of some social category and away from the perception of self as a unique person' (Turner et al. 1987: 50). In other words, social identities are categorizations of the self into more inclusive social units that *depersonalize* the self-representation. In this sense, depersonalization does not mean a loss of individual identity, but rather a change from the personal to the social level of identity, with consequent change in the nature and content of salient self-concepts.

When a particular social identity is made salient, individuals are likely to think of themselves as having characteristics that are representative of that social category. Social identity, in other words, leads to **self-stereotyping** (Simon and Hamilton 1992). This effect was demonstrated in an experiment by Hogg and Turner (1987) involving gender identity. In this study, male and female college students participated in a discussion under one of two conditions. In the personal identity condition, the discussion was between two people of the same sex and the two discussants held different positions on the issue under consideration. In the social identity condition, the discussion group consisted of four people – two males and two females – and the sexes differed on the issue. The latter arrangement was intended to make categorization by sex particularly salient in the setting, and to increase the probability that participants would think of themselves in terms of their gender identity. Following the social interaction, participants in the social identity condition characterized themselves as more typical of their sex and attributed more masculine or feminine traits to themselves than did those in the personal identity condition.

The Hogg and Turner experiment demonstrates that stereotypical traits that may not be particularly relevant to personal identity become central to the self-concept when social identity is activated. When a woman's female identity is not salient, she may think of herself in terms of personal traits that are not relevant to the masculinity–femininity distinction (for example as organized, neat and politically conservative). When her identity as a member of the female category is made salient, however, this same woman may think about herself in terms of those characteristics that make her more like other women and distinct from most men (for example nurturant and dependent).

Consistent with this perspective, other experimental research has demonstrated that activation of the 'private' self-representation increases retrieval of self-cognitions that are quite different from self-cognitions retrieved when the 'collective' self aspect is activated (Trafimow et al. 1991). These results led Trafimow, Triandis and their colleagues to speculate that private and collective self-concepts are stored in separate locations in memory.

BEHAVIOURAL CONSEQUENCES OF GROUP IDENTITY

The parallel between egocentrism/personal identity on the one side and ethnocentrism/social identity on the other supports the idea that identification with a social group entails a transformation of the sense of self from the individual to the group as a whole (Brewer 1991). When group identification is engaged, goals and motivational biases that function to preserve and enhance the self/ego (Greenwald 1980) are applied to the ingroup. The implication here is that the transformation goes beyond cognitive representations and self-descriptions. A shift in level of self-definition also has profound effects on motives, intentions and behaviour. In its more dramatic manifestations, the activation of social identities may lead individuals to behave in ways that are contrary to personal self-interest, even at the cost of personal survival.

The potential conflict between individual and collective self-interest is most vividly demonstrated by acts of self-sacrifice associated with warfare or heroic altruism. Individuals dying on behalf of group goals represent an extreme in the difference between behaviour directed toward preservation and enhancement of the personal self and behaviour motivated by group identification. Less dramatic, but nonetheless significant, evidence of disparities between personal and social identity has been obtained in a number of experimental studies. Some of these differences are reviewed below.

Speech style

Although individuals differ in their facility with different languages, dialects and accents, we are all capable of altering aspects of our style of speech to suit various social occasions (Hymes 1967). Choice of words, certain affectations, use of colloquial expressions, grammatical constructions, and so on, can vary depending on how we choose to present ourselves to others. In most social situations, the language we use reflects the aspect of identity that is most salient in that setting (Giles 1978; Giles et al. 1980; Giles and Johnson 1981; Sachdev and Bourhis 1990). For bilingual individuals, in particular, language and social identity are closely related (Giles and Byrne 1982).

Experimental research on evaluative ratings of individuals with different dialects or speech styles indicates that hearing 'ingroup' speech elicits positive affect toward the speaker (Edwards 1985; Ryan et al. 1989). When a region or nation is divided into two or more ethnolinguistic communities, it is often the case that choice of language signals identification with groups that differ in power or status. In general, the language or linguistic style associated with the dominant group is more prestigious, and speech patterns of the subordinate group are derogated or devalued. Under these conditions, members of subordinate ethnic or lingustic groups often exhibit 'speech accommodation' (Giles and Smith 1979) in interactions with members of the dominant group, modifying their language style to converge with that of the other speaker.

In contrast to the dynamics of speech accommodation, ethnolinguistic identity theory (Giles and Johnson 1981) focuses on the use of divergent speech patterns on the part of subordinate group members, as a method of asserting or expressing distinctive group identity. Bourhis and Giles, for instance, found that adults in Wales accentuated their Welsh accent after hearing a speaker of standard, non-regional English (Giles et al. 1977). Similar results were obtained among Flemish speakers in Belgium (Bourhis et al. 1979). These findings are particularly interesting when one takes into account the fact that members of low-status groups gain advantages as individuals when they exhibit accommodation in their speech patterns (Bourhis et al. 1975; Giles and Smith 1979). Nonetheless, when group identity is at stake, divergent speech is exhibited despite the social costs incurred.

Polarization of beliefs and attitudes

Self-cognitions include more than abilities and personality traits that we attribute to ourselves. They also include the beliefs and attitudes that we hold as expressions of our values and theories about the world. Decades of research on social influence, conformity and group decision making have documented the importance of social group membership in shaping attitudes and beliefs (Turner 1991). Of most relevance here is evidence of the effect that social categorization alone can have on the salience, extremity, and commitment with which individuals hold positions on specific social or political issues.

An extremely important outcome of group behaviour is the phenomenon of **group polarization**. Positions on issues adopted following a period of group discussion and consensus formation tend to be significantly more extreme than the average positions advocated when individuals express their personal opinions prior to group discussion (Myers and Lamm 1976; Isenberg 1986). This polarization of attitudes associated with group formation has been demonstrated across a wide range of attitude issues and decision tasks.

Most analyses of the group polarization phenomenon focus on the informational and normative social influence that takes place during group discussion. However, some experimental research indicates that the effect of discussion on extremitization of an individual's own attitude is mediated by social identification processes. When the arguments generated in group discussion are tape-recorded and then played to individual participants (who are alone while they listen to the tape), changes in their attitudes depend on whether the individuals on the tape are identified as members of the listener's ingroup or not. When discussants are not categorized as ingroup members, attitude change, if any, is in the direction of moderate positions expressed in the discussion. However, when the tape is believed to be a discussion among ingroup category members,

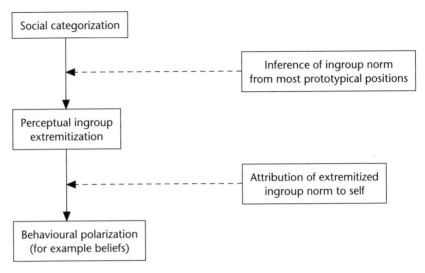

Figure 2.1 Social categorization theory of group polarization
Source: Ng (1989: 7). Reproduced by permission of New Zealand Psychological Society, Inc., copyright holder, *New Zealand Journal of Psychology*.

participants shift their own attitudes in the direction of the more extreme positions represented on the tape (Mackie and Cooper 1984; Mackie 1986; Wetherell 1987). Further, the listeners perceive the content of the discussion to be more polarized when they think the discussants are ingroup category members than when they do not (Mackie 1986).

These results are consistent with a social identity interpretation of group polarization, which holds that shared identification with a group is a precondition for group polarization (Turner et al. 1989). Ingroup formation is associated with differentiation between ingroup and outgroup categories. On attributes where ingroup and outgoup differ, the ingroup is represented in terms of relatively extreme positions in order to enhance the contrast between groups. Group members then accommodate to the perceived ingroup position as an expression of their social identity (see Figure 2.1). Hence, attitudes associated with salient social identities may be more polarized than personal attitudes, even in the absence of communication or direct social influence. Even when members of the ingroup are not present, focusing attention on group performance or group values can lead to extremitization of individual attitudes (Mackie 1986: Experiment 2; Ng and Wilson 1989).

Bases of attraction

In the research literature on interpersonal attraction, liking between two individuals is strongly related to the similarity between them (Byrne 1971; Byrne et al. 1986). People are likely to become friends or lovers to the extent that they perceive that they are similar to each other in preferences, attitudes and values. At this interpersonal level, attraction seems to be a function of the two individuals' personal traits and the degree of match between their individual identities.

On the other hand, research on social categorization and ingroup preference suggests that positive evaluations and liking for other individuals can be induced simply by the knowledge that they share a common group identity. Ingroup members tend to be liked more than outgroup members even when we know nothing about their personal characteristics. In general, we tend to assume that fellow ingroup members are similar to each other, but in this case liking and similarity seem to be a consequence of group formation rather than its cause (Hogg and Turner 1985). As a consequence, **ingroup favouritism** can occur in the absence of interpersonal attraction or its antecedents.

To represent the idea that liking is sometimes based on group membership alone, Hogg (1992, 1993; see also Hogg and Hardie 1991) draws a distinction between idiosyncratic personal attraction and depersonalized **social attraction**. Personal attraction is based on personal identities of the individuals involved, and similarity of personal interests, attitudes and values is the primary basis for this form of liking. Social attraction, on the other hand, is based on preferential liking for ingroup over outgroup members. To the extent that a particular group member exemplifies the characteristics that are distinctive or important to that group, that individual will be socially attractive to other ingroup members, regardless of interpersonal similarity.

Figure 2.2 depicts the distinction drawn by Hogg between personal and social attraction. Because these two forms of attraction have different origins, it is possible to display preference for an ingroup member we do not like very much, and to discriminate against a member of an outgroup even if we like that individual personally. Because of this distinction in sources of attraction, it is possible for groups to work together as cohesive units even when members do not like each other interpersonally, a phenomenon that has been demonstrated in laboratory groups (Hogg and Turner 1985) and in real-life groups such as sports teams (for example Lenk 1969).

Research by Prentice et al. (1994) has also verified the distinction between group identification that is based on direct attachments to the social category and identification based on interpersonal attachments among group members. In studies of various campus groups, they found that members of groups based on common-identity (such as the staff of the school newspaper) were more attached to the group than to fellow group members, whereas members of groups based on interpersonal bonds (such as members of social clubs) were more attached to members of the group overall, and showed a stronger relationship between identification with the group and evaluation of individual group members.

Deprivation and social justice

The distinction between interpersonal relations and intergroup relations is also reflected in the judgements that people make about whether they are being treated fairly or justly. The 'relative deprivation' theory of justice

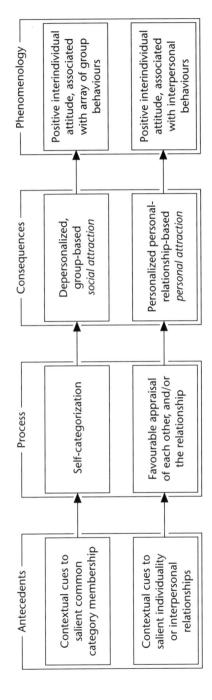

Figure 2.2 A model of personal and social attraction
Source: Hogg (1992: 101). Reproduced by permission of the author and Prentice Hall International, Ltd.

(Davis 1959; Runciman 1966) holds that individuals' perceptions of the fairness of their lot in life derives not from the actual value of their outcomes but from comparisons between what they have and what they expected to have. If I have a lot but expected much more, I will feel unjustly treated. If I have very little but expected little, my outcomes will seem fair. Expected outcomes are determined in part by social comparisons between myself and others. If others have more than I do, I feel deprived. If everyone else is equally deprived, I do not feel so bad. Hence, the experience of deprivation is relative.

A few years ago, India was troubled by a wave of suicides among teenage members of the upper castes in protest against government programmes designed to open more jobs to the poor from lower castes. By objective standards, the Brahmin, Kshatriya and Vaishya upper castes were still doing very well, regardless of programmes designed to benefit the disadvantaged castes; nor were the young people or their families in any personal danger of losing wealth or status. Yet the perception that their own caste was losing position relative to the lower castes created a sense of comparative deprivation that was sufficient to motivate dramatic protest at the cost of individual life.

Incidents such as this led relative deprivation theorists (discussed in Chapter 1) to draw a distinction between perceived deprivation at the personal level and fraternal deprivation (Runciman 1966; Vanneman and Pettigrew 1972). Fraternal deprivation arises from comparisons between the outcomes of one's ingroup as a whole and those of other groups, particularly more advantaged outgroups. Fraternal deprivation is more closely associated with ethnic identification than are perceptions of personal deprivation (Petta and Walker 1992).

What makes the fraternal deprivation concept particularly interesting is the pervasive finding of a consistent discrepancy between perceptions of discrimination among members of disadvantaged social categories at the individual versus the group levels of comparison. Members of disadvantaged groups report high levels of discrimination against their ingroup. However, the same individuals report significantly lower levels of discrimination when asked to indicate whether they personally have been discriminated against on the basis of their category membership (Crosby 1982; Taylor et al. 1990). There is an apparent discontinuity between perceived discrimination at the personal and social levels of identification. But it is discrimination against one's group that is more closely associated with perceived social injustice and desire for social change (Guimond and Dubé-Simard 1983; Walker and Pettigrew 1984; Kawakami and Dion 1993). As a consequence, it is only when individuals are acting in terms of their social identities that they are willing to initiate or participate in collective action in the interests of group welfare (Wright 2001).

Engaging social identities also influences perceptions of social justice and justice motives in general. Recent research provides evidence that group identification limits the scope of people's concerns for distributive justice (Tyler 2001). For instance, Wenzel (2000) found that only East and West Germans who strongly identified with the inclusive category 'German' were likely to apply norms of equality to entitlements of all citizens (east and west) of the country. Similarly, Tyler and his colleagues have found that individuals who are highly identified with a group or organization are more likely to defer to authorities and to be concerned with procedural fairness (Huo et al. 1996; Tyler et al. 1996). And people appear to be *less* concerned about distributive or procedural justice for actions related to outgroups in intergroup contexts than they are in interpersonal contexts (Bruins et al. 1995; Platow et al. 1997). As we shall discuss in Chapter 3, this transformation of the rules of justice or fairness when ingroup identities are activated plays an important role in justifying intergroup discrimination.

Cooperation and competition

Group membership also plays an important role in how individuals respond to others when they are in a situation of mutual interdependence. In socially interdependent situations, each person's outcomes are affected by how the others behave. In Chapter 1 we discussed the different kinds of social motives that individuals might bring to such situations. Most important is whether the individual has a cooperative orientation (where the goal is to satisfy the needs and motives of everyone in the group), or a competitive orientation (where the individual is attempting to maximize their own outcomes relative to the others).

The distinction between cooperative and competitive intentions is particularly critical in what are called 'mixed-motive' situations (Rapoport and Chammah 1965) – relationships in which cooperation between two or more individuals is necessary in order to maximize mutual interests, but where there is also temptation for participants to act competitively in order to serve their individual self-interests. In these situations, if one individual cooperates while the other competes, the competitor comes out ahead and the cooperator loses. However, if both individuals compete, both are worse off than they would be if both cooperated. Thus, competition is a losing strategy in the long run, but cooperation requires trust and concern for the common welfare.

The classic example of a mixed-motive situation is the so-called **prisoner's dilemma**, in which each of two individuals must decide whether to cooperate or compete without knowing what the other will do. The name comes from an anecdote in which two suspected criminals are arrested and placed in separate rooms where they are isolated from each other. Then each is given the following choice: if you confess and the other guy does not, then you will go free and he will be sent to prison for 20 years; if you do not confess but he does, then you will be the one sent to prison and he will go free; if you both confess, both of you will get 10 years in prison. However, if neither of you confesses, you will both get only five years on a reduced charge. Clearly, in this dilemma, the two criminals are best off if they do not confess. But each individual must make this decision without knowing what the other is doing – if one holds out and does not confess while the other one makes a confession, the hold-out will be severely penalized. If there is any element of distrust between the two criminals, both will confess. (This is obviously what the sheriff in this story has in mind!)

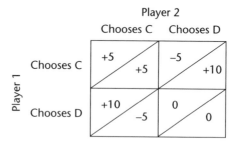

Figure 2.3 The prisoner's dilemma game
Note: Value to the left of each diagonal represents the outcome to Player 1, value to the right is outcome to Player 2.

Social psychologists have turned this choice dilemma into a 'game' situation in which players are faced with the decision represented in Figure 2.3. Choosing C provides the best possible outcomes for both players combined, but choosing D gives each player a chance to win while the other loses. However, if both choose D, both come out worse than if they had chosen C.

Years of experimental research with the prisoner's dilemma paradigm has helped to identify under what conditions pairs of individuals will develop mutual cooperation in response to the dilemma, and when they will 'lock in' to competitive responding in which both lose in the long run (Oskamp and Perlman 1965; Rapoport and Chammah 1965). One factor that seems to influence choices in the dilemma situation is the category membership of the two participants. Even though the players are strangers to each other, if they know that they share some common ingroup membership they are more likely to enter into cooperative responding than if they do not have a shared category membership (Wilson and Kayatami 1968; Dion 1973; Prentice and Miller 1992). Apparently, just knowing that another individual is a member of the same ingroup is sufficient to increase the level of trust and cooperation.

The effect of ingroup membership on cooperative behaviour has been observed beyond the two-person situation. When the prisoner's dilemma is generalized to groups of more than two people, it is known as a **social dilemma** (Messick and Brewer 1983). Social dilemmas are choice situations in which individuals acting in their own self-interest make decisions that lead to collective disaster. Many real-world problems such as conservation of scarce resources, environmental pollution, waste disposal and depletion of the ozone layer are examples of large-scale social dilemmas. In social dilemmas individuals are, in effect, faced with a conflict between their own individual self-interest and collective welfare. In laboratory experiments involving social dilemma choices, group identity has been found to make a significant difference in individual behaviour. When a collection of individuals believe that they share a common ingroup membership they are more likely to act in the interest of collective welfare than individuals in the same situation who do not have a sense of group identity (Kramer and Brewer 1984; Brewer and Kramer 1986; DeCremer and Van Vugt 1999).

Table 2.1 Prisoner's dilemma game: cooperation by individuals versus groups

		Mean no. cooperative plays	Mean joint cooperation	Mean joint competition
McCallum et al.	*Individuals*	13.70	5.57	1.87
(1985) Experiment 1	*Pairs*	7.57	2.07	4.37
McCallum et al.	*Individuals*	14.94	6.25	1.12
(1985) Experiment 2	*Pairs*	9.25	3.37	4.00
Insko et al.	*Individuals*	18.68	9.45	0.21
(1987)	*Three-person groups*	12.77	5.41	3.18
Insko et al.	*Individuals*	19.00	—	—
(1990) Study 2	*Three-person groups*	9.86	—	—

Identification with ingroups, then, can elicit cooperative behaviour even in the absence of interpersonal communication among group members. Within the ingroup category, individuals develop trust and a cooperative orientation toward shared problems. What happens, however, when dilemmas involve two or more groups of individuals? In an important programme of research, Insko and his colleagues have demonstrated a significant discontinuity between individual and group behaviour in social dilemma situations. When two unrelated individuals make decisions in a prisoner's dilemma setting they are much more likely to make cooperative choices than when decisions are made by individuals who represent two different social categories (McCallum et al. 1985; Insko et al. 1987, 1990).

As can be seen in Table 2.1, decisions made by groups are consistently and significantly more competitive than decisions made by lone individuals in the same setting. The same competitive orientation is obtained when individuals make decisions on behalf of, or as representatives of, a social group (Insko et al. 1987). A similar effect has been found in laboratory experiments on social dilemmas. When a collective is divided into distinct subcategories, individuals behave less cooperatively (and are more likely to destroy the collective welfare) than when the group is undifferentiated (Kramer and Brewer 1984).

The clear implication of this research is that social identity has very different effects on cooperation depending on whether the interdependence is within or between social groups. When social identity is salient, individuals adopt a cooperative orientation toward fellow ingroup members and are likely to behave in ways that promote group welfare rather than individual self-interest. On the other hand, they are also more likely to adopt a competitive orientation toward individuals who are members of outgroups, even when they face a common problem (Brewer and Schneider 1990). When individuals interact in terms of their social identities, it makes a big difference whether the situation is an intragroup or an intergroup exchange.

Summary

The evidence from a number of different domains of social behaviour supports a distinction between behaviour motivated by identification with social groups and behaviour motivated by personal self-interest. When a particular group identity is engaged, individuals act in ways that represent and maintain distinctive group characteristics, even when that behaviour is not consistent with individual egocentric motives. On the one side, social identity enhances liking, trust and cooperation toward fellow ingroup members, and actions that promote collective welfare. On the other hand, social identity also engages preferential biases, extreme attitudes and competitive orientation toward members of outgroups – all conditions that promote the likelihood of intergroup conflict.

Thus, motives and behaviours that derive from attachment and loyalty to ingroups have important implications for intergroup relations. Before we turn to intergroup settings, however, we should give some attention to various theoretical perspectives that have been advanced to explain why we become attached to ingroups in the first place.

THEORIES OF GROUP IDENTIFICATION

Human sociobiology

Theories of human evolution must take into account the overwhelming evidence that the human species evolved in the context of group living (Caporael and Brewer 1991). Much of the speculation about species-specific traits and abilities derives from analysis of the survival requirements associated with living in hunter-gatherer societies (for example Buss 1990, 1991). Sociobiological models of the evolution of human social behaviour rest heavily on the notion of inclusive fitness. These models assume that the gene is the basic unit of selection, and that selection favours genes that produce behaviour benefiting anyone who carries those genes, including other individuals who possess the same genes by common descent or kin relationships (Archer 1991).

One implication of this model of evolution is that there is a genetic disposition to behave differentially toward 'insiders' (kin and extended family likely to share common genes) and 'outsiders' (non-kin, outgroups). This idea is the basis for a 'sociobiology of ethnocentrism' (van den Berghe 1981; Reynolds et al. 1987), which holds that ethnocentric behaviour derives from self-interested pursuit of inclusive genetic fitness. Cooperation between individuals will occur only to the extent that they have a high proportion of shared genes, since helping one's close relatives perpetuates one's own genes. Conversely, the likelihood of conflict between individuals or groups of individuals increases as the proportion of shared genes decreases (van den Berghe 1981: 7).

According to the sociobiological view, the primal ethnic group is the small band of 100–200 related individuals, within which the human propensity for cooperative social arrangements is presumed to have evolved.

Ethnocentric preference is extended to larger social groups through the development of 'markers' (skin pigmentation, hair and facial features, mannerisms and so on) which signal genetic relatedness among unfamiliar individuals (Johnson 1986, 1989). One model goes so far as to postulate an evolved 'identification mechanism' that provides for selective attachment to large groups that best promote the interests of the nucleus (kin-based) ethnic group (Shaw and Wong 1989).

Other biological models of ethnocentrism and xenophobia preceded the sociobiological perspective, including ethological theories of territoriality and aggression (for example Eibl-Eibesfeldt 1979). More recently, sociobiological theorizing has been linked to the idea of a genetic predisposition to **social dominance** (Sidanius and Pratto 1999). Collectively, these theories link ingroup formation to ethnocentric aggression and the inevitability of warfare, both of which are discussed further in later chapters.

Psychodynamic theories

Freudian theory departs somewhat from evolution-based biological models in assigning a greater role to experience and development in the origin of ethnocentric identification. Freud's own theory of group identification centred on the role of the group leader as the object of identification (Freud [1921] 1960). Neo-Freudian 'object relations theory' (Klein 1975; Ashbach and Schermer 1987) extended the theory to incorporate all symbolic representations of the group as objects of identification. According to this view, social identity is the product of projection of the self onto external objects and introjection/incorporation of objects into the sense of self.

Freud also coined the phrase **narcissism of minor differences** to refer to the apparent preoccupation of group members with small or trivial distinctions that maintain differentiation between groups (Freud [1912] 1957). Volkan (1988) used this as a basis for a theory of identity formation that holds that individual identity is achieved through a universal process of defining 'allies' and 'enemies'. The process begins in the first few months of life as the infant bonds with the primary caretaker and learns to distinguish familiar others from strangers. This process of we–they differentiation (along with associated affect) continues as a basis for achieving a stable definition of self.

An extension of psychoanalytic approaches to understanding group identity is **terror management theory** (Solomon et al. 1991) which is based on the idea that when human beings evolved the capacity for self-awareness, this included awareness of mortality and the inevitability of one's own death. Given the universal instinct for self-preservation, this awareness creates a high level of anxiety which could lead to paralysing fear if not sufficiently suppressed. According to the theory, human societies have evolved shared worldviews and cultural values as an adaptation to cope with this anxiety over death. By subscribing to this worldview and living up to cultural values, individuals achieve a sense of validation, self-worth and a type of psychological immortality that serves to suppress mortality terror.

One implication of terror management theory is that if thoughts of mortality are made salient, an individual will respond by reaffirming their own cultural worldview, with intolerance toward different values or cultural views. A number of experiments have demonstrated just such a relationship between mortality salience and ingroup bias (for example Greenberg et al. 1992; Harmon-Jones et al. 1996; Nelson et al. 1997). When participants in these studies are induced to think about the prospect of their own death (as compared to other possible negative experiences, such as a painful dental procedure), ingroup preference, intolerance of others, and intergroup bias are significantly increased.

Unlike sociobiological explanations, psychoanalytic theories of group identification assume that self-relevant groups are defined by experience and culture rather than kinship. Nonetheless, the psychoanalytic version of social identity formation is an intensely individual one in that groups are essentially projections of the personal self, a product of individual development and interpersonal experiences. In these theories, social identity is in the service of protecting personal self-esteem and self-concept (see Gaertner et al. 1999).

Social comparison theory

Moving to more truly social psychological perspectives, a classic theory of group formation is provided by Festinger's (1954) social comparison theory of affiliation. Prior to the publication of the formal theory of social comparison, Festinger published an earlier version of the theory which focused on the processes of communication and consensus formation in small groups (Festinger 1950). His purpose in this earlier paper was to explain why members of groups tend to be so similar in attitudes, values and behaviour.

A basic premise of Festinger's explanation was the idea that people need a sense of subjective validity for their beliefs about themselves and the world around them. Much of our knowledge or understanding about the world we live in does not come from direct personal experience. We may come to learn that ice is cold and walls are solid by direct contact with these objects, but much of our knowledge about what is right or true – especially our knowledge about social groups and social behaviours – has no such objective referent. In order to achieve a sense of validation of such beliefs, people engage in **social reality** testing. Beliefs are seen as valid or appropriate when they are shared by similar others, that is by members of appropriate reference groups. The more uncertain an individual is about the correctness of a belief or attitude, the more important it becomes to find consensual support for that belief. Similarity to reference groups induces stability and confidence in one's own perceptions.

The effect of uncertainty on seeking the company of similar others was first demonstrated experimentally in a classic study by Schachter (1959). In this experiment, female students arrived at the research laboratory and learned that their participation would involve receiving a series of electric shocks. In one experimental condition, the participant was reassured in advance that the shocks would be mild and safe. In the alternative experimental treatment, the description of the upcoming shocks was somewhat more ominous. What Schachter was trying to do with these experimental variations was to induce different levels of fear and uncertainty in the research participants. Those who were given reassurances about the nature of the electric shock were assumed to be in a state of low uncertainty and little fear. Those who had been led to anticipate something more severe were assumed to be in a state of relatively high fear and uncertainty about what would happen to them.

At this point in the experiment the researcher explained to the student that it would take about 10 minutes to set up the laboratory equipment and that during that time she could wait in another room. Each participant was given a choice between waiting alone in a separate waiting room, or in a classroom down the hall 'with some of the other girls here' who were participating in the same experiment. As expected on the basis of Festinger's social comparison theory, women in the high fear/uncertainty condition showed more desire to be with others than did those in the low fear condition. Out of 32 participants in the high fear condition, 20 expressed a clear preference to wait with others, whereas only 10 out of 30 in the low fear condition had such a preference.

Schachter believed that uncertainty led to the need to be with others, but only with others who were similar to themselves, facing the same situation. This was demonstrated in a later version of the experiment in which participants, after being put through the high-fear condition, were again given a choice between waiting alone or with others down the hall. But this time, the others were not participants in the experiment but students waiting for an exam. With that option, none of the research participants chose to wait with others. Apparently affiliation to reduce uncertainty is selective – only the ingroup will do.

Agreeing with members of one's ingroup apparently increases certainty and subjective validity of beliefs and attitudes (Darley 1966). Finding out that others disagree reduces certainty – but only if those others are ingroup members. Learning that outgroupers do not share our opinions or values does not shake our confidence in the correctness of those beliefs (Orive 1988). On many issues of values and preferences we expect to agree with ingroup members but not necessarily with everyone. Thus, only ingroup members count as sources of validation, at least for subjective judgements (Gorenflo and Crano 1989). As a consequence of this relationship between ingroup membership and feelings of certainty, ingroup identification increases under conditions of uncertainty and doubt (Hogg 2000).

Social identity and self-categorization theory

Social comparison theory is essentially an interpersonal theory of group formation and attachment. According to such theories, individuals seek similar others to satisfy needs for social reality and self-definition; ingroups are derived from this process of mutual affiliation among individuals. Social identity theory provides an alternative account of group formation and social influence (Turner 1991).

As originally articulated by Tajfel and Turner (Tajfel 1981; Turner 1984; Tajfel and Turner 1986), social identity theory was largely a response to the prevailing interpersonal models of group formation, such as social comparison theory (Hogg 1992). The basic premise of social identity theorists was that ingroup–outgroup distinctions arise from social categorization processes. Accentuation of category differences, combined with a need for positive distinctiveness (**intergroup social comparison**), results in ingroup favouritism. The important point is that ingroup classification precedes rather than derives from interpersonal processes.

Further elaboration of the cognitive underpinnings of group formation and ingroup preference is represented by Turner's **self-categorization theory** (SCT) (Turner et al. 1987). From this perspective, personal and social identity differ in that they represent different levels of abstraction (inclusiveness) for self-categorization. There is, of necessity, a functional conflict between different levels of categorization of the same stimulus situation. Since categorization results in accentuations of similarity within categories (assimilation) and of differences between categories (contrast), the salience of one level of categorization reduces or inhibits perceived similarities and differences at other levels. Thus, self-categorization at the group level (social identity) is incompatible with categorization at the personal level. A shift toward social identity entails a depersonalization of individual self-perception, perceiving oneself as a representative of the ingroup category possessing those characteristics that distinguish the ingroup from relevant outgroups (the self-stereotyping effects cited earlier in this chapter). According to SCT, it is this depersonalization of self-perception that underlies basic group phenomena, including ethnocentrism, cooperation, emotional contagion, and conformity to group norms (Turner 1985; Turner et al. 1987).

Motivational theories of social identification

As a version of social identity theory, SCT is heavily cognitive, emphasizing the categorization processes underlying group identification to the exclusion of most motivational and affective processes (Hogg and Abrams 1993). Other variations of social identity theory accept the basic premise of categorization but add various motivational components to account for the emotional and behavioural consequences of ingroup identification.

Common fate

Jacob Rabbie has criticized social identity theory (and SCT more specifically) for failing to recognize perceived interdependence among individual members of a collective as the defining characteristic of a social group (Rabbie and Horwitz 1988; Rabbie et al. 1989). Perceived interdependence derives from experiencing **common fate**, which Rabbie regards as a precondition for the emergence of group norms, group identification, and shared social identities. In this view, social identity derives ultimately from self-interest, under conditions in which each individual's outcomes are linked to the outcomes of others. Positive interdependence produces cooperation and ingroup formation. Negative interdependence produces conflict and differentiation.

It is not always clear from the experimental procedures that Rabbie uses to induce common fate whether shared outcomes necessarily involve true interdependence. Interdependence means that one person's outcomes are affected directly by the behaviour of another individual in achieving their own outcomes. In a highly interdependent situation such as a team sport, each individual's opportunities and successes are determined in part by the actions of other team members, and the coordination among their actions. However, individuals can share the same outcomes without interdependence in that sense. For example, three people standing at the same bus stop in the rain are experiencing the same fate (getting cold and wet) without their outcomes being in any way determined by the behaviour (or outcomes) of the other group members. If one member of the group chooses to come in out of the rain, this does not affect how wet the others get. Similarly, members of a specific social category may receive the same treatment from some external body without creating interpersonal interdependence among category members. Yet if this kind of common fate can produce ingroup identification – as the results of Rabbie's own experiments suggest it can (Rabbie and Horwitz 1969) – then interdependence is not a necessary condition for group formation. Perceived interdependence may be a product of common fate, rather than its source.

With or without actual interdependence, perceptions of shared interests or common fate do seem to be crucial to the emergence of collective identity. Gurin and Townsend (1986) found that a sense of common fate (perceived common treatment and outcomes as a function of category membership) proved to be the most important predictor of collective orientation in a study of gender consciousness and political activism. And Prentice and Miller (1992) argue that identification can be based on bonding produced by distinctive shared experiences, such as having the same birthday.

Self-esteem

Even more controversial than the issue of interdependence is that of the role of social identity in maintenance of positive self-esteem (Abrams and Hogg 1988; Crocker et al. 1993; Gaertner et al. 1999). There seems little doubt that individuals do derive benefit from their group's successes and achievements, even when that individual has not contributed directly to the group's accomplishment (Cialdini et al. 1976). One experiment found that after sports fans watched a live basketball game, their estimates of their own personal skills were influenced by the outcome of the game. When their team was successful, fans predicted that they would perform better in a later experimental task than when their own team had lost (Hirt et al. 1992). This is consistent with social identity theory's contention that an individual's sense of self-worth is enhanced by positive distinctiveness of their ingroup. In general, individuals have been found to identify more strongly with experimentally created groups that are successful and have high status (Ellemers et al. 1988).

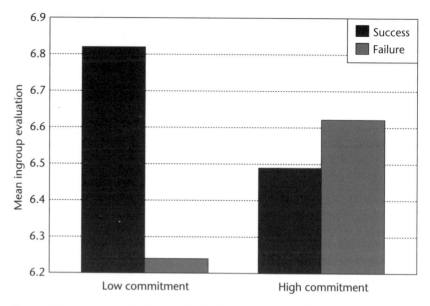

Figure 2.4   Ingroup attachment following success or failure
Source: Turner et al. (1984). Experiment 1.

Findings such as these have led some theorists to conclude that group identification is motivated by the need for self-enhancement. In other words, individuals seek to identify with high-status groups in order to repair or maintain positive self-esteem. However, there is little direct evidence that the need for self-enhancement underlies ingroup identification. For one thing, individuals with low self-esteem do not value ingroups more positively than individuals whose self-esteem is already high – if anything, it is the other way around, with high self-esteem individuals showing greater ingroup identification (Crocker and Schwartz 1985; Crocker et al. 1987).

The self-esteem explanation is further undermined by evidence of strong identification with disadvantaged or low-status ingroups (Crocker et al. 1994; Doosje et al. 1995). Some experimental research indicates that social identification with a group may actually be increased when the group is threatened or stigmatized. Results of an experiment by Turner and his colleagues (1984) demonstrated that when individuals are committed to group membership, ingroup defeat produced even higher levels of ingroup preference than did success (see Figure 2.4).

These results from laboratory experiments parallel findings from field studies of members of disadvantaged or stigmatized groups. Many studies now indicate that identification with such groups is associated with high rather than low individual self-esteem (Rosenberg 1979; Cross 1985; Crocker and Major 1989). Overall, research in this area supports the idea that positive ingroup evaluation and collective self-esteem is the product of group identification rather than its cause.

Self-verification

Apart from enhancement of positive self-esteem, recent theories of self-development postulate a number of other motivational factors that influence the construction of an individual's self-concept. Foremost among these is the need for **self-verification** (Swann 1987), the drive to establish and maintain a consistent, coherent self-image. Abrams and Hogg (1988; Hogg and Abrams 1993) propose that it is this need for self-definition that is the primary movational basis for social identification.

Like Festinger's social comparison theory, this version of social identity theory assumes that group formation ultimately derives from the need to reduce uncertainty. However, instead of interpersonal social comparison as the basis for self-definition, this theory focuses on the role of group consensus as the basis for coherence and subjective certainty. As Hogg and Abrams (1993: 189) put it, 'uncertainty-reduction is an individual motivation, but one that inevitably can only be realized by group belongingness'. This accounts for the strong tendency to polarize representations of the ingroup on dimensions that distinguish it from other groups, and for group members' willingness to conform to group norms and stereotypes in the interests of maintaining intergroup distinctions.

Hogg and Abrams (1993) go so far as to suggest that enhanced self-esteem is a consequence of the uncertainty-reduction achieved through group consensus and social identity. From this perspective, subjective certainty is the primary motive underlying social identification and positive self-esteem is a secondary or derivative motivation. At the level of social identity, self-enhancement and self-verification are not competing motives but aspects of a single motivational process.

Optimal distinctiveness

For group membership to satisfy an individual's need for meaning and coherence, the clarity of the boundary that separates ingroup membership from non-membership becomes particularly important. Therefore, theories based on self-verification call attention to the importance of the distinctiveness of social categories as a factor in group identification. Distinctiveness incorporates both category salience and the exclusiveness of group membership as properties of specific social categories. In a variation of self-categorization theory, Brewer (1991) provided a model of the psychological motives underlying the preference for distinctive social identities.

Brewer's **optimal distinctiveness** theory (ODT) postulates that human beings have two powerful social motives: a need for inclusion which is satisfied by assimilation of the self into larger collectives, and an opposing need for differentiation which is satisfied by distinguishing the self from others. Groups that are exclusive rather than highly inclusive engage more attachment and identification because they satisfy both of these needs simultaneously. Distinctive social identities meet the individual's need for inclusion (intracategory assimilation) while at the same time serving the need for differentiation between self and others (intercategory contrast). According to this model, distinctive social identities should be more satisfying than personal identity as the preferred level of self-categorization.

Experimental evidence in support of optimal distinctiveness theory has shown that when the balance between inclusion and differentiation is threatened, individuals respond by increasing their preference for distinctive ingroups. When participants are made to feel *either* highly different from everyone else *or* that their identity is the same as everyone else, ingroup identification and self-stereotyping increases (Pickett et al. 2002a, 2002b).

Status versus distinctiveness

Optimal distinctiveness theory accounts for the pervasive finding that social identification and ingroup favouritism are greater for members of minority groups than among majority group members (Mullen et al. 1992). This group size effect has been obtained in both laboratory and field studies, although effects in the real world are complicated by the frequent confounding of minority status with other social disadvantages. However, experimental evidence indicates that when the need for differentiation is activated, individuals value minority category membership more than membership in majority groups, regardless of other status differentials between ingroup and outgroup (Brewer et al. 1993).

Because minority size is often associated with disadvantages in status or power, in many contexts group distinctiveness and positive evaluation may be negatively related. Members of low-status minorities may face a conflict between group identification based on optimal distinctiveness and preference for positive social identity. Similarly, for members of stigmatized groups, self-verification of social identity may conflict with the need for self-enhancement. In the study cited earlier by Hogg and Turner (1987), for instance, when categorization by sex was made highly salient both male and female participants accentuated the sex-typicality of their own self-perceptions. However, for females this self-categorization resulted in lowered self-esteem, compared to conditions in which sex categorization was not so salient.

To protect self-esteem, individuals may actively distance themselves from their group identity, at least with respect to those attributes that are contained in the negative group stereotype (Gibbons 1985; Gibbons et al. 1991). On the other hand, negative attributes may have less impact on individual self-esteem if they are perceived as group characteristics rather than distinctive personal traits (Coates and Winston 1983; Crocker and Major 1989). In that case, self-esteem may actually be enhanced by self-stereotyping as a typical group member since it alters the context in which negative traits or experiences are evaluated. Minority group members can embrace their distinctive group identity, but sometimes at the cost of rejecting or defying majority criteria for positive evaluation (Steele 1992).

The conditions under which members of disadvantaged minorities will adopt a strong group identity and commit themselves to collective action on behalf of group interests have long been of concern to social and political psychologists (for example Gurin et al. 1980; Tajfel and Turner 1986; Wright et al. 1990). We shall consider further research and theory on this issue in later chapters.

DO INGROUPS REQUIRE OUTGROUPS?

Discussion of the importance of meaningful intergroup differentiation as a determinant of social identification raises the issue of the social context within which ingroups are defined. Defining what the ingroup is also requires defining what it is not (Allen et al. 1983). As Tajfel and Forgas (1981: 124) put it, 'we are what we are because they are not what we are...' But who constitutes this ambiguous 'they'? Are relevant others limited to members of specific contrasting groups, or could 'they' refer to all other human beings who are excluded from membership in the ingroup?

Both theory and research are ambiguous on this issue of the need for specific outgroups as a factor in ingroup identity. Almost all initial experimental research on social identity was undertaken in the context of specific ingroup–outgroup comparisons, and the notion of 'positive distinctiveness' is usually understood to mean comparisons between the status of the ingroup and specific, relevant outgroups. Ingroup attraction and perceived similarity have both been found to be enhanced when ingroup members are evaluated in the context of salient outgroups (Wagner and Ward 1993). Further, there is evidence that the presence of symbols of an outgroup is sufficient to arouse awareness of ingroup identity (Wilder and Shapiro 1984), demonstrating the reciprocal relationship between ingroup and outgroup salience.

But although specific intergroup comparisons may enhance ingroup awareness, this does not mean that such contrasts are a necessary condition for social identification. More recent experimental work being undertaken with respect to self-categorization theory is exploring the effects of group formation per se, in the absence of any explicit intergroup context (Turner et al. 1987; Hogg 1992). In an earlier review of ingroup bias research, Brewer (1979) suggested that the existence of an identifiable outgroup may not be essential to ingroup favouritism. The perception of common fate and shared distinctiveness may be achievable without reference to specific outgroups, although the presence of outgroups may influence the nature or intensity of affect or emotions attached to ingroup membership. More importantly, the effects of ingroup bias and favouritism may occur in the absence of any hostility or antagonism toward other groups (Brewer 1999, 2001). As we shall see in Chapter 3, preferential treatment of those who are in the ingroup produces biases and discrimination even without any negative prejudices against the outgroup. By the same token, however, some biases and discrimination may be motivated by outgroup hatred, rather than ingroup love. The analysis of such outgroup hostility is the subject of Chapter 4.

FURTHER READINGS

Brewer, M.B. (1991) The social self: on being the same and different at the same time, *Personality and Social Psychology Bulletin*, 17: 475–82. The optimal distinctiveness theory of the motivations underlying group identification.

Crocker, J. and Major, B. (1989) Social stigma and self-esteem: the self-protective properties of stigma, *Psychological Review*, 96: 608–30. A review of the role of group identification in protecting individuals from the negative effects of stigmatization.

Hogg, M.A. and Abrams, D. (eds) (1993) *Group Motivation: Social Psychological Perspectives*. London: Harvester Wheatsheaf. An edited volume of papers on the motivations underlying group behaviour.

Turner, J.C., Hogg, M., Oakes, P., Reicher, S. and Wetherell, M. (1987) *Rediscovering the Social Group: A Self-categorization Theory*. Oxford: Blackwell. A cognitive theory of group identification and self-concept.

THREE

INTERGROUP DISCRIMINATION: WHAT IS JUST TO US IS UNFAIR TO THEM

Key concepts: minimal intergroup situation, discrimination, ingroup bias, intergroup schema, positive distinctiveness, outgroup bias, collective movements

In 1970, high school boys in Bristol, England, took part in a series of social psychological experiments that changed dramatically the future of research on intergroup relations. The experiments, conducted by Henri Tajfel and his colleagues (Tajfel 1970; Tajfel et al. 1971), consisted of two phases. In the first phase, eight boys from the same high school were brought together in a lecture room and told that they would be participating in a study of visual judgement. A series of 40 slides consisting of large clusters of dots were flashed in a screen briefly and participants wrote down their estimates of the number of dots that appeared in each cluster. Their judgements were then collected and taken away for scoring while the researcher explained that some people consistently overestimate the number of dots in this judgement task while others consistently underestimate the actual number.

While the dot estimates were being 'scored', the boys were taken into separate rooms for the second phase of the experiment. At this point they were each assigned a code number (in order to keep their personal identity unknown to others in the session) and then told whether their total number of guesses in the dot estimation task had been among the four highest in the session (the overestimators) or among the four lowest (underestimators). In actuality, these assignments were made randomly. The dot estimation task was used simply to divide the eight participants into two distinctive categories on an arbitrary basis.

The second phase of the experiment consisted of a different decision task involving assignment of monetary rewards or penalties to other participants in the session. Every participant was given a booklet containing 18 pages of allocation matrices. On each page of the booklet there was a

Allocation to:

Ingroup member	18	17	16	15	14	13	12	11	10	9	8	7	6	5
Outgroup member	5	6	7	8	9	10	11	12	13	14	15	16	17	18

Figure 3.1   A choice matrix from the minimal intergroup experiments
Source: Tajfel (1970: 97).

matrix consisting of a series of number pairs, as illustrated in Figure 3.1. The pairs represented alternative allocations of points (worth money), with the upper number going to the person whose group label and code number was indicated on the top row, and the bottom number going to another person whose label and code were attached to the bottom row. Each page of the booklet consisted of such a set of choices for a different pair of recipients.

Now let us consider the decision being made by participants in these experiments when they were called upon to allocate points on behalf of two other individuals. On what basis could such a decision be made? Keep in mind that the decision never involved the decision maker directly (the code numbers always referred to two participants other than the decision maker himself) and he did not know the identity of the two recipients except by code number. Under such circumstances it is generally assumed that the fairest decision rule is to allocate each recipient as close to an equal number of points as possible. In the case of the choice matrix illustrated in Figure 3.1, this would mean selecting one of the options that assigned 12 points to one and 11 to the other (choice no. 7 or 8).

When making allocations for individuals who belonged to the same category (that is, both were labelled 'overestimators' or both 'underestimators') participants did tend to choose the most equal point distribution. However, Tajfel and his colleagues were particularly interested in what would happen in those cases when the two target individuals belonged to different categories (that is, one 'overestimator' and one 'underestimator'). In this case, one of the targets would be identified as belonging to the same category as that of the decision maker (an ingroup member) while the other would be identified as an outgroup member. Under these circumstances, category membership *did* make a difference in allocation decisions. Decision makers consistently deviated from the point of maximum fairness in order to assign more points to the member of their own ingroup. In the first experiment conducted by Tajfel and his colleagues, 26 out of 32 participants gave more points to ingroup targets than to outgroup targets. Rarely did they go so far as to allocate the maximum possible to the ingrouper and the minimum to the outgrouper, but they did deviate significantly from an equal distribution. In the matrix depicted in Figure 3.1, for instance, participants allocated an average of 13 points to ingroup targets and only 10 to outgroup targets.

DISCRIMINATION IN THE MINIMAL INTERGROUP SITUATION

The behaviour of the decision makers in the Tajfel experiments illustrates intergroup discrimination. Fellow participants were treated differently by the decision makers on the basis of their group membership alone. Apparently allocators felt justified in making decisions that discriminated in favour of ingroup members and against outgroup members, even though they did not know anything about the individuals personally. Since 1970, this finding has been replicated in many experiments using different types of allocation matrices and different bases of group categorization (Brewer 1979; Turner 1981; Diehl 1990; Mullen et al. 1992).

The results of the original Tajfel experiments surprised social psychologists because social discrimination was exhibited on such an arbitrary basis. The experimental procedures involve what is called a **minimal intergroup situation**. Participants are classified into separate categories that have no prior meaning (before coming to the research setting, students had never heard of 'overestimators' and 'underestimators'). Further, category members are unknown to each other; there is no group interaction, no history of intergroup conflict; and participants have no self-interest in the allocations they make. Yet they make decisions that discriminate in favour of members of one category over the other.

Prior to the publication of these experiments, most social psychologists had assumed that such discrimination was the result of existing prejudice and hostility that developed over time in the course of intergroup relations. Now we know that intergroup discrimination can be produced by mere categorization into separate groups, in the absence of any history of intergroup contact or conflict. This discovery not only had a profound effect on theories of intergroup behaviour, but also had important methodological implications. More than had ever been realized before, it became clear that important intergroup processes could be studied in the laboratory under experimentally controlled conditions. This greatly enhanced social psychologists' ability to test theories about the processes underlying intergroup discrimination.

Discrimination and the rules of fairness

The thing that is most surprising about the results of the Tajfel experiments is that participants were willing to allocate rewards in a way that favoured one individual (an ingroup member) over another (an outgroup member) without any apparent justification for the inequality. The fact that point allocations in the minimal intergroup situation deviate from equal distribution suggests that ingroup–outgroup distinctions alter concepts of what is 'fair' or 'just' (Messick et al. 1985; Messé et al. 1986; Platow et al. 1990).

Equality as a rule of fairness assumes that individuals are the same in all relevant respects and hence deserve the same outcomes. Other rules of fairness take individual differences into account in determining outcome distributions. The rule of equity, for instance, holds that individuals should receive outcomes proportional to their inputs (Walster et al. 1978). Those who contribute more in terms of abilities or efforts should also receive more, according to the principle of equity. One explanation for the presence of ingroup favouritism in the minimal intergroup situation is that participants assume that members of their own group are higher in ability or aptitude than members of the outgroup (an interesting form of ingroup bias in its own right). Differences in competence provide one justification for awarding somewhat more points to some individuals than others. When groups actually do differ in status or power, the tendency to discriminate in favour of the ingroup is especially strong for members of the higher status or dominant group (Sachdev and Bourhis 1991).

To test the influence of equity considerations in intergroup allocations, some experiments have given participants explicit information about individual differences in performance or contribution at the time allocations are made (Ancok and Chertkoff 1983; Ng 1984; Lerner and Grant 1990). Participants are first divided into two categories and then take part in a task that earns money for the group as a whole. At the end of the experiment they are given the opportunity to distribute part of the earnings between two other members of the group. According to feedback provided about individual contributions to the group task, one of these members was more productive than the other. When the category identity of the two members is not known, participants typically make an allocation in line with equity principles – the more productive member is allocated somewhat more points than the less productive member. When the two group members belong to different social categories, however, the allocation rule is altered. If the more productive individual also happens to be a member of the decision maker's own ingroup, even more is allocated to that individual. The principle of equity is used as a justification for enhancing the ingroup member's outcomes.

But what happens if the ingroup member is less productive than the outgroup member? Does the rule of equity still apply? Apparently not, because in this case participants tend to make more equal allocations between the productive outgroup member and the less productive ingroup member (see Table 3.1). Which rule of fairness is applied seems to be influenced by category membership. If equity can be applied to the benefit of an ingroup member, rewards are distributed differentially. However, if

Table 3.1 Studies of equity in intergroup allocation

	Differential allocation to more productive worker	
	More productive worker = ingroup member	More productive worker = outgroup member
Ancok and Chertkoff (1983)	+1.53	+1.00
Ng (1984)	+3.63	−0.53
Lerner and Grant (1990)	+3.40	+2.00

equity does not work to the ingroup's benefit, allocators shift toward an equality distribution rule. Ingroup bias apparently precedes selection of rules of fairness.

Implications for affirmative action

Both equity and equality are rules of fairness that refer to the distribution of outcomes that results from some system of allocation. It is clear from the findings of experimental studies of intergroup allocations that the use and interpretation of these outcome fairness rules are influenced by ingroup favouritism. When ingroup outcomes exceed those of outgroups, it is apparently easy for group members to justify and accept this differential in terms of some application of equity principles. However, when outcomes favour the outgroup, the same differential is likely to be evaluated as unfair and unjustified – something closer to equality seems more 'fair' in this circumstance.

An interesting experimental test of differences in perceived justice was conducted by Azzi (1992) with students in the USA and South Africa. Participants were given the task of dividing political power between two simulated ethnic groups that differed in size. Some participants were given instructions to identify with, or take the position of, members of the majority group in the simulation, while others were told to identify with the minority. Those representing the majority were more likely to adopt a proportionality rule for the allocation of power and resources, with resources distributed in accord with number of individuals in each group. Those representing a minority group, on the other hand, were more likely to adopt an intergroup equality principle of distributive justice, and this was particularly true for experimental participants who themselves were members of real ethnic minorities.

It is not difficult to extrapolate from these findings why affirmative action policies should be perceived so differently by members of advantaged and disadvantaged groups. The latter are most likely to focus on the pre-existing outcome differentials that favour the outgroup unfairly, and perceive affirmative action as a mechanism for bringing the intergroup outcome distribution closer to equality. Members of the advantaged group, on the other hand, are less likely to see pre-existing differences as unfair but more likely to perceive affirmative action in terms of unfair outgroup advantage. Attitudes toward affirmative action policies are strongly influenced by whose view of fairness one accepts (Nacoste 1990; Crosby et al. 2001).

The positive–negative asymmetry

Although the initial experiments by Tajfel et al. (1971) claimed that ingroup bias in the minimal intergroup situation occurred for allocations of both positive and negative outcomes, subsequent research suggests that when the outcomes to be distributed are negative or harmful, the usual intergroup discrimination may be lessened or may disappear all together. Hewstone et al. (1981) modified the normal paradigm by asking group members to subtract money from ingroup and outgroup recipients. Although some ingroup bias was observed in this context, the levels were lower than those obtained with the standard allocation matrices. Mummendey et al. (1992) extended this finding by asking participants to distribute different durations of an unpleasantly high-pitched tone to ingroup and outgroup members. With harm as an outcome, ingroup bias was generally eliminated and strategies to equalize or minimize the amount of aversive stimulation were observed.

Mummendey and Otten (1998) have suggested that the **positive-negative asymmetry** in intergroup discrimination is explained by normative constaints that make it more difficult to *justify* differential allocations that harm others directly rather than just benefit some more than others. As long as everyone obtains some benefit, it is relatively easy to find justification for why the ingroup might be entitled to benefit more than the outgroup. There is even evidence that such ingroup benefiting is considered normative in its own right (Platow et al. 1995; Blanz et al. 1997). Thus, allocations that favour the ingroup over the outgroup may be motivated primarily by intentions to be a 'good' ingroup member. Inflicting harm, however, is not sanctioned so directly. It is more difficult to justify protecting the ingroup if it comes at the expense of inflicting harm on others (Mummendey and Otten 1998).

SOME POSSIBLE MECHANISMS: REASONS FOR INGROUP BIAS

Once the phenomenon of ingroup bias even in minimal intergroup situations had been well established, social psychologists turned attention to theories about why the bias occurs. One implication of the minimal intergroup findings was that intergroup conflict and competition could not be accounted for solely in terms of the structural relationships between groups, as purported by **realistic group conflict theory** (Sherif 1966a, 1966b; LeVine and Campbell 1972: Chapter 2). Instead, the search was for psychological mechanisms that might account for ingroup favouritism and competitive orientation toward outgroups even in the absence of conflict over scarce resources. Of course, these theories are not intended to explain only minimal intergroup behaviour. The same psychological mechanisms are presumed to underlie ethnocentric biases and discrimination among real-world social groups, where structural factors may also play an important role.

Ethnocentric attributions

One psychological mechanism that sustains different perspectives on fairness is the attributions that are made about the causes of other persons' good or bad fortunes. If an individual performs well or succeeds because of personal effort, ability and integrity, then they are perceived to deserve

positive outcomes. Conversely, if failure is attributed to personal dispositions such as laziness, incompetence or dishonesty, then poor outcomes
are deserved. However, the relationship between behaviour and outcomes
is altered if the behaviour is attributed to external factors, such as caused
by circumstances outside the individual's control. When good performance is attributed to luck or external aid, positive outcomes are not deserved. And poor performance that was caused by bad luck or handicapping
circumstances does not deserve bad outcomes.

Attributions are often made in ambiguous circumstances. It is not
always clear whether behaviour reflects the individual's personal dispositions or is being caused by the situation they are in (Jones 1979), so
causal attributions are often a matter of subjective judgement. The attributions that are made for another person's behaviour can be influenced
by knowledge of the social group to which that individual belongs. In
general, failure and negative behaviours exhibited by an outgroup member are more likely to be attributed to internal, dispositional causes than
the same negative behaviour by an ingroup member (where it is more
likely to be attributed to external or situational causes). Conversely, positive acts and success are more likely to be attributed to internal causes for
ingroup members than for members of an outgroup. As we discussed in
Chapter 1, this ethnocentric pattern of attributions was labelled the 'ultimate attribution error' by Pettigrew (1979); it has been demonstrated in
studies of attributions made by members of different ethnic groups, sports
teams, schools and gender categories (Hewstone 1990).

The ethnocentric attribution bias has also been demonstrated in a laboratory setting using artificial social categories. In an experiment by Weber
(1994), participants were arbitrarily divided into two social categories
(overestimators and underestimators – as in the minimal intergroup experiments). Following an initial phase of ingroup formation, all participants viewed a videotape depicting an interaction between teams of
underestimators and overestimators. At one point in the videotape, the
members of the overestimator team approach the leader of the underestimator team with a request for help. In one version of the tape, the
overestimator responds positively to the request; in an alternative version,
he abruptly and rudely refuses the request for help. Half of the participants saw the positive behaviour version of the tape, and half saw the
negative behaviour version.

After viewing the video, participants were asked to give causal explanations for why the underestimator leader had behaved as he did. Consistent with the intergroup attribution bias, explanations differed depending
on whether the behaviour was positive or negative and whether the actor
was a member of the perceiver's ingroup or an outgroup member. Specifically, the negative behaviour was attributed to internal dispositions when
exhibited by an outgroup member, but the same behaviour was attributed
to external, situational causes when the actor was an ingroup member.
This tendency was particularly strong when overestimators and underestimators were in a competitive relationship with each other. In such
intergroup contexts, negative or hostile behaviours on the part of the
ingroup are perceived as justified by the circumstances and not indicative
of any negative personality traits.

Ethnocentric attributions are a form of ingroup bias in their own right. Ingroup members are given the benefit of the doubt in ways that are not extended to outgroup individuals. These beliefs, in turn, sustain and justify other forms of intergroup discrimination. Intergroup attribution biases serve to justify differential outcomes that favour the ingroup. In effect, ingroups are credited more for successes and positive actions than are outgroups, and are less likely to be held accountable for failures or negative actions. This can explain why ingroup members are rewarded more when they outperform an outgrouper, but the same performance is not rewarded as highly when produced by an outgroup member.

The intergroup schema

In Chapter 2 we described a series of experiments conducted by Insko and his colleagues demonstrating that in situations in which either cooperation or competition is possible, people are consistently more competitive in intergroup contexts than in interpersonal exchanges. Insko and Schopler have suggested several interesting explanations for this so-called **discontinuity effect** (Insko and Schopler 1987; Insko et al. 1990, 1992; Schopler and Insko 1992). The primary explanatory concept is the existence of a 'group schema', learned by individuals through experience in intergroup contexts. (Interestingly, the group schema notion is not too different from an earlier idea raised by Tajfel. In describing the results of the initial minimal intergroup experiments, Tajfel (1970) speculated about a 'generic norm' of intergroup behaviour that prescribed outgroup competition.)

Relative trust

As developed by Insko and his colleagues, the group schema has at least two important components. The first is **schema-based distrust**, the learned belief or expectation that intergroup relations are competitive and therefore the outgroup is not to be trusted and the ingroup's welfare must be protected. Anticipated competition tends to create a self-fulfilling prophesy (Kelley and Stahelski 1970). When one believes that the other party has competitive intent, the only reasonable action is to compete oneself in order to avoid potential loss. Since competition begets competition, the expectancy is confirmed. Indeed, in the Insko experiments with the prisoner's dilemma game, mutual competition is the dominant response pattern in intergroup contexts. This is also consistent with Ng's (1981) equity explanation for intergroup allocation biases. Ng assumes that participants in the minimal intergroup paradigm see themselves in a mutual control situation with an outgroup member, where each jointly determines how much the ingroup and outgroup gets. If participants expect that the outgrouper will make a biased choice in favour of the outgroup, then the individual's own allocations will be biased toward the ingroup in order to maintain equity. In this view, ingroup bias is a strategy for maintaining equity by compensating for anticipated bias on the part of the outgroup.

Schema-based distrust is similar to Campbell's notion of the **universal stereotype** that is attributed to all ingroups vis-à-vis outgroups (Campbell

1967; LeVine and Campbell 1972: Chapter 10). Whatever other content group stereotypes may contain, ingroups are believed to be trustworthy, cooperative, peaceful and honest, while outgroups are perceived to be untrustworthy, competitive, quarrelsome and dishonest. These stereotypes, according to Campbell (1967), have a 'grain of truth' because they reflect the individual's actual experiences with ingroup and outgroup members. Since internal relations within groups are characterized by loyalty and favouritism toward fellow group members, individuals experience their own group as cooperative and friendly. However, encounters with outgroup members involve external relations, which are less cooperative and more suspicious. Hence the perception that outgroupers are quarrelsome and untrustworthy (even though those same outgroup individuals may be perfectly friendly and trusting in intragroup contexts).

In a test of the universal stereotype conducted as part of a survey study of intergroup attitudes among ethnic groups in East Africa, Brewer and Campbell (1976) found that 27 out of 30 ethnic groups rated themselves as more positive on these traits than any of 29 outgroups. In an experimental test of the schema-based distrust hypothesis, Insko et al. (1990) found that group discussion preceding intergroup prisoner's dilemma play was characterized by frequent references to the potential untrustworthiness of the other group, and that there was a strong negative correlation between the amount of recorded distrust during discussion and later cooperativeness in prisoner's dilemma games. Further, groups more than individuals chose withdrawal from play when that option was made available, where withdrawal indicates fear that the other player will compete.

The idea that intergroup encounters are more competitive than interpersonal encounters because they are associated with learned distrust is interesting and well supported, but somewhat circular. If we approach intergroup encounters competitively because we have learned that intergroup contexts are competitive, how did the competitiveness get started in the first place? If we look at Campbell's analysis of the universal stereotype, it is clear that the trust–distrust perception is a product of ingroup favouritism rather than its cause. What this suggests is that competition and distrust are the universal 'default' expectations applied to strangers in general (Insko et al. 1998), but put aside in the case of interpersonal relationships within ingroups. In other words, it is not so much that we learn to distrust outgroups but that we have come to trust the ingroup.

Furthermore, anticipated distrust does not account fully for biased allocations in favour of ingroup members. Allocations that discriminate in favour of the ingroup have been obtained even when respondents are led to expect that the outgrouper plans to make a fair/equal allocation (Diehl 1989), and when the participant alone has full control over the final outcomes (Platow et al. 1990). These findings indicate that ingroup favouritism is motivated by something more than fear of the outgroup.

Relative gain

The second aspect of Insko's 'group schema' concept is that intergroup contexts are associated with different social motives, or social values, than interpersonal exchanges. More specifically, intergroup relations entail a shift from maximizing the absolute value of one's outcomes to the goal of maximizing the relative value compared to the outcomes of another. To understand the difference between an absolute and relative gain orientation, consider the following choices among distributions of outcomes:

Outcomes to	Choice A	Choice B
Self/us	12	9
Other/them	14	7

If one's goal is to get as much as possible for oneself or one's group, then Choice A is the preferred option. From this perspective, Choice B makes no sense because we wind up with less value than we get from Choice A. However, with Choice A, the other person or group gets even more than we do. If we value our outcomes relatively, this is not satisfactory. From this perspective, Choice B is the preferred outcome because our outcomes are higher than the others' outcomes. Choosing B involves sacrificing total outcomes for the sake of getting more in comparison to the other. With a relative gain orientation, all exchanges are competitive because both players cannot achieve the goal of maximizing relative gain at the same time. If I win, you lose, and vice versa.

Results of experimental studies confirm that people are more concerned with relative gain when choosing on behalf of their group than as individuals (Insko et al. 1992). Moreover, individuals with a strong cooperative (joint gain) value orientation do not exhibit significant allocation biases in intergroup settings (Platow et al. 1990). The importance of relative gain orientation as a factor in intergroup discrimination is consistent with several other explanations for ingroup bias, as discussed below.

Positive distinctiveness and self-esteem

Social identity theory, at least in its early formulations (for example Turner 1975; Turner and Brown 1978), placed a heavy emphasis on **social competition** for positive distinctiveness as the basis for ingroup bias. Biased allocations in the minimal intergroup situation were interpreted as an attempt to create a positive advantage for the ingroup over the outgroup, thus enhancing the ingroup's value in comparison to that of the outgroup. The minimal intergroup situation was particularly suited for eliciting such biases because of the absence of any pre-existing value differences between the artificially created social categories. With no positive distinctiveness already inherent in the categorization itself, participants take advantage of the allocation task to create a positive differential in favour of the ingroup over the outgroup. This interpretation is bolstered by experiments demonstrating that discrimination is even greater when the outgroup is similar to the ingroup, rather than dissimilar on dimensions such as attitudes or interests (Diehl 1988; van Knippenberg and Ellemers 1990). Presumably, there is less need for establishing positive distinctiveness relative to outgroups that are either already distinctly different or not directly comparable to one's own group.

As an explanation for ingroup bias, the positive distinctiveness hypothesis rests on two basic assumptions. The first is the assumption that group evaluation is based primarily on intergroup social comparison. On most dimensions of evaluation, the intrinsic value of the group's outcomes or position cannot be assessed except in comparison to the position of other groups on the same dimension. Hence, the positivity of the ingroup depends on its standing relative to comparison outgroups so that relative gain orientation dominates evaluations in intergroup settings.

Second, social identity theory assumes that positive distinctiveness serves the more fundamental need for a positive self-esteem in the form of a positive social identity. This has been interpreted by some researchers to mean that ingroup evaluation derived from comparisons at the intergroup level has direct implications for personal self-esteem at the individual level. (See Chapter 2 for further discussion of this point.) If this is the case, then the underlying motive for discrimination in favour of ingroups over outgroups is to enhance personal self-esteem.

Research on the role of self-esteem in intergroup discrimination has taken two different directions. One line of research investigates whether discriminating in favour of ingroups and against outgroups has the effect of enhancing global self-esteem (Oakes and Turner 1980; Lemyre and Smith 1985). Other researchers have focused on the question of whether low self-esteem motivates ingroup–outgroup discrimination (Wills 1981; Crocker and Schwartz 1985; Brown et al. 1988).

The fact that self-esteem can be investigated both as cause and effect of discrimination leaves the overall relationship between self-esteem and ingroup bias somewhat ambiguous (Abrams and Hogg 1988; van Knippenberg and Ellemers 1993). As an effect, the relationship between discrimination and resultant self-esteem should be a positive one. As a cause, the relationship is assumed to be negative, with low self-esteem leading to more discrimination. Results of research on both directions of effect are equivocal (Abrams and Hogg 1988; Rubin and Hewstone 1998), but in general there is more evidence that ingroup favouritism enhances self-esteem than there is that low self-esteem individuals are more prone to discrimination than those high in self-esteem. In fact, if anything, it is those who are high in personal self-esteem who show greater ingroup bias (Hogg and Abrams 1990; Crocker et al. 1993; Aberson et al. 2000).

Two important distinctions in the self-esteem literature can help to clarify the otherwise murky research findings on self-esteem as a cause of intergroup discrimination. The first involves recognizing the difference between high or low self-esteem as a general, chronic characteristic of an individual's overall self-concept (trait self-esteem) and temporary loss or threat to self-esteem caused by experiences of embarrassment or failure (state self-esteem). Most of the research demonstrating a relationship between low self-esteem and discrimination has involved an experimental manipulation of temporary, state esteem. For instance, Cialdini and Richardson (1980) found that college students who had been told they performed poorly on a test of creativity rated their own university more highly and a rival university more negatively than did students who had been given more positive feedback.

In a different experimental context, Meindl and Lerner (1984) manipulated participants' self-esteem temporarily by rigging an accident. At the beginning of the experimental session, the researcher asked the participant to retrieve a missing chair from a next-door office. The chair was arranged in such a way that when the participant moved it, a large stack of computer cards spilled in disarray on the floor – computer cards that contained essential data from a graduate student's dissertation research. Following this incident, the participants (who were all English-speaking Canadians) took part in an attitude survey in which they were instructed to respond as members of the English-speaking majority in Canada. The survey included a series of questions on the 'Quebec issue', in which respondents were asked to express attitudes toward French-speaking Quebec. Participants who had just experienced the esteem-lowering accident expressed significantly more negative attitudes towards French-speaking Canadians than did those who had not had such an experience.

Such experiments support the idea that favouring ingroups or derogating outgroups relative to the ingroup may serve to restore self-esteem when it has been threatened or temporarily lowered. Moreover, recent findings in the self-esteem literature indicate that it is individuals with generally high self-esteem who are most likely to engage in self-enhancing social comparisons when their positive self-image is threatened or damaged (Taylor and Brown 1988). When self-esteem is positive and secure, high self-esteem individuals may not show much propensity to exhibit intergroup discrimination and instead value both ingroups and outgroups positively. However, when self-esteem is threatened, it is high self-esteem individuals who are most likely to respond by enhancing ingroups relative to outgroups (Brown et al. 1988). It is those who think positively of themselves in general who are most likely to be able to subscribe to the belief that their ingroup deserves favourable advantage.

A second important distinction is that between personal self-esteem and collective self-esteem (Crocker and Luhtanen 1990; Luhtanen and Crocker 1991, 1992). Most of the research linking self-esteem and intergroup discrimination has assessed self-esteem at the level of the individual, personal self-concept. Yet if one subscribes to the distinction between personal identity and social identity, it is not at all clear that self-esteem derived from evaluations of the individuated self-concept should be the same as that derived from evaluations of the ingroup. Attempts to measure collective self-esteem separately from private self-esteem indicate that self-esteem at the two levels are positively correlated, but only moderately so (Luhtanen and Crocker 1992). It is likely that collective self-esteem is more closely related to ingroup bias than just personal self-esteem (Rubin and Hewstone 1998).

Threats to intergroup distinctiveness

The optimal distinctiveness theory of social identity discussed in Chapter 2 suggests that group members are concerned not only with the esteem in which their ingroups are held but also with the extent to which the ingroup can be clearly *differentiated* from other groups. Positive evaluation is less meaningful if it is not also distinctive. Although membership in a majority group may hold advantages with respect to power and resources, it has disadvantages with respect to identity needs. This helps to account for why members of small, distinctive groups tend to show more ingroup bias than members of large majority groups (Mullen et al. 1992; Simon et al. 2001). If majority group members are less identified with their ingroup, they have little basis for ingroup bias. This idea is supported by findings that members of majority groups *do* exhibit ingroup bias when identification has been increased (Leonardelli and Brewer 2001). When ingroup identification is high, discrimination provides a way of increasing intergroup differentiation and distinctiveness between the majority ingroup and minority outgroups.

The desire for distinctiveness means that heightened intergroup similarity poses a potential threat to ingroup integrity. When an outgroup is perceived to be too similar to the ingroup, bias and discrimination serve to restore differentiation (Roccas and Schwartz 1993; Jetten et al. 1996, 1997). On the other hand, when the outgroup is found to be highly similar to the ingroup, ingroup–outgroup boundaries may disappear. Jetten et al. (1998) found evidence of a curvilinear relationship between intergroup difference and discrimination in both laboratory and natural groups. Bias was strongest against an outgroup that was similar to, but still distinct from, the ingroup. Bias was relatively low when ingroup and outgroup were either very similar or very dissimilar.

Intergroup status and power differentials

The importance of intergroup comparison and differentiation highlights the fact that social groups are embedded in multi-group networks or social systems. Many such social networks are organized hierarchically, with some groups accorded more status and power than others. In fact, Sidanius (1993; Sidanius and Pratto 1999) has gone so far as to argue that hierarchical arrangement is a universal characteristic of all intergroup structures. Where such structural relationships do exist, psychological needs such as self-esteem and positive distinctiveness will interact with enduring power and status differences between groups to determine the degree of intergroup discrimination and the form that it takes (Hagendoorn 1995).

Experimental studies of **intergroup power** and status differentials that have been conducted in laboratory settings support the contention that these aspects of intergroup relationships play an important role in moderating intergroup bias and discrimination.

Status

In early versions of social identity theory, status differentials are critical to understanding intergroup relationships (Tajfel and Turner 1986). According to this view, the goal of intergroup discrimination is to achieve or maintain status differences in favour of the ingroup, a goal activated in any context where particular ingroup–outgroup distinctions are salient and attended to (Abrams 1985).

The focus on positive status differences as the motivation for intergroup discrimination raises many of the same issues as those related to self-esteem. On the one hand, high-status ingroups may sustain and justify discrimination against lower-status outgroups on equity grounds. On the other hand, groups that have already achieved positive status differentials should have less need for intergroup discrimination and low-status ingroups may exhibit greater disrimination in the interests of redressing unfavourable status differentials.

As with self-esteem, the findings from research on the relationship between ingroup status and intergroup discrimination are mixed. In a meta-analysis of a large number of laboratory studies, Mullen et al. (1992) found that, overall, members of groups that had been accorded high status exhibit greater ingroup bias than those assigned to low-status conditions (see also Sachdev and Bourhis 1987, 1991). However, this status effect is qualified by important factors related to the nature of the status differences between groups and the way in which discrimination is measured.

Discrimination on the part of high-status groups is related to the relevance of the dimension of discrimination to the nature of the status differences (van Knippenberg and van Oers 1984; Mummendey and Simon 1989). In general, individuals tend to exaggerate differences between groups on those dimensions of evaluation that are favourable to their own group, but to minimize the difference when the comparison is not so favourable to the ingroup (Brewer 1979; Spears and Manstead 1989). As a consequence, there is a consistent interaction between the status of the ingroup and the status-relevance of the dimension of discrimination as determinants of ingroup bias (Mullen et al. 1992).

In experimental studies of intergroup status effects, the experimenter usually introduces status differentials by providing feedback that members of one social category generally perform better than the other category on some dimension of ability, competence, or creativity. Not surprisingly, then, members of the higher status group tend to show strong ingroup bias on evaluations of competence and creativity, while the lower status group members show little or no ingroup bias on these dimensions. Similarly, members of the higher status group discriminate more in allocations to ingroup over outgroup when the allocations are seen as related to group differences in competence or ability (Sachdev and Bourhis 1987, 1991).

On other dimensions of evaluation, however, which are irrelevant to the nature of the status difference between groups, differences between high- and low-status groups in the degree of ingroup bias are eliminated or reversed. When evaluating groups on traits such as likeability, friendliness, and cooperativeness, members of both high- and low-status groups rate their ingroup more positively than the outgroup (Sachdev and Bourhis 1991). In fact, on these dimensions low-status groups often show greater ingroup favouritism than high-status groups (Mullen et al. 1992; Brewer et al. 1993), possibly as compensation for unfavourable ingroup comparisons on status-relevant dimensions. When members of lower status groups are committed to their group identity, they express ingroup bias in those domains where the ingroup can be compared favourably to the higher status outgroup.

Power

In intergroup contexts, social power can be defined as the degree of control that one group has over its own fate and that of outgroups (Jones 1972). Based on this definition, the allocation task used in the minimal intergroup experiments can be seen in terms of assignment of power to determine the outcomes (fate) of group members (Ng 1982a). When members of both groups are given allocation choices, the groups have mutual power (mutual fate control). When allocation decisions are made by members of only one of the social categories, that group has unilateral power (fate control).

In experiments where allocation power is assigned independently of status differences between groups, members of high power and equal power categories discriminate more against outgroups than do members of low power groups (Sachdev and Bourhis 1985, 1991). Intergroup discrimination is particularly high on the part of high-power minority groups (Sachdev and Bourhis 1991). Groups with unilateral power discriminate as much as or more than groups that share mutual fate control, indicating that discrimination in favour of the ingroup is not just a defensive reaction to outgroup power (Diehl 1990).

As Sachdev and Bourhis (1991) point out, power is a necessary condition for effective discrimination. Members of low-power groups may prefer allocations and status differentials that favour their ingroup, but without fate control over both ingroup and outgroup their preference will not be expressed in actual allocations. One explanation for why low-status groups show little ingroup bias on status-relevant dimensions is that they feel powerless to affect or redress the status differential between groups. When low-status groups are given unilateral power to control allocation outcomes, they do show significant ingroup favouritism (Cole and Bourhis 1990; Sachdev and Bourhis 1991).

Effects of instability

When experimenters assign status and power differentials to experimentally created social categories, those differences are usually assumed to be stable and legitimate. Both dominant and subordinate groups can be expected to respond differently when the status system is perceived to be unstable or subject to change. Clear-cut, stable intergroup status relations tend to reduce the salience of intergroup comparisons, but instability in the status hierarchy enhances comparison salience and intergroup discrimination on the part of both high- and low-status groups (Tajfel and Turner 1986; van Knippenberg and Ellemers 1990).

Tajfel and Turner (1986) distinguish three different ways in which status relationships among groups may be subject to change. These are the perceived **permeability** of group boundaries and the perceived *stability* and *legitimacy* of the status differences between groups. Permeability refers to the extent to which group members can expect to be able to move from one group to another, or shift their social identity, on an individual basis. According to social identity theory, under conditions of high permeability members of lower status groups will tend to prefer membership in the higher status outgroup and seek social mobility as a strategy for improving positive social identity (van Knippenberg and Ellemers 1993). Experimental studies have confirmed that manipulations of perceived permeability interact with **group status** to affect ingroup identification. Members of low-status groups express more dissatisfaction with their group membership and less ingroup preference when group boundaries are permeable rather than impermeable (Ellemers et al. 1988). However, when individuals could potentially change their group affiliation (high permeability), members of high-status groups increase their commitment to their current group membership. Under the risk of losing their attractive group membership, members of permeable high-status groups express significantly stronger ingroup identification than when group membership is fixed (Ellemers et al. 1992).

Permeability creates instability of group membership but does not necessarily alter the status relationships between the groups as a whole. More important for social identity is the perceived stability or security of the status or dominance hierarchy itself (Tajfel and Turner 1986; Sidanius 1993; van Knippenberg and Ellemers 1993). When status differentials are perceived to be unstable or illegitimate, members of lower status groups exhibit significantly stronger ingroup identification than when status relationships are stable (Caddick 1982; Ellemers et al. 1990). Although perceived injustice at the personal level often motivates individuals to dissociate from low-status ingroups, perceived collective injustice enhances group identification and efforts to improve the status position of the group as a whole (Taylor et al. 1987; Wright et al. 1990; Ellemers et al. 1993).

At the same time, perceived instability of the status hierarchy threatens the positive distinctiveness of high-status groups. In experiments manipulating both group size and group status, discrimination in intergroup allocations is particularly high for minority high-status groups (Mullen et al. 1992). Sachdev and Bourhis (1991) argue that this is because when the dominant group is in the minority, the status structure is inherently more unstable than when the majority is dominant. Secure status differentials may reduce the salience of intergroup comparisons and discrimination, but insecurity heightens the motivation to maintain status distinctions on the part of high-status group members. Thus, conditions of social change increase the motivation for intergroup discrimination for groups in all positions of the dominance hierarchy.

Reverse discrimination and outgroup bias

Although discrimination that favours the ingroup over outgroups is by far the dominant pattern in intergroup relations, the existence of power and status differentials between groups provides the context in which outgroup bias can also occur. Discrimination that favours an outgroup over the ingroup is particularly interesting because it seems to violate the universality of ethnocentric bias and the drive for positive distinctiveness (Hinkle and Brown 1990).

Outgroup bias is most frequently discussed in connection with members of low-status or disadvantaged groups. In both experimental and field studies, low-status groups have been found not only to exhibit less ingroup bias than high-status groups but sometimes to favour the outgroup over the ingroup (Mullen et al. 1992). Examined more closely, however, this effect is found to occur almost exclusively on status-relevant dimensions of evaluation (Mullen et al. 1992; Brewer et al. 1993). Considering this factor, the effect should probably not be labelled a 'bias' at all. Instead it reflects acknowledgement of outgroup superiority on consensually defined status dimensions. To the extent that members of low-status ingroups minimize the degree of outgroup superiority, this minimal outgroup discrimination can be a form of ingroup bias (Brewer and Campbell 1976). Further, when consensual support for status differences between groups is removed (when they are perceived to be unstable and illegitimate), outgroup bias on the part of low-status groups disappears, even on status-relevant measures (Turner and Brown 1978; Levin et al. 2002).

As an indicator of ingroup identification, outgroup favouritism on status-relevant dimensions on the part of low-status group members is ambiguous. On the one hand, it may reflect dissociation from the low-status ingroup and true preference for and identification with the higher-status outgroup (as discussed earlier in the case of permeable intergroup boundaries). On the other hand, it may simply reflect a strategic response to the dominant group in the face of secure status and power differentials (Ellemers 1993: Ellemers et al. 1999). What has to be looked at is how low-status group members evaluate ingroup and outgroup on status-irrelevant dimensions. If members are dissociated from their ingroup and seeking social mobility, outgroup preference should be exhibited on all dimensions. If outgroup favouritism is strategic, it should be limited to status-relevant dimensions while members express ingroup identification and favouritism on other measures. Most often, low-status ingroups do show ingroup bias on status-irrelevant dimensions (Mullen et al. 1992; Brewer et al. 1993), but this is moderated by the perception of permeability of intergroup boundaries (Ellemers et al. 1988).

Further supporting the strategic explanation of outgroup favouritism is the finding that relative bias on status-relevant and status-irrelevant dimensions is reversed on the part of high-status group members. When status differentials are secure and legitimate, high-status groups show most ingroup bias on status-relevant measures and less ingroup preference – and sometimes outgroup favouritism – on irrelevant dimensions (Bettencourt et al. 2001). When outgroup favouritism is exhibited by members of high-status, dominant groups, it is referred to as **reverse discrimination**, suggesting that it is motivated by a desire to compensate for existing status inequities.

In some cases, reverse discrimination may reflect a value conflict between preservation of status differentials that favour the ingroup on the one hand, and egalitarian values on the other. The more a behaviour is recognized as discriminatory, the more a member of an egalitarian society will 'bend over backwards' not to exhibit such behaviour toward members of a disadvantaged group (Dutton 1973). When individuals who wish to believe they are unprejudiced are made aware of discriminatory behaviour, they deliberately avoid it, sometimes demonstrating reverse discrimination in the process.

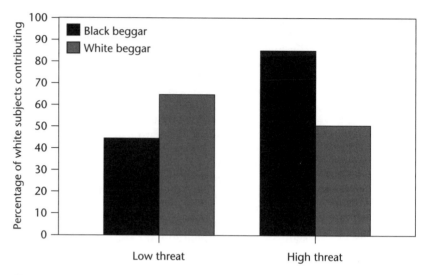

Figure 3.2 Contributions following threat to one's self-image as a non-prejudiced person
Source: Dutton and Lake (1973).

This is well illustrated by the results of a study by Dutton and Lake (1973) in which white students who rated themselves as not racially prejudiced took part in what they believed to be an experiment on autonomic responses. In the course of the experiment, electrodermal activity and pulse rate of the participant was allegedly monitored as they watched a series of slides of social scenes, which included some scenes of interracial interactions. Feedback on their autonomic response was provided to participants as they viewed each slide, presumably an indication of the degree of negative arousal they experienced in response to each. For half of the participants, the false feedback provided in response to the interracial scenes was neutral, indicating no negative arousal. But for the remaining viewers, the feedback indicated they were experiencing high arousal, suggesting that they had unconscious racial prejudice.

When participants had completed this experiment, the researchers arranged that they would be approached as they left the laboratory by a black or a white beggar who requested spare change for food. Participants' response to this request was significantly affected by the race of the confederate and the feedback they had just received. Those who had received neutral feedback about their responses to interracial scenes were somewhat more likely to help and to give more money to a white than a black beggar. But when students had been threatened by evidence of their own prejudice, their reactions were reversed and they gave significantly more to the black than to the white confederate (see Figure 3.2). By the same token, when members of high-status groups give favourable ratings to low-status groups on evaluations unrelated to the status differential, they may be doing so to avoid seeing themselves as prejudiced or discriminatory.

Reverse discrimination on the part of high-status group members may also be a case of a more general 'magnanimity' effect studied by

Mummendey and her colleagues (for example Mummendey and Schreiber 1983, 1984; Mummendey and Simon 1989). Results of this research indicate that social groups seek positive distinctiveness on dimensions that are defined as important to ingroup identity and differentiation from outgroups. Once favourable comparisons have been achieved on important dimensions, ingroup bias is less likely to be exhibited on unimportant dimensions. Outgroup favouritism (magnanimity) is most likely to be displayed on dimensions of comparison that are important to the outgroup, but unimportant to the ingroup (Mummendey and Schreiber 1984; Mummendey and Simon 1989). This strategy allows both groups to be seen as 'better,' just in different ways. (Of course, this does not work so well for dimensions that are important to *both* groups.)

Mummendey and Schreiber (1984) point out that biases which favour the outgroup in unimportant comparisons may be an indirect or subtle form of justifying ingroup favouritism on important dimensions. Such magnanimity may be a particularly important strategy for high-status groups as a form of appeasement of lower-status groups, in the interests of preserving the stability of the overall status hierarchy (Sidanius 1993). When the power of the dominant group is reduced or threatened, high-status groups exhibit much less intergroup discrimination (Ng 1982b; Sachdev and Bourhis 1991), possibly to avoid further instability of status relationships.

Figure 3.3 provides a schematic representation of variations in the degree and direction of intergroup discrimination as a function of status differences between ingroup and outgroup, and the perceived stability of those status relationships. The expression of ingroup bias depicted for each condition represents the interaction between ethnocentric preferences and loyalty to the ingroup, on the one hand, and strategic considerations dictated by the group's position in the dominance hierarchy, on the other.

Summary

The initial experiments with the minimal intergroup situation demonstrated that ingroup–outgroup categorization alone can produce intergroup discrimination, even in the absence of pre-existing structural relationships between the groups. However, the experiments reviewed in these last sections indicate that the degree of ingroup bias, or the form that it takes, are clearly influenced by the introduction of meaningful differences between groups in resources, status, or power. When these contextual factors are brought into play, the expression of ingroup bias may reflect strategic considerations, as well as perceptual and emotional processes (Ellemers 1993; Ellemers and Barreto 2001).

SOCIAL IDENTITY AND COLLECTIVE MOVEMENTS

Research on status and power differentials between social groups gives rise to questions about when and how members of a social category

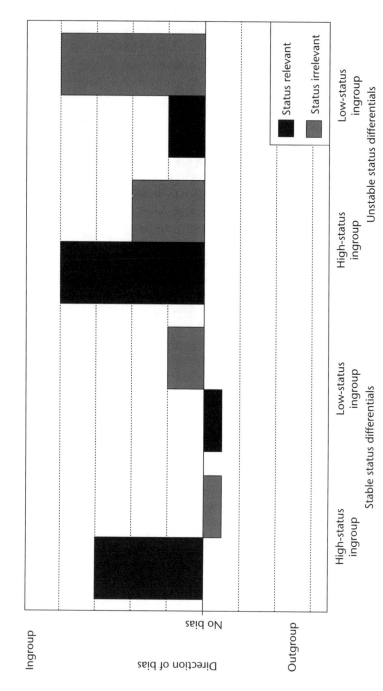

Figure 3.3 The joint effects of ingroup status, stability and dimension of evaluation on degree of ingroup bias

– particularly members of low-status or relatively disadvantaged social groups – will engage in collective action to change the existing status relationships within a given society. Theories of social identity, social comparison and relative deprivation (see Chapter 1) all suggest that members of lower-status groups will be discontented with the resources and valuation attached to their collective identity and will be motivated toward social change. Yet it seems to take a great deal more than perceived discrepancies and status differentiatials to mobilize collective action.

In reviewing the options available to members of low-status social categories for achieving positive distinctiveness, Tajfel and Turner (1986) distinguished three different avenues of response to negative social identity, each with different implications for collective movements:

- *Individual mobility*: with this option, individuals dissociate themselves from the lower-status ingroup and seek identification with the higher-status outgroup. This route to achieving positive social identity is most likely in social systems characterized by permeability of group boundaries and high opportunity for upward social mobility.
- *Social creativity*: group members may achieve positive distinctiveness by redefining the bases of intergroup comparison, choosing new dimensions on which the ingroup can be assigned higher values than relevant outgroups, or changing the valuation attached to existing comparisons. The 'black is beautiful' movement in the United States is an example of this latter strategy. This option essentially leaves the social relationships between groups unchanged, but alters the implications for group self-esteem.
- *Social competition*: finally, low-status group members may seek to change the structure of intergroup dominance and status differentials by engaging in direct competition with higher-status outgroups. The research on instability and legitimacy reviewed above suggests some of the conditions under which the motivation for social change will be aroused. However, there are a number of psychological barriers that seem to work against collective mobilization for social change, even under conditions where relative disadvantage is evident at the intergroup level.

The perception of illegitimate relative disadvantage depends on individuals making comparisons at the intergroup rather than interpersonal levels. When personal identities, rather than social identities, are made salient, individuals are less likely to perceive relative disadvantage or to engage in collective action (Kawakami and Dion 1993; Kelly and Breinlinger 1996).

In a conceptual review of the psychology of *entitlement*, Major (1994) outlined three important factors that influence the choice of targets of comparison for members of disadvantaged groups. First is the proximity or availability of comparison groups in the immediate environment. When social categories are geographically or occupationally segregated (as is the case in most status-differentiated systems), intergroup comparisons are less salient than intragroup comparisons within the disadvantaged group itself. A second factor is the preference for making comparisons with similar others, those who are perceived as relevant targets of comparison for purposes of self-evaluation. The greater the status dissimilarity between one's own social category and outgroup categories, the less relevant comparisons between the self and members of those categories are likely to be. Finally, comparison targets are influenced by the motivation underlying social comparison in the first place. To the extent that individuals are motivated to achieve positive social comparisons, they will avoid contrasting themselves with those much more advantaged than themselves and prefer comparisons with less advantaged others. All of these factors converge to bias disadvantaged group members toward interpersonal, intragroup social comparisons rather than intergroup comparisons with better-off outgroups.

Another important factor in motivating social change is the availability of perceived *social mobility* as an alternative mechanism for achieving positive social status. If members of disadvantaged social groups believe that they have the possibility of moving, individually, into higher-status categories, the motivation for collective action may be diffused. Of particular importance here is the potential role of *tokenism* as a subtle but powerful force in maintaining status structures. Even a small number of highly visible representatives of disadvantaged categories who 'make it' into the advantaged statuses may preserve the perception of social mobility as a viable option. The impact of token representation on group behaviour has been demonstrated in laboratory experiments by Wright et al. (1990).

In order to study the effects of tokenism in a laboratory context, Wright and his colleagues first developed a framework for categorizing the possible responses available to members of a disadvantaged group and then designed an experimental paradigm to determine which responses were most likely to be chosen. The response alternatives included five broad categories of behaviour:

- acceptance of the disadvantaged position
- attempting individual upward mobility through normative means
- individual counter-normative actions
- collective actions through normative means
- counter-normative collective action.

Participants in the experiment were placed in a decision-making group with initially low status, but with the promise that performance on the decision-making task could potentially earn them 'promotion' to the higher-status category. (Members of the high-status group were eligible for participation in a $300 lottery, while those in the low-status group were relegated to chances of winning a $30 lottery.) Participants were then given a decision-making test, and feedback on the results of the test were used to create different experimental conditions. Of particular interest were conditions in which the participant's performance was allegedly sufficient to qualify for the high-status category, but where access to entry in that category was restricted. In the 'closed' condition, participants were told that a panel of high-status group members had decided not to allow any of the low-status group into membership, regardless of performance. In the 'partially closed' condition, participants were told that 30 per cent of the qualified low-status group members would be admitted, and the participant themself was denied admission. Finally, in the 'token' condition, only 2 per cent of the low-status category members were permitted access to the high-status group.

After receiving this information on the basis of their being denied access to the high-status category, participants were asked to rate their preferences among the five response options designated by the researchers. Available options were

- accept the decision
- write an individual protest
- request an individual retest
- request a retest for the whole group
- organize a collective protest.

Participants in the partially closed condition responded to their disadvantage by accepting the outcome or seeking individual mobility (the personal retest). By contrast, those in the closed condition were most likely to endorse collective action. However, participants in the 'token' condition did not seek collective means of redress. Instead, they were more likely to prefer individual action, either normative or counter-normative, that did not involve collective mobilization.

Results such as these support the idea that it takes more than the perception of unfair disadvantage at the group level to motivate collective movements (Gurin et al. 1980; Wright 2001). A more elaborate theory of the psychological and structural conditions required for collective behaviour is the five-stage model of intergroup relations developed by Taylor and McKirnan (1984) and Taylor and Moghaddam (1994). The stages of the model are outlined in Figure 3.4. Note that although the model starts with recognition of stratified intergroup relations, it suggests that members of the disadvantaged strata (particularly the elite representatives of those groups) must move through various individualistic orientations before the stages of consciousness-raising and collective action are reached.

The five-stage model integrates aspects of social identity theory with research on collective movements to describe conditions under which intergroup comparisons, perceptions of social justice, and the need for positive distinctiveness will converge to lead members of disadvantaged groups to seek social change. As discussed previously in this chapter, however, members of advantaged social categories are likely to respond to collective mobilization that threatens existing status structures with increased social identification, as well. Thus, the conditions of social change are also those most likely to engender intergroup conflict, distrust and heightened discrimination.

CONCLUSIONS

In this chapter we have reviewed the effects of intergroup comparison on attitudes and behaviour towards ingroup and outgroup members. Overall, the results of research in this area suggest that social competition, relative deprivation and social instability are enhanced by making comparisons between groups salient, and these are all factors that contribute to intergroup discrimination and conflict. However, the studies reviewed in this chapter suggest that ingroup bias and discrimination are often motivated

Figure 3.4 The five-stage model of collective behaviour
Source: Taylor and Moghaddam (1994: 142), reprinted by permission of
Greenwood Publishing Group, Inc. copyright 1994.

by positive favouritism toward the ingroup (being a 'good' ingroup member) rather than by any direct antipathy or hostility toward outgroups (Brewer 1999, 2001). Thus, intergroup discrimination is constrained when there is no direct motivation to harm or derogate the outgroup. These are the constraints that are lifted when outgroups are viewed with hatred or contempt – emotions that justify outgroup harm above and beyond ingroup benefit. Yet outside of the laboratory, the world is full of evidence of the existence of such self-justified harm toward outgroups, even at great costs to the ingroup. A desire for positive distinctiveness can account for preferential hiring of ingroup members over outgroup members and for selective investment in projects that benefit one's own group over others. But wars of conquest, pogroms and ethnic cleansing require explanation that goes beyond that of achieving positive distinctiveness for the ingroup. In Chapter 4 we turn attention to social psychological research that is focused directly on prejudice and hate toward outgroups.

FURTHER READINGS

Abrams, D. and Hogg, M.A. (1988) Comments on the motivational status of self-esteem in social identity and intergroup discrimination, *European Journal of Social Psychology*, 18: 317–34. A review and critique of the role of self-esteem as an explanation for intergroup discrimination.

Brewer, M.B. (1979) In-group bias in the minimal intergroup situation: a cognitive-motivational analysis, *Psychological Bulletin*, 86: 307–24. A review of the early experimental studies employing the minimal intergroup situation.

Schopler, J.W. and Insko, C.A. (1992) The discontinuity effect in interpersonal and intergroup relations: generality and mediation, in W. Stroebe and M. Hewstone (eds) *European Review of Social Psychology*, Vol. 3. Chichester: Wiley. A review of the research documenting the difference in competitive orientation evidenced in interpersonal compared to intergroup situations.

Tajfel, H. (1970) Experiments in intergroup discrimination, *Scientific American*, 223(2): 96–102. The original report of ingroup bias in the minimal intergroup situation.

FOUR

OUTGROUP PREJUDICE: NEGATIVE AFFECT AND HOSTILITY

Key concepts: prejudice, intergroup affect, aversive racism, aggression, intergroup emotions

In the aftermath of the attack on the World Trade Center in New York City by al Qaeda terrorists on 11 September 2001, the question that was raised all across the USA was 'why do they hate us so much?' The idea that people are emotionally attached to their ingroups and give preference to ingroups over outgroups is understandable (if not always acceptable) to most people. But the kind of antipathy toward another group that could lead to an unprovoked attack on anyone in the population apparently requires further explanation. The difference between ingroup love and outgroup hate is apparent when individuals are willing to engage in behaviour that harms the outgroup without any apparent benefit to the ingroup.

Although (as we have reviewed in Chapter 3) ingroup favouritism can lead to discriminatory behaviour that disadvantages outgroups, it is not necessarily motivated by hostility toward the outgroup. In fact, intergroup discrimination is significantly reduced if negative outcomes are involved (Mummendey et al. 1992). In most cases, it is easy to justify benefiting one's own group more than others, but harming others is not so readily accepted. Based on these findings, Mummendey and Otten (2001) have differentiated among three different types of intergroup discrimination:

- **mindless ingroup favouritism**: discriminatory bias that arises from automatic positive evaluations of the ingroup, without much thought or attempt to justify the differential benefits
- **ambivalent discrimination**: differential treatment that is inconsistent with explicit norms of equality and fairness but rationalized by beliefs and stereotypes so as to be justified
- **intentional discrimination**: deliberate differential treatment (usually negative toward an outgroup) that is perceived to be normative and deserved.

The difference between the second and third types of intergroup discrimination is the difference between 'subtle prejudice' against outgroups and more overt or 'blatant prejudice' (Pettigrew and Meertens 1995; Pettigrew et al. 1998). In this chapter we shall focus particularly on the role of affect and emotion in creating and justifying both forms of outgroup prejudice.

INTERGROUP AFFECT AND PREJUDICE

Since the mid-1960s, the dominant approach to understanding reactions to outgroup members has focused on cognitive process, with a particular emphasis on how we attend to, interpret and remember information about outgroups or members of outgroups (see Devine et al. 1994). More recently, however, interest has begun to shift toward affective and emotional responses, in an attempt to understand how cognition is affected by other internal states such as negative and positive mood, emotions, and levels of anxiety or arousal. As elegantly stated by Hamilton and Mackie (1993):

> contemporary thinking about cognition and affect emphasizes a more integrative relationship between these two systems. Cognition has its impact on affect by constituting the appraisal processes that regulate the social and cultural interpretation of experienced emotion. At the same time, affect has its effects on judgments and behavior through its impact on cognitive processes. Affect activates motivations or goal states, which in turn influence the extent and nature of further processing. In addition, arousal level and affective states influence what information is attended to and what contents will be activated from memory, thereby exerting control over the raw material that becomes the grist for the information processing mill. Thus, affect and cognition are mutually interactive components of a broader system.
>
> (Hamilton and Mackie 1993: 4–5)

Figure 4.1 presents a model depicting this interplay of cognition and affect as determinants of outgroup attitudes. Note that cognition and affect mutually influence one another, as well as having effects on attitudes and behaviour toward the outgroup. Note too that situational factors are shown as moderating the effects of cognitions and affect on these attitudes and behaviour. In this section, we shall review some of the social psychological research illustrating different aspects of this model and its implications for intergroup aggression.

The effects of arousal and mood on responses toward the outgroup

Physiological arousal can tax cognitive resources. In the early days of experimental psychology, Easterbrook (1959) proposed that an increase in arousal causes selective attention toward the most salient cues in a situation. This restricted, selective attention has the effect of altering interpretation

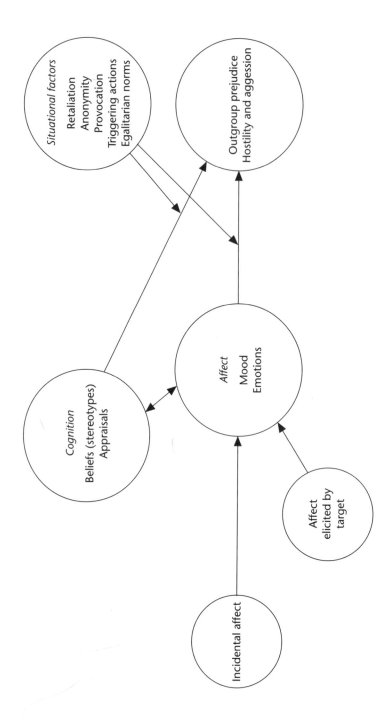

Figure 4.1 A theoretical model of the interrelationships among cognition, affect and situation as determinants of outgroup orientation

of the total situation. In social situations, arousal and the concomitant narrowing of attentional focus can increase reliance on stereotypes, which may lead one toward negatively biased inferences based on incomplete information.

Imagine, for instance, that two college friends are walking toward campus to take an exam. Eddie is in a neutral mood, but Steve is in a highly aroused state because he does not feel well prepared for the important exam he is about to take. As they walk, a black man, running quickly, bumps Steve slightly. A moment later the friends hear the sound of a police siren. Two policemen approach and explain that a silent burglar alarm has sounded in the building the friends had just passed. They query the two, asking if they saw anything suspicious. Steve, who is agitated, tells the policemen of the black man, wearing dark clothing, who ran by a moment earlier. Focusing on this limited information, the policemen look to Eddie for corroboration. Recall, however, that Eddie was unaroused and therefore had more cognitive resources for noticing not only the central cues relevant to the man and the situation, but also the details, or the peripheral cues. He remembers that the man was wearing a navy blue business suit and tie, was carrying an expensive looking attaché case, and seemingly was running to catch a bus that had just pulled away before he could reach the bus stop. Eddie's unaroused (or neutral) state allowed him to attend more carefully, and to process and remember the peripheral cues that, in this case, might have considerably lessened the suspicions of the police.

Experiments show that the source of the arousal – whether it is physical or psychological – is irrelevant in producing these effects. Stereotypic processing can be increased even from arousal that is produced by recent physical exertion. Kim and Baron (1988) demonstrated this in an experiment involving stereotypes of occupational groups. Four sets of adjectives were selected that were rated as characteristic of each of two occupations: librarians (practical, wise, serious) and airline cabin crew (comforting, modern, stylish), along with a set of neutral adjectives that were not associated with either stereotype. Using these 16 adjectives, the researchers created sentences, each of which described a woman by her first name, gave her occupation, and gave two other trait adjectives. No two adjectives were paired together more than once, nor were two adjectives that had been judged as characteristic of the same occupation paired together in any one sentence. Thus, a typical sentence read, 'Sue, a librarian, is wise and stylish.' Note that 'wise' is part of the librarian stereotype, but 'stylish' is part of the cabin crew stereotype.

Level of physiological arousal was manipulated in this experiment by having half of the participants exercise on a stationary bicycle prior to reading the sentences. Then all participants read the full set of sentences (presented for five seconds each with a slide projector) and were asked to estimate the frequency with which adjective–occupation pairs occurred within the sentences. Those in the high arousal condition were not only less accurate in their frequency estimates of the adjective-occupation pairs that were presented, but in their errors they overestimated the frequency of occupation-consistent (stereotypic) traits.

The anxiety often associated with being among outgroup persons (Stephan and Stephan 1985) provides another source of arousal that might influence perceptions. We tend to feel uncomfortable in strange settings. We feel apprehensive when we are unsure about what will happen next, and strangeness or unfamiliarity is often a precursor of anxiety. Because we are less familiar with outgroup persons, imagining or being with them is likely to trigger anxious thoughts (Wilder and Shapiro 1989a) which, in turn, limit cognitive processing and enhance stereotyping.

Incidental affect and affective priming

Bodenhausen (1993) distinguished between two sources of emotional arousal that can be elicited in intergroup situations. When emotional responses are aroused directly by actual or anticipated contact with outgroup members, the arousal is labelled **integral affect**, because it is inherent in the contact situation itself. When the source of emotional arousal is not directly related to the intergroup contact but caused instead by other factors that are unrelated to category membership, it is termed **incidental affect**. Emotional arousal of both types has been found to influence the course of intergroup interactions.

Incidental affect biases ingroup–outgroup interactions by limiting the cognitive resources that are available in the situation. In addition, however, the valence (positive or negative) of the affect is important. Numerous studies provide evidence of **affective priming**, or mood-congruency effects in which mood facilitates responses that match the valence of one's mood and inhibit those that oppose it in valence. For instance, when judging an interviewee in a videotaped interview between an employer and a job applicant, participants induced to be happy, as compared to those made sad, will see more positive and more skilled behaviours, but also, fewer negative and unskilled behaviours. These effects are particularly consistent in studies of social judgements (Forgas 1990; Bower 1991) and in the learning of mood congruent information (Bower 1981).

In accord with affective priming effects, if one approaches a social interaction while in a bad mood, attention toward negative (as opposed to neutral or positive) aspects of the situation is increased (Higgins and King 1981), and more negative information is noticed, processed and available to influence the valence of attributions and actions. Stereotypes about outgroups most often are predominantly negative, and consequently lead to expectations that are likely to organize our interaction with a previously unknown member of the outgroup in ways that promote hostility, rejection or conflict. Our negative stereotypes will lead us to expect negative behaviours from that stranger. Thus, it is not surprising that interactions with an outgroup member can often go badly. What is important with respect to the role of incidental negative affect, however, is that even if that stranger approaches us with positive intentions, the effect of a negative mood acts to increase the likelihood that we shall interpret that person's ensuing behaviour as confirming our negative expectations – the friendly intention can be seen as evidence of pushiness; the inquisitive interest, as nosiness; or the reserved and tactful approach, as snobbishness and insincerity. In other words, whatever the form that the truly positive intentions of the outgroup stranger may take, their manifestations in his or her behaviour can readily be interpreted negatively (Campbell 1967).

In addition to the effects just described, some negative mood states, such as sadness, increase attention toward self (Carlson and Miller 1988). Such inward focus further acts to limit available cognitive capacity for unbiased information processing. This means, for example, that if one is in a sad or depressed state and is evaluating in a short period of time an array of well-qualified prospective employees, each of whom presents substantial relevant background information, the information-processing needed for an unbiased evaluation will be impaired. This will increase reliance on stereotypic information linked to the social category memberships of the applicants.

In sum, a negative mood biases perception in two ways. First, it takes up valuable cognitive resources. This effect occurs independently of whether the evaluated individual is an ingroup or an outgroup member (Griffitt 1970; Gouaux 1971; Veitch and Griffitt 1976). Second, it directs attention to negative aspects of the situation. But in the case of an outgroup target, negative stereotypic beliefs are more likely to be available and called upon when attention is occupied by one's negative mood (Stangor and Ford 1992) and, moreover, the same stereotypic trait can be evaluated more negatively when the perceiver is in a bad mood (Esses et al. 1994).

But what about the effects of incidental positive feeling states on perceptions of group characteristics? Though less consistent, such studies yield findings similar to those for negative feeling states. Happy participants, too, show more evidence of stereotyping than those in a neutral mood, particularly with respect to negative group attributes (Isen and Daubman 1984; Mackie et al. 1989). In the minimal intergroup situation discussed in Chapter 3, putting participants in a positive mood prior to the allocation task has been found to increase ingroup bias (Forgas and Fiedler 1996).

If we assume that happiness primes positive feelings, why should this effect obtain? Like other forms of arousal, happiness uses precious cognitive resources. One needs to pay attention to one's good mood in order to maintain it (Wegener and Petty 1994). Again, this limits the breadth of cues that one uses in order to understand or evaluate other persons and situations. Thus, the effect is similar to others that limit our cognitive capacity. It causes more superficial information processing and, thereby, greater reliance on categorization and stereotyping. If we assume that discrimination in the minimal intergroup situation is often of the 'mindless ingroup favouritism' variety, these findings are consistent with the idea that positive affect reduces thoughtful processing and increases reliance on simple biases.

Integral affect

It is also important to consider the consequences of emotion that is elicited as a direct result of contact with members of the outgroup. For some outgroups, difference in and of itself is likely to invoke negative affect. That is, strangeness or unfamiliarity may produce a negative feeling state even in the absence of negative conditioning, negative affective priming, or prior negative outcomes with members of that outgroup. For example, it has been found that white infants at the age of 4 to 24 months show more frequent anxious-avoidant responses to black, as opposed to white, strangers (Feinman 1980). Additionally, as strangers move closer to the infant, anxiety increases more if the stranger is black. In the same study these white infants showed more receptive or welcoming responses to white, as opposed to black, strangers. This and other studies suggest that a primitive type of person categorization separates persons who are similar and familiar from those who are different or strange.

Automatic affect

The capacity of a salient outgroup to elicit negative affect and associated negative cognitions was shown in an interesting series of studies by Dovidio and his colleagues. In one study (Dovidio et al. 1986) white subjects saw brief flashes of the word 'white', 'black' or 'house' on a video screen. Subjects were then asked to think about the typical black person, white person or house. Then, they were asked to indicate separately for each adjective in a series, whether it could or could not ever truly characterize the initially presented categories. Thus, for each adjective, subjects first saw one of the three category primes and were then presented with a test adjective. The test adjectives consisted of positive and negative words that had been pretested as being stereotypically characteristic of the two racial categories. For instance, practical and musical were among the positive words for whites and blacks respectively, whereas stubborn and lazy were among the negative adjectives for each group respectively.

The speed with which the white subjects pressed a computer button indicating whether an adjective could ever be characteristic of the category showed that the cue 'white' facilitated the processing of positive traits that were part of the white stereotype, whereas 'black' facilitated the processing of negative traits comprising the black stereotype. These results showed that when an outgroup category is made salient, it facilitates the processing of affectively negative, but not positive material that is consistent with the stereotype of that outgroup. In other studies Dovidio and his colleagues produced similar results (Perdue et al. 1990). Priming or cueing with an ingroup designator ('we') produced more positive associations than did an outgroup designator ('they'). Using a somewhat different priming task, Fazio and his colleagues have found that exposure to black facial photographs facilitates responding quickly to subsequent negative adjectives and inhibits responding to positive adjectives, in comparison to response following exposure to a white face (Fazio et al. 1995). As we discussed in Chapter 1, this type of automatic negative affect has been used as a way to assess unconscious prejudices (see Wittenbrink et al. 1997).

The implication of these experiments with automatic evaluations is that for many individuals, the mere appearance of an outgroup member may arouse negative affect that may influence subsequent perceptions without the individual being consciously aware of the affect itself. Taken together, these findings suggest that outgroup status in and of itself, and in the absence of the experience of prior negative consequences, induces integral affect that is negative in valence. Moreover, this process often takes place outside of conscious awareness.

Intergroup anxiety

As previously suggested, researchers have noted that **intergroup anxiety** is a frequent consequence of outgroup contact (Stephan 1992; Stephan and Stephan 1993). For example, a woman walking into a work setting consisting of six men is likely to be very aware of her own outgroup and minority status, as well as the social category distinction between herself and the others in the setting. Consequently, she is likely to be somewhat anxious. Though she may be unaware of psychological studies which show that men, in fact, do tend to interrupt speakers more frequently than do women (Eakins and Eakins 1978), she may nevertheless be sensitive to that issue. She may hold the stereotypic view that males are harsh on females in business, and fear that they will evaluate her negatively and discount her ideas. Her discomfort and anxiety may be even higher if her previous experiences with other all-male groups has also been negative. Stephan and Stephan (1985) posit that the anxiety experienced in anticipation of interaction with an outgroup member has the same cause as other types of anxiety, that is, anticipated negative outcomes for oneself.

There are several reasons why anxiety might be elicited in anticipation of, or during intergroup contact. For instance, the ingroup member may be aware of cultural differences between self and other, as when Dutch nationals interact with Turks (Dijker 1989). Often, one does not know how to behave when confronted with such differences. When Americans interact with Japanese, they are likely to feel embarrassed by the bowing behaviour of the Japanese, not having learned what is appropriate in response to it. Further, familiarity with the customs and ways of one's culture and unfamiliarity with those of the outgroup often result in judgements of moral superiority of the ingroup relative to the outgroup (Sande et al. 1989). This, in turn, is likely to result in feelings of distrust regarding the intentions of the outgroup (Schopler and Insko 1992). In line with the previously discussed tendency to attribute one's own attitudes to others, this feeling of distrust is likely to be projected onto the outgroup, further augmenting existing feelings of anxiety because one assumes that if I distrust them, they too must distrust me. Additionally, as Pettigrew showed in the mid-1970s, the prejudiced behaviour of whites toward blacks in the southern part of the USA was to a substantial degree a manifestation of conformity to community norms (Pettigrew 1975). Consequently, when manifesting positive behaviour toward members of the outgroup, concern about ingroup rejection can be another source of anxiety.

As previously indicated, higher levels of anxiety, along with other states of affective arousal, occupy our limited cognitive resources and cause more superficial information processing. In turn, this fosters a greater reliance on stereotyping and categorization, and a less detailed and thorough view of each individual. Anxiety causes assimilation of judgements about the members of social categories, amplifying the ordinary tendency to minimize differences within categories (Stroessner and Mackie 1993;

Wilder 1993a). Likewise, anxiety amplifies the characteristic tendency of accentuation of differences between categories (Wilder 1993b).

Ambivalence/amplification

Another potential source of integral affect experienced in intergroup contact situations is emotional ambivalence associated with arousal of negative affect in situations where positive attitudes are desirable. The theory of **ambivalence amplification** (Katz and Hass 1988; Hass et al. 1991) refers to a complex motivational state that applies particularly to the relation between a dominant, politically powerful group (such as whites in the USA) and a less powerful or disadvantaged minority group (such as blacks). It emphasizes the conflict between egalitarian values and anti-pathy toward the outgroup. On the one hand, whites hold pro-black feel-ings that stem from the endorsement of egalitarianism and fairness as societal values and they simultaneously perceive that blacks are disadvan-taged. Concomitantly, these same whites possess anti-black feelings that arise from early socialization and stereotypes, including the perception that blacks deviate from the traditional cultural values, such as the Protes-tant work ethic. In turn, these ambivalent feelings motivate exaggerated evaluations of blacks.

According to the ambivalence-amplification model, in comparison with how whites respond to other whites, their conflicting feelings about black Americans lead them to evaluate them more extremely – either more extremely positive or more extremely negative, depending on the situ-ation. Thus, when a black individual and a white individual exhibit the same positive behaviour, the black will be evaluated more positively than the white; conversely, a black behaving negatively will be evaluated more harshly than a white who behaves in that same manner. And the more strongly a white American simultaneously holds these conflicting motives toward blacks, the more extreme these evaluations will be.

Aversive racism

The ambivalence associated with internal conflicts between egalitarian values and negative affect toward outgroups plays a role in a number of theories of prejudice and racism. In 1991, survey data in the USA, for instance, supports the view that white Americans' attitudes toward black Americans has become more accepting (Schuman et al. 1997). In 1989, within the National Research Council, the Committee on the Status of Black Americans concluded that, 'white attitudes concerning black–white relations have moved appreciably toward endorsement of principles of equal treatment' (Jaynes and Williams 1989: 155–6). This emphasis on egalitarian values typically exerts pressure on members of the dominant group to behave in a non-prejudiced manner toward members of the disadvantaged group. However, theories of 'aversive' (Gaertner and Dovidio 1986), 'modern' (McConahay and Hough 1976; McConahay 1986), 'sym-bolic' (Sears 1988; Sears and Funk 1991), or 'regressive' racism (Rogers and Prentice-Dunn 1981) argue that there is a conflict between egalitarian values and the antipathy toward outgroup members that is caused by the many processes that we have discussed, such as accentuation of group differences, the ultimate attribution error, the processing of and attention to stereotype consistent information, incidental and integral affect, and outgroup status as a prime for negative affect.

Simply stated, **aversive racism** is the tendency of white respondents in the USA to mask overt expression of prejudice toward black Americans. Among the propositions of aversive racism (Gaertner and Dovidio 1986, 2000) is that the salience of egalitarian values influences the expression of racial bias. When the salience of egalitarian values is high, there will be no overt display of racial discrimination. When it is low, discrimination may appear, particularly in subtle forms. According to the model, prejudice influences behaviour via an indirect process whereby the race of the other person enhances the salience of elements in a situation that would justify or rationalize a negative response to that individual. In interactions between ingroup and outgroup members, then, egalitarian values may typically exert pressure to behave in a non-prejudiced manner. However, when there is a justifying cause that can rationalize a negative response, that will legitimize negative behaviour toward outgroup members, resulting in amplified negative responses and prejudice that is not recognized as such by the actor.

For example, in an experiment conducted by Frey and Gaertner (1986), white participants were put into a situation in which they had to decide whether or not to give help to another individual in a task involving forming words from anagrams. After the participant and their partner had been working on the task for a while, the participant received a note from the partner requesting help to form enough words to win valuable bonus points. The person requesting help was either black or white, and the experiment varied the reason why this individual needed assistance. In one condition, the partner needed help because they had been assigned a particularly difficult set of anagrams (more difficult than the participant's own task), and although they had been working hard at it, had not been able to form enough words to win the bonus points. In another condition, the partner had a relatively easy set of anagrams but had been playing around rather than working at the task and had not formed enough words.

Consistent with aversive racism theory, when the partner had worked hard and was clearly deserving of help, participants helped a black or a white partner equally – almost 100 per cent gave help in either case. However, when the partner was not so deserving (and the appropriateness of helping was more unclear), participants chose to help a black partner significantly less often than when their partner was white (30 per cent versus 90 per cent). When the situation made helping clearly appropriate, no discrimination was evident. But when the requirement to help was more ambiguous, whites could feel justified in withholding help from an outgroup member while still maintaining a nonprejudiced self-image.

Another explanation for the consequences of ambivalence or aversive racism is that conflict of values affects resources available for cognitive processing. Devine (1989), for instance, argues that because prejudicial responses are well learned from early childhood, two processes are necessary for suppression of prejudiced behaviour: first, inhibition of automatically

activated negative stereotypes and second, activation of 'controlled information processing' that makes salient those associations that are consistent with egalitarian values. Thus, circumstances in which egalitarian values
are salient will allow an individual to inhibit negative associations and
behave in a manner consistent with them. If, however, either time or processing capacity are limited or constrained, biased behaviour emerges as
a consequence of over-learned negative racial associations. This suggests
that biased behaviour can occur unintentionally, even in one who sin-
cerely embraces egalitarianism.

In these models, it is the circumstance that determines the overt expression of racial bias. Thus, to inhibit the expression of outgroup hostility
circumstances must clearly promote the salience of egalitarian values.
Factors that serve this function include moral and religious exhortation to
extend egalitarian principles to outgroups of all types; media emphasis on
the inappropriateness of displaying ethnocentric attitudes; and endorsement of egalitarian attitudes by high-status persons such as teachers,
political and business leaders, and parents. It is not enough simply to
suppress negative responses toward outgroups. Instead, negative attitudes
and beliefs must be replaced by competing, positive value systems.

AFFECT AND AGGRESSION

In the research discussed to this point, the key dependent measures have
been perceptions and evaluative judgements, or decisions whether to help
or benefit another individual or not. More potent forms of prejudice
involve the expression of overtly hostile or harmful behaviour that is
exhibited in the context of face-to-face interaction. Experimental studies
of aggression provide an opportunity to examine hostile behavioural effects induced by outgroup status in social interaction settings. Often such
studies have employed the *teacher–learner paradigm*, which typically pro-
ceeds as follows.

Two participants enter the laboratory. Unknown to the true subject,
however, the other participant is not an actual experimental participant,
but a confederate of the experimenter. Allegedly, the experiment concerns
the effects of punishment on learning. A coin is tossed, and the real participant is assigned the role of 'teacher' while the confederate takes the role
of 'learner'. The teacher then receives instructions on how to control the
duration and intensity of the electric shocks that they will deliver to the
learner when the learner makes errors. Sometimes the participant receives
a small shock from the experimenter, ostensibly 'to have direct experience
with the sensation', which serves to augment the credibility of the setting.
The confederate is then connected or strapped to the (bogus) shock ma-
chine and given a task to learn. The experimental instructions require the
teacher-participant to deliver a shock each time the learner makes a mis-
take, but the participant is free to select both its intensity level (from an
array of shock buttons) and the duration for which it is depressed.

In this paradigm, shock intensity is interpreted as an expression of direct
(blatant) aggression against the confederate, whereas shock duration is

thought to reflect indirect (subtle) aggression in that participants receive no instruction about duration and are less aware of the degree to which they vary the duration of the shocks they apply to the learner across trials.

Factors that moderate the expression of direct and indirect aggression

Although outgroup members receive higher levels of aggression than ingroup members in some studies (for example Donnerstein and Donnerstein 1978), further experiments have isolated several variables that interact with group membership to affect the level of aggressive responding. Specifically, potential consequences of aggression, such as threat of retaliation, anonymity, and the potential for future censure are key factors. Depending on the circumstance, these factors may work to either exacerbate or inhibit the expression of aggression toward outgroup members. Interestingly, however, manipulation of these same factors often has no effect on the expression of aggression expressed toward ingroup members.

Consequences for aggressing

In some experiments, the threat of retaliation was manipulated by telling participants at the start of the experiment that the roles of teacher and learner would be reversed after the first learning task (Donnerstein et al. 1972; Donnerstein and Donnerstein 1973, 1975). Whereas threat of retaliation had little effect on the expression of aggression by white subjects toward other ingroup members, when aggression toward outgroup members was measured, retaliation influenced the type of aggression expressed. Under the threat of retaliation, white male subjects expressed less direct aggression toward black males than toward ingroup members, but at the same time, they expressed higher levels of indirect aggression toward outgroup members.

Anonymity

Manipulating anonymity and censure produces an interaction similar to that produced by threat of retaliation (Donnerstein and Donnerstein 1973, 1978). Specifically, when white participants believed they were identifiable or threatened with the potential for future censure, they expressed less direct aggression toward black targets in comparison to white targets, but, as in the retaliation studies described above, they expressed more indirect aggression. In an anonymous condition, however, these results were reversed. As with the results of previous studies, these same variables did not affect the expression of aggression toward ingroup members. Taken together, these data imply that although anti-outgroup hostility may in fact be present, it is expressed only when certain prerequisite conditions for its inhibition are absent. That is, threat of retaliation, lack of anonymity, and threat of future censure, all inhibit the direct, but not the indirect, expression of aggression toward outgroup members.

Provocation

In the studies previously discussed, the reader may have felt that there was a lack of correspondence with real world situations in that people typically behave aggressively toward others after they have been attacked or provoked, or when they think another person has offended or abused them. By contrast, many experimental studies have assessed aggression in the absence of any prior or perceived provocation. Within the experimental research on aggression, however, there is a large literature that examines the effects of prior provocation. In many of these studies, the source of provocation subsequently becomes the target toward whom aggressive responding is observed. Researchers have induced such provocation by having the target (a confederate) insult the subject (Richardson et al. 1994) or evaluate their performance as poor or below standard (Baron 1972). Not surprisingly, provocation consistently increases aggression relative to that exhibited by unprovoked control subjects.

As with other processes discussed above, however, it is likely that a provoking event which elicits negative affect will interact with whether its source is an ingroup or outgroup member, affecting the valence and intensity of attributions about it and subsequent actions that may result. That is, the same act will be interpreted differently when performed by an ingroup or outgroup member. As we have previously argued, outgroup status is likely to prime negative cognitive associations and affect, and thereby increase the likelihood that an outgroup member's action will be perceived as intentional or hostile. It follows, then, that after one has been provoked by another, the level of retaliation will be higher if that other is an outgroup as opposed to an ingroup member. Perceptual, cognitive and attributional processes combine such that even a trivial or accidental action by an outgroup member may elicit exaggerated negative attributions and strong negative affect which, in turn, induces aggressive responding. Conversely, when the instigating source is an ingroup member, the provoking event must be more clearly and unambiguously hostile to exceed the threshold for aggression and elicit a retaliatory response.

Baron (1979) used insult to examine the effect of provocation on the disinhibition of aggression by white subjects toward ingroup and outgroup members. Prior to their introduction to the teacher–learner paradigm, half of the subjects overheard the black or white learner (in reality a confederate of the experimenter) directly insult the subject. Although hearing a white target insult them had no effect on participants' levels of direct or indirect aggression (as expressed through shock intensity and duration respectively), it did have a disinhibiting effect on the expression of aggression toward a black target. In addition, in the no-insult condition, subjects expressed significantly less aggression toward black targets than toward white targets. That is, when not angered, white participants in this experiment displayed a type of reverse racism wherein they expressed greater aggression toward ingroup members than toward outgroup members. When angered, the level of aggression expressed toward ingroup members did not increase significantly, but that toward outgroup members was reliably greater than that expressed in the no-insult condition.

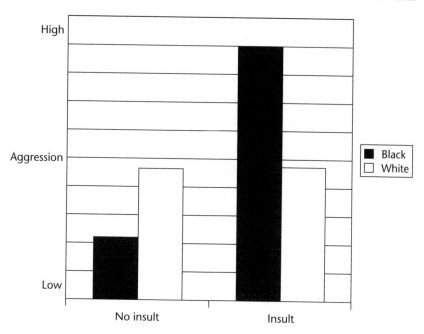

Figure 4.2 Group aggression as a function of insult and target race
Source: Adapted from Rogers and Prentice-Dunn (1981).

A variation of this experiment examined the effect of provocation on aggression, but placed the participants in a group setting in which their responses were supposedly indistinguishable from the other three members of their group (Rogers and Prentice-Dunn 1981). White male participants were told that the shock level that each of them set for the target learner would be averaged with the levels set by three others to determine the intensity and duration of shock that would be delivered to the target, thereby making each individual subject's actions anonymous. The results of this study paralleled those of the Baron study three ways: in the no-insult condition, less direct and indirect aggression was displayed toward the black outgroup targets than toward ingroup targets; provocation did not affect the levels of direct or indirect aggression that white subjects expressed toward ingroup targets; and lastly, provocation augmented the level of aggression expressed toward outgroup members. Moreover, in the provocation condition the level of aggression expressed toward outgroup targets, whether direct or indirect, reliably *exceeded* that expressed toward ingroup targets (see Figure 4.2).

Apparently the anonymity conferred by collective action was important in unleashing the greatest amount of aggression against outgroup members. The interaction between the presence or absence of provocation and the race of the target – ingroup or outgroup member – emerged more strongly in the group setting. Taken together, research suggests that when people in a crowd are emotionally aroused by a provocation, both blacks (Wilson and Rogers 1975) and whites will readily aggress against outgroup targets (Miller and Dollard 1941: 218). These findings are consistent with the concept of aversive racism described earlier. When aggression is not clearly justified by the circumstances, most individuals do not display discriminatory aggression against outgroup members (and may show more aggression toward another ingrouper than toward an outgroup target). But when aggression can be justified by provocation or other circumstances, so that it does not appear to be motivated by prejudice, aggression against outgroup members in particular is greatly increased.

Displaced aggression

The studies we have just described examined retaliation, which is aggression directed against the person who is perceived to have provoked it. Although retaliation against the provocateur is a common form of aggression, sometimes aggression is instead displaced onto a target other than one who instigated the anger. This may be necessary because retaliation is feared, as, for example, when the provocateur is powerful – they are the boss and have the ability to fire you. The unavailability of the perceived cause of the provoking act may also set the stage for **displaced aggression**. For example, the offending person may be unavailable in the immediate environment – a hit-and-run driver left a dent in your parked car. Finally, in many instances, the source of one's annoyance is unknown, intangible or impersonal. For example, a pneumatic drill pounding outside may be giving you a headache, or there has been a power failure and you have lost all the work that you have entered into your computer during the preceding hour.

When circumstances prevent direct retaliation, aggression may be redirected toward more available displacement targets (Dollard et al. 1939). Displaced aggression, then, is an act of harm directed at a target other than the original source of provocation. Thus, previously elicited, but inhibited or unexpressed anger or hostility lies dormant behaviourally, but has been primed and may persist ruminatively until some future time. Here, our previous discussion of types of provocation that emanate from a source other than the target of aggression is relevant. A meta-analysis (a quantitative integration and summary) of this literature shows that displaced aggression is a reliable effect (Marcus-Newhall et al. 2000).

Of special interest here, however, is the role of triggering acts on the part of the displacement target in augmenting displaced aggression and in how the source of a triggering act moderates its effect. Although there is no research on this issue, the data and arguments we have presented in this chapter argue that even minor acts of provocation on the part of an outgroup member can be a very potent instigation for the display of displaced aggression. The cueing functions of outgroup membership and the attributional distortions that characterize the interpretation of outgroup behaviour, when allied with the priming effect of a negative mood induced by a previous provocation from another source, are likely to result in stronger aggressive action. Consider for instance, the likely result when a gang member who was just 'chewed out' by his boss, comes home to hear his well-loved grandmother say 'your shoes sure look funny'. Imagine instead, the consequences of the same remark when uttered by a rival gang member. Although the grandmother's remark may elicit some anger, it may just as likely be interpreted as benign, or even as teasing, but loving and friendly attention. When uttered instead by a rival gang member (in the same intonation) the negative cognitive and motivational factors that are ordinarily mobilized by outgroup category membership are likely to be given explosive fuelling by the mildly provocative, if not ambiguous comment. We suspect that such triggering of displaced aggression can be seen in collective intergroup dynamics, as well as in ingroup–outgroup interaction at the interpersonal level.

INTERGROUP EMOTIONS

The idea that racial prejudice represents a motivational conflict has led social psychologists to a renewed interest in the affective or emotional component of attitudes toward outgroups in general. It has long been recognized that intergroup attitudes are a complex mixture of affective, evaluative and cognitive responses, but social psychological research has been dominated more recently by a focus on the cognitive component (stereotypes) to the relative exclusion of the more emotional underpinnings of prejudice. Although feelings and emotions toward specific outgroups are certainly connected to beliefs about those groups, these components are conceptually and empirically separable (Esses et al. 1993).

Zanna and Rempel (1988) have suggested that an attitude can be defined as an overall evaluation of a social group that is based on a combination of cognitive information (beliefs and stereotypes) and affective information (feelings and emotions). Attitudes toward different groups may reflect different weightings of affective and cognitive components. For some individuals, prejudice toward a specific group may be primarily emotion driven, while for other individuals or other groups, prejudice is primarily a matter of beliefs and values (Esses et al. 1993). Further, emotional states may directly affect the beliefs and evaluations associated with an outgroup.

Emotional reactions to a particular outgroup can include positive emotions (for example admiration, respect) as well as a range of negative emotions (for example fear, disgust, anxiety and hate). In Dijker's (1987) examination of the relation between emotions and attitudes toward two minority groups in the Netherlands, although both types of emotion predicted evaluation of the outgroups, positive emotions were more predictive of attitudes toward one group and negative emotions were more predictive of attitudes toward the other. Similarly, in an investigation of the relation between positive and negative emotional responses toward seven minority groups in the USA, both types of emotion predicted prejudice toward these groups (Stangor et al. 1991: Study 1).

The emotional component of prejudice is made more complex when one realizes that positive and negative affect may be held independently (Larson and Diener 1992; Cacioppo and Berntson 1994). If positive and negative emotions are potentially independent, the reduction of extreme negative affect toward a particular outgroup does not necessarily result in increased positive affect. Pettigrew and Meertens (1995) have suggested that, although 'blatant' forms of prejudice against outgroups involve strong negative affect, more 'subtle' forms of prejudice involve the absence of positive emotional reactions toward the outgroup, rather than the presence of negative emotions. For many outgroups, prejudice comes in the form of relative indifference and exclusion from the benefits of positive affect and leniency accorded to ingroup members. Antipathy-based prejudice and discrimination occur only against outgroups that arouse strong negative emotions.

Differentiating negative emotions

In addition to distinguishing between positive and negative emotions as components of intergroup attitudes, researchers have begun to recognize the importance of distinguishing among different types of negative emotions in intergroup contexts. As we discussed in Chapter 1, distinct emotions reflect different underlying causes and lead to different types of behaviour. E.R. Smith (1993) has suggested that five specific emotions are most likely to be aroused in intergroup situations: fear, disgust, contempt, anger and jealousy. Of these, fear and disgust can be distinguished as emotions that imply avoidance or movement away from the outgroup, whereas contempt and anger imply movement against the outgroup (although fear can also elicit the attack response if the perceiver feels trapped or cornered and unable to effectively flee the source of fear). Attitudes that are driven by the former emotional states are likely to have different cognitive contents and behavioural implications than attitudes that are associated with the latter forms of emotion.

Mackie and colleagues (2000) demonstrated, across three empirical studies, that for groups that are defined by a basic value conflict, anger and fear can be differentiated as distinct negative emotional responses to the outgroup. Appraisals of relative ingroup strength determine the degree of reported anger towards the outgroup, and level of felt anger mediates the relationship between strength appraisals and participants' desire to confront, oppose, or attack members of the outgroup. Based on these findings, Mackie et al. (2000) conclude that intergroup attitudes and behaviour are channelled by the specific emotions that are elicited in response to appraisals of a particular outgroup in relation to the ingroup.

According to appraisal theories of emotion, the type of emotion directed toward outgroups may be a function of the degree of conflict of interest that is perceived to exist between the outgroup and the ingroup. When perceived conflict or threat is relatively low, negative emotions toward outgroups are likely to be associated with appraisals of status and legitimacy. The perception that the outgroup is different from the ingroup in ways that are devalued or illegitimate gives rise to feelings of moral superiority, intolerance, and concomitant emotions of contempt and disgust toward relevant outgroups. The emotions associated with moral superiority may justify some negative discrimination against outgroups, but do not necessarily lead directly to hostility or conflict. In various contexts, groups have managed to live in a state of mutual contempt over long periods without going to war over their differences. The emotions of contempt and disgust are associated with avoidance rather than attack, so intergroup peace may be maintained through segregation and mutual avoidance.

As perceived conflict increases, avoidant emotions such as anxiety and disgust may be replaced by emotions such as anger which instigate active hostility and aggression. This relationship was indicated by results of a study of the attitudes of Israeli citizens towards members of an ultra-orthodox sect (Struch and Schwartz 1989). Two types of intergroup attitudes were assessed, one measuring aggressive intent against the outgroup, the other measuring more conventional ingroup–outgroup evaluative ratings. The strongest predictors of ratings on the aggression measure were perceived conflicts of interests and values between the respondent's own religious group and the outgroup sect. However, these conflict measures did not predict the more traditional evaluative ratings, and these two measures of outgroup attitude were essentially uncorrelated.

Threat and social change

The shift from contempt to anger and hate as dominant intergroup emotions may be particularly likely under conditions of social change, when previously subordinated groups challenge an existing power or status hierarchy. Historically, for instance, the status and power relationship between whites and blacks in the USA was one in which there was general consensus that whites held the advantaged position over blacks on both dimensions. To the extent that whites still perceive that black Americans are lower in power, resources and status than white Americans, the appraisal of blacks would be that of an inferior and dependent outgroup, and the primary intergroup emotion should be that of contempt or disgust. If blacks are perceived as weak and ineffective, they are not directly threatening to ingroup interests and thus associated with low levels of fear or anger. This **dependent image** of blacks and the associated emotions reflect the content of traditional or 'old-fashioned' forms of racism in the USA.

Many Americans believe that the traditional status hierarchy between blacks and whites in the USA has been effectively challenged and that the nature of intergroup relations is changing. Perceived changes in any of the dimensions of relationships between the two groups – relative status, power, or goal compatibility – should be accompanied by changes in emotions and images elicited by the respective outgroups. If whites believe that greater equality in status and power between blacks and whites reflects cooperative efforts toward a more egalitarian society, then contempt should be replaced with more positive emotions. On the other hand, if whites believe that blacks are still culturally inferior but gaining in power and control, threat appraisals and anger will be aroused. Such perceptions of increasing black power may explain the shift from 'old-fashioned' images or stereotypes to the current, hostile image of blacks held by modern racists (McConahay and Hough 1976).

Blacks may also respond to perceived changes in the structure of intergroup power and status by changing images of whites and associated
emotions. Again, the perception that blacks and whites have mutually
compatible goals for a more egalitarian society should be associated with
positive emotions of admiration and trust. On the other hand, if blacks
and whites are seen as having incompatible goals and interests, perceived
increases in the power and resources of the ingroup (blacks) should un-
leash anger and a corresponding image of whites as the enemy.

These hypotheses about the relationship between appraisals of social
power and intergroup emotions were supported in a survey study of the
mutual images and emotions that white and black high-school students
hold of each other, given their understanding (appraisals) of the nature of
black–white relationships in the USA today (Brewer and Alexander 2002).
Comparisons between black and white perceptions revealed that both
groups perceived some degree of goal incompatibility (conflict of interests) between whites and blacks and both groups perceived that status
differentials in the USA are in favour of whites relative to blacks. Thus, on
these two dimensions of appraisal, black and white students viewed the
intergroup situation in essentially the same way. On evaluations of relative power, however, perceptions of the two respondent groups tended to
diverge. Although both groups agreed that whites have more control of
politics and wealth than do blacks, blacks evaluated this differential as
more extreme than did white respondents, and in the other direction,
whites perceived blacks as gaining power to a greater extent than blacks
did. Consistent with these appraisal differences, the dominant emotions
that white students felt toward blacks were fear and anger, and perceived
black power was negatively correlated with positive emotions (trust and
admiration) and positively correlated with the degree of fear and anger.
For black respondents, appraisals of power also proved to be meaningful,
with emotions of envy and resentment increasing the more powerful
whites were perceived relative to blacks. Thus, perceived outgroup power
played a critical role in intergroup emotions for both groups. For black
students, however, power and status differences were associated with resentment rather than fear. For whites, the perception of increasing black power
elicited threat, fear and anger – the most volatile of intergroup emotions.

CONCLUSION

Although ingroup attachment and favouritism clearly has an affective
component, the study of affect and emotions has proved to be particularly important to our understanding of prejudice and hostility toward
outgroups. As depicted in Figure 4.1 at the beginning of this chapter,
there is a complex interplay of cognitive and affective factors involved in
predicting intergroup attitudes and behaviour. On the one hand, affective
states (both incidental and integral affect) influence cognitive processing
and interpretation of situations involving ingroup and outgroup members.
On the other hand, the interpretation and appraisal of such situations
determine what emotions are aroused which in turn have a powerful

influence on intergroup behaviour. The fear and anger elicited by the perception that the ingroup is under threat plays an important role in converting ingroup love into outgroup hate (Brewer 2001).

FURTHER READINGS

Devine, P.G. (1989) Stereotypes and prejudice: their automatic and controlled components, *Journal of Personality and Social Psychology*, 56: 5–18. Experiments on automatic stereotype activation and the conscious control of prejudice.

Gaertner, S.L. and Dovidio, J.F. (1986) The aversive form of racism, in J.F. Dovidio and S.L. Gaertner (eds) *Prejudice, Discrimination and Racism*. Orlando, FL: Academic Press. A review of research on aversive racism and the indirect expression of racial prejudice.

Pettigrew, T.F. and Meertens, R.W. (1995) Subtle and blatant prejudice in Western Europe, *European Journal of Social Psychology*, 25: 57–75. A cross-national survey study of the negative and positive affective components of prejudice.

Smith, E.R. (1993) Social identity and intergroup emotions: toward new conceptualizations of prejudice, in D.M. Mackie and D.L. Hamilton (eds) *Affect, Cognition and Stereotyping*. San Diego, CA: Academic Press. A taxonomy of emotional responses in intergroup situations.

FIVE

INTERGROUP CONTACT, COOPERATION AND COMPETITION: DOES TOGETHERNESS MAKE FRIENDS?

Key concepts: contact hypothesis, superordinate goals, realistic group conflict, decategorization, recategorization, subcategorization, dual identity, cross-categorization, pluralism

See that man over there?
Yes.
Well, I hate him.
But you don't know him.
That's why I hate him.
    (Allport 1954: 265)

This little parable from Allport's 1954 book was intended to illustrate the idea that lack of familiarity with others can breed hostility and contempt. Mutual avoidance precludes opportunities for acquiring information that might disconfirm perceptions of the other's motives and character, thus promoting what Newcomb (1947) called 'autistic hostility'. Misperceptions and distrust between groups are also fed by lack of contact between members of different social categories. Hostile groups tend to maintain high social distance, avoiding interactions with outgroup members and perpetuating a cycle of further hostility and avoidance.

INTERGROUP CONTACT: THE SOCIAL PSYCHOLOGY OF DESEGREGATION

According to Allport, this cycle captures the reasoning behind the so-called **contact hypothesis** of intergroup relations. If ignorance and unfamiliarity promote hostility, then opportunities for personal contact between members of opposing groups should reduce hostility by increasing mutual knowledge and acquaintance. This idea played an important role in shaping race desegregation policies in the USA.

When the US Supreme Court agreed to review the case of *Brown v. Board of Education of Topeka* (1953), it had among the documents in the case a paper entitled 'The effect of segregation and the consequences of desegregation: a social science statement', which was submitted as an appendix to the plaintiff's legal briefs. The statement had been drafted by social psychologists Isidor Chein, Kenneth B. Clark and Stuart Cook, and was signed by 32 social scientists, including anthropologists, psychologists and sociologists who were experts in race relations.

At the time, 17 states in the USA either required or permitted local school districts to provide segregated schooling for black and white children. Until 1953, the US Supreme Court had accepted the notion that 'separate but equal' facilities for schoolchildren of different races did not violate Fourteenth Amendment rights to equal protection under the law. The Brown case challenged that notion. The social science statement focused on psychological and social research documenting the negative effects of legally sanctioned segregation on the self-esteem of black children and the perpetuation of prejudice and negative stereotypes. The statement also made some recommendations regarding the potentially positive effects of desegregation, citing field research on desegregation in public housing, employment, and military units to support the conclusion that under the right conditions desegregation could promote positive intergroup relations and reduce unfavourable attitudes (for example Deutsch and Collins 1951).

When the Supreme Court rendered its decision in the case in 1954 it reversed the 'separate but equal' doctrine and ruled that segregated schooling was unconstitutional. We have only indirect evidence that the social science statement influenced this opinion, but some of the wording justifying the decision resembles arguments presented in the statement (Cook 1984). The opinion read in part:

> To separate them from others of similar age and qualifications solely because of their race generates a feeling of inferiority as to their status in the community that may affect their hearts and minds in a way unlikely ever to be undone ... Segregation of white and colored children in public schools has a detrimental effect upon the colored children. The impact is greater when it has the sanction of the law; for the policy of separating the races is usually interpreted as denoting the inferiority of the Negro group. A sense of inferiority affects the motivation of a child to learn. Segregation with the sanction of law, therefore, has a tendency to retard the educational and mental development of Negro children and to deprive them of some of the benefits they would receive in a racially integrated school system. Whatever may have been the extent of psychological knowledge at the time of Plessy v. Ferguson, this finding is amply supported by modern authority.
>
> (*Brown v. Board of Education* 1954: 494)

Some qualifying conditions

Of course, social scientists were not so naive as to believe that physical proximity alone would be sufficient to eliminate intergroup conflict and these negative effects of segregation. The contact hypothesis has been carefully qualified to specify the conditions under which intergroup contact should promote positive relations (Amir 1969). The conditions that are expected to influence the effectiveness of personal contact as a method of reducing intergroup hostility were most recently summarized by Cook (1985). According to his review, contact can produce favourable attitudes when:

- the situation promotes equal status interactions between members of the social groups
- the interaction encourages behaviours that disconfirm stereotypes that the groups hold of each other
- the situation involves cooperative interdependence among members of both groups
- the situation has high 'acquaintance potential', promoting intimate contact between participants
- the social norms in the situation are perceived as favouring intergroup acceptance.

One way to understand the conditions associated with the contact hypothesis is to think of it as an application of the principles of dissonance theory (Festinger 1957). Dissonance theory suggests that an effective way to change people's attitudes is to first change their behaviour. Avoidance and social distance from members of specific groups are forms of negative social behaviour that are consistent with hostile attitudes and distrust. If individuals with such negative attitudes find themselves in situations in which they engage in positive social interactions with members of the despised group, their behaviour is inconsistent with their attitudes toward the group as a whole. It is just this sort of inconsistency that dissonance theory predicts will result in changes of attitudes to justify the new behaviour (Leippe and Eisenstadt 1994). However, contact alone does not guarantee that positive interactions will occur. The contact situation must be structured in a way that promotes positive social behaviour without coercion if dissonance-induced attitude change is to take place.

Robbers Cave: a classic experiment in intergroup relations

A clear demonstration that contact alone is not sufficient to reduce intergroup conflict was obtained in a classic field study conducted by Muzafer Sherif and his colleagues in the summer of 1954 (Sherif et al. 1961; Sherif 1966b). At that time, 22 11-year-old boys arrived by bus at a campsite in Robbers Cave, Oklahoma, to participate in a three-week summer camp session. The boys, all from white, middle-class backgrounds, were unaware that their camping experience would be part of a series of field studies conducted by social psychologist Muzafer Sherif and his colleagues to test their theory of intergroup conflict and conflict reduction.

Before beginning the summer camp session, the boys (who were all previously unacquainted) were arbitrarily divided into two subgroups. The two groups arrived at the camp on separate buses and were settled into cabins at a considerable distance from each other. For the first week of the session, contact between the two groups was prevented. During this time, the members of each group engaged in cooperative activities that contributed to group formation. To further the development of group identity, the boys were encouraged to adopt a group name. One group chose to call themselves the 'Rattlers', the other became the 'Eagles'.

When contact between the two groups did occur, beginning in the second week, it was under conditions of intergroup competition, primarily in the form of competitive sports events. But the hostilities that ensued extended well beyond the playing field. After being defeated in one game, for instance, the Eagles burned a banner left behind by the Rattlers. The next morning, the Rattlers seized an Eagles flag, and from that point on raids on each other's campsites were frequent, along with name-calling and fist fights. Conversations and the content of posters drawn by group members documented highly derogatory images of the other group. By the end of this stage, cohesiveness within groups had increased, and both groups expressed strong preferences not to have any further contact with the other group, even if it meant forgoing pleasant activities such as movies if members of the other group were to be present.

At this point, the researchers had succeeded in demonstrating that groups with no cultural, physical or status differences between them, composed of boys selected for good psychological adjustment and sociability, could become warring factions based on the presence of competing group interests alone. The competition that had been introduced was a **zero-sum situation** – one group's win was always the other group's loss. Once the groups had experienced this form of competition on the playing field, they continued to define all further intergroup interactions in competitive, zero-sum terms.

Having created two rival groups with hostile attitudes and negative images of each other, the researchers' final task was to find conditions that would reduce the intensity of intergroup conflict. As an initial step toward conflict reduction, the groups were brought into contact with each other under conditions that were pleasant but involved no objective competition. These events included things like a common banquet, Fourth of July fireworks and movies. Instead of reducing conflict, these events simply served as opportunities for mutual name-calling and attack. The common meals, for instance, were marked by shoving and contests over which group would be first in line for food. So much food and paper was thrown around that the meals became known as 'garbage wars'.

After demonstrating the failure of contact alone to reduce intergroup hostility, the researchers then introduced a new feature into the situation – the presence of **superordinate goals**. The general idea was that if incompatible group goals (that is, competition) produced hostility, then common goals should reduce it. Superordinate goals were defined as important needs shared by members of both groups that could by met only by mutual cooperation. Common goals were created by facing the Rattlers and Eagles with several urgent situations that required cooperative effort.

One such situation was the breakdown of the water supply system to the camp. The flow of water, which came through pipes from a tank about a mile away, was interrupted and the boys from both groups had to work together to locate the source of the problem. On a second occasion a truck that was needed to fetch food supplies to a camp picnic refused to start and all of the boys had to join in a coordinated effort to pull the truck by rope until it started. Yet a third opportunity arose when members of both groups had a particular movie high on their list of preferences for showing at the camp. They were told that the movie was too expensive to acquire and both groups wound up contributing money in order to rent it.

None of these incidents alone was sufficient to eliminate the strong intergroup hostilities, but the cumulative effect of the series of joint activities did have a significant influence (Gaertner et al. 2000). During the final week of the camp session name-calling and shoving in meal lines had stopped and some friendships were formed across group lines. On the last day, the Rattlers and the Eagles elected to ride home together on the same bus rather than take separate buses (and even stopped along the way for shared refreshments, purchased by one group's remaining prize money).

School desegregation: the record

When one reviews the qualifications of the contact effect, it is clear that many contact situations do not meet all or most of the qualifying conditions. Superficial contacts in formal settings, for instance, or contacts between employers and servants, would not be expected to have any favourable effects on intergroup attitudes; nor would forced contact in situations where local authorities clearly do not support the contact effort. And, indeed, research indicates that contact under these circumstances does little to alter prevailing social stereotypes or intergroup hostility (Pettigrew 1998; Pettigrew and Tropp 2000).

Since the historic 1954 Supreme Court ruling, school desegregation in the USA has had a controversial history. The original case dealt with legislated segregation, where segregated schools were mandated by law, often requiring that black children be bused from their own neighbourhoods in order to attend segregated black schools at a distance. Since then the courts have also ruled against de facto segregation of neighbourhood schools, sometimes requiring the development of busing programmes in order to desegregate schools within and across districts. As a consequence, the effects of desegregation in school settings have been tested under a great variety of favourable and unfavourable circumstances.

What is the effect of school desegregation on intergroup relations? Reviews of field studies in the USA and elsewhere reveal that the answer is 'mixed' (Gerard and Miller 1975; Cook 1984; Miller and Brewer 1984; Stephan 1986). Studies in some settings have documented positive racial attitudes under desegregation. The most notable long-term effect is increased likelihood that blacks from desegregated schools will enrol in integrated colleges, live in integrated neighbourhoods and work in integrated employment settings (Braddock 1985). On the other hand, many studies have found that white prejudice against blacks increased following desegregation or showed no improvement. In addition, observational studies have documented the phenomenon of 'resegregation', whereby blacks and whites in racially mixed schools rarely interact either because of student preferences in friendship choices (Schofield and Sagar 1977) or because of teaching practices that track or stream children into racially homogeneous groupings (Epstein 1985). Research in both the USA and Israel indicates that streaming on the basis of academic abilities seriously undermines the immediate and long-term positive influences of desegregated schooling (Schofield 1979; Schwarzwald and Cohen 1982).

The fact that school desegregation, as practised, did not have uniformly positive effects on intergroup relations has led some to criticize the validity of the 1953 social science statement (for example Gerard 1983). Defenders, however, point out that the statement was directed primarily at the negative effects of legally mandated segregation that existed at the time, and could not have been expected to anticipate all of the forms of mandated desegregation that later developed (Cook 1984). Further, the statement was very careful in specifying the conditions under which desegregation could be expected to be successful. The results of 30 years of field and laboratory experiments on intergroup contact have clearly validated the importance of those qualifying conditions (Schofield and Eurich-Fulcer 2001).

CONTACT EXPERIMENTS: DEFINING THE LIMITS

The full version of the contact hypothesis reflected the outcomes of early experience with intergroup contact in natural settings. One aspect of the hypothesis (cooperative interdependence) was systematically tested in the Robbers Cave experiment and since then many of the other features of the contact hypothesis have been tested in controlled experiments. The results of those experiments have both confirmed and expanded the list of factors that are critical to the effectiveness of contact in promoting positive intergroup relations.

Amount of contact

Most successful integration efforts involve contact over an extended period of time or multiple cooperative interactions. In the Robbers Cave study, a single cooperative incident did not do much to alter intergroup hostility, but several such experiences did make a difference. Some of the first laboratory experiments on interracial contact found that it took intensive interactions between prejudiced whites and a black co-worker over a 20-day period in order to attain significant reductions in prejudicial attitudes towards that co-worker (Cook 1985). Laboratory experiments with artifically created groups have also found that reduction of ingroup bias is a function of the frequency and duration of intergroup interaction (Worchel et al. 1977; Wilder and Thompson 1980).

The number of independent contacts with different members of the outgroup also has a significant effect on intergroup perceptions. It takes exposure to many diverse group members to break down stereotypes and perceived homogeneity of outgroups (Weber and Crocker 1983; Islam and

Hewstone 1993). In an experiment with young children, Katz and Zalk (1978) found that exposing white children to multiple black faces reduced prejudice more than face-to-face contact with two specific black children. In general, a variety of contact experiences produces more generalized change than experiences that are limited to a few group members or a single interaction setting.

Intergroup anxiety

In Chapter 4 we discussed the important role that negative affect, such as anxiety, plays in maintaining intergroup prejudice. Social psychologists have recognized that intergroup contact itself is often an anxiety-provoking experience (Stephan and Stephan 1985; Wilder 1993b). Experiments by Wilder and Shapiro (1989a) provide evidence for a direct link between experienced anxiety and the outcomes of intergroup contact. Anticipated contact with outgroup members in a competitive environment produced intergroup anxiety. When anxiety was high, an encounter with a positive outgroup member did not improve intergroup attitudes. Instead, judgements of the positive outgrouper were assimilated to the negative stereotypes of the outgroup as a whole. When intergroup anxiety was reduced within a cooperative context, however, a positive encounter with an outgroup member did produce more positive evaluations of the outgroup.

In a field study of intergroup contact among Hindu and Muslim religious groups in Bangladesh, Islam and Hewstone (1993) confirmed the role of anxiety in mediating the effects of contact on intergroup attitudes. Various measures of the quality of contact between Bangladesh respondents and members of the outgroup proved to be related to reported feelings of anxiety during occasions of interaction with members of the religious outgroup. More experiences with voluntary, pleasant, cooperative and intimate contact with members of the outgroup produced lower levels of anticipated anxiety. Lower levels of anxiety were, in turn, predictive of more positive attitudes toward the outgroup as a whole. As with many studies of contact effects, it proves to be the nature and quality of contact experiences, rather than the frequency of contact, that makes the biggest difference in intergroup attitudes. Of particular importance to the quality of interactions is whether or not the contact occurs in a cooperative environment.

Cooperation

Sherif's demonstration that intergroup conflict is reduced in the presence of superordinate goals requiring cooperative effort has been replicated in a wide variety of settings. Blake and Mouton (1986) report experiments involving 150 groups of executives from industrial organizations with results that parallel those of the Robbers Cave study. In each experiment a phase of intergroup competition was followed by a series of cooperative tasks that reduced the negative effects of the earlier competitiveness. Effective cooperation involves at least two important conditions of interdependence: shared goals (if one gains, we all gain) and shared effort (we must work together in order to achieve our goals).

Cooperation in the classroom

Probably the most extensive application of Sherif's findings has been the implementation of cooperative learning programmes in desegregated classrooms. In cooperative learning exercises, children work through lessons or assignments in small groups, teaching each other as they go along. A number of different methods of cooperative learning strategies have been devised, but all incorporate basic principles of the contact hypothesis (Slavin 1985). One form of cooperative learning is the 'jigsaw' technique which was developed by social psychologist Eliot Aronson and has been studied in ethnically mixed elementary school classrooms in Texas and California (Aronson et al. 1978; Aronson and Gonzalez 1988). In the jigsaw method, children are assigned to six-member groups that are academically and ethnically diverse. The material for a particular unit (for example a geography lesson) is divided into six parts and each child is given an opportunity to become an 'expert' on one section of the unit. In effect, each group member is given one piece of the puzzle. It is then that child's responsibility to 'teach' what they know to the other members of the group so that they all can do well on later tests of the material. The idea is to create an environment in which each child has something to gain by learning from each of the others, in a form of positive interdependence. This is in stark contrast to the usual competitive atmosphere in classrooms where children score points by performing at the expense of classmates.

Reviews of the effectiveness of implementing cooperative learning strategies such as jigsaw indicate that group learning is associated with increases in liking for classmates, increased cross-ethnic interactions and generalized reduction in ethnic prejudice (Sharan 1980; Johnson and Johnson 1981; Slavin 1985). The success of cooperative learning methods has been acclaimed as one of the most important contributions of social psychology principles to education. As Slavin (1985: 60) put it, 'thirty years after Allport laid out the basic principles, we finally have practical, proven methods for implementing contact theory in the desegregated classroom. These methods are effective for increasing student achievement as well as improving intergroup relations.'

Status equality

An important qualification to the effectiveness of cooperative contact as a method of improving intergroup relations is that the conditions promote equal-status interaction among the participants. In many racially and ethnically mixed settings this is not so easily achieved since participants come into the situation with pre-existing status differences based on group membership. Even if there are no formal status differentials within the cooperative setting, ethnic identity may serve as a generalized cue for expectations of differences in ability and competence. As a consequence, members of higher status groups may be unwilling to learn from or be influenced by members of lower status groups, and their expectations of lesser competence may be reinforced (Cohen 1982, 1984). Under these conditions, the relative positions of members of the cooperative work group are not truly 'equal'. Cooperation may be undermined when the contributions of the two groups are not well balanced (Garza and Santos 1991).

Cooperative learning strategies attempt to override status expectancies by providing group members with specialized knowledge that makes each member critical to the group's success. But attempts to compensate for initial status disadvantages must strike a delicate balance. We discuss in Chapter 3 how advantaged or high-status groups may react to direct threats to ingroup status differences. However, even though status compensation may be regarded as 'unfair', it may be a necessary step toward successful intergroup contact, as was demonstrated in an important laboratory experiment by Norvell and Worchel (1981). In the initial phases of this experiment, participants were arbitrarily divided into two groups who then competed on a series of tasks. In one condition, no information was given on who won the competition, but in the other condition, one group was consistently announced as the winner. This manipulation served to establish a 'history' of status differential between the two groups.

In the second phase of the experiment, the two groups were brought together to work on a cooperative task. In some cases, one of the groups was provided with a special advantage – extra information that would help in the cooperative endeavour. In other cases, no special information was conveyed to either group. The effect of this special status advantage on intergroup attitudes following cooperation varied depending on the nature of initial group differences. If the groups had previously been equal, the special information created a status imbalance that reduced intergroup attraction compared to the no advantage condition. However, when the two groups were different in status, cooperation did not improve intergroup attraction unless the initially low-status group had the special advantage (see Figure 5.1). The special information served to compensate for status inequalities and improved intergroup relations even though the advantage was perceived as 'unfair' in all conditions.

The results of this experiment have interesting implications for policies involving affirmative action for disadvantaged groups. Such policies are often regarded as unfair because they violate principles of 'procedural justice' (Barnes-Nacoste 1992). But in the long run such policies may improve intergroup relations because they satisfy desires for distributive justice (equal or equitable outcomes for members of all groups) and promote conditions for equal-status contact (Crosby et al. 2001).

THEORETICAL PERSPECTIVES ON CONTACT AND COOPERATION

The contact hypothesis and its qualifying conditions were largely derived empirically, from experience with intergroup relations in real-world contexts. However, more general theoretical perspectives have since been

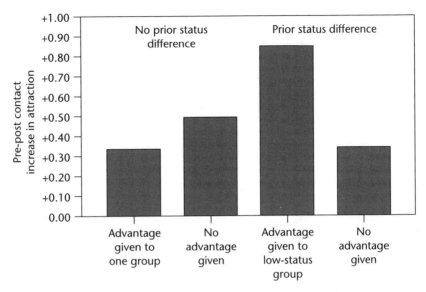

Figure 5.1 Effects of inequality on liking for outgroup members
Source: Adapted from Norvell and Worchel (1981).

brought to bear on understanding the mechanisms through which contact may alter intergroup attitudes and the conditions under which contact will be most effective. Of these theoretical frameworks, the two that have had the most impact are *realistic group conflict theory* (LeVine and Campbell 1972: Chapter 3) and theories of social categorization and social identity.

Realistic group conflict and intergroup relations

Sherif and his colleagues set out to demonstrate a number of points about the nature of intergroup relations in their summer camp experiments. Their work was conducted within the framework of realistic group conflict theory which holds that the nature of group relations is determined by the actual or perceived relationship between ingroup and outgroup interests. When one group can attain its goals (for resources, status or power) only at the expense of another group, intergroup conflict is the inevitable consequence. Conflict can be reduced only by the acceptance of shared, superordinate goals in place of competing interests.

As discussed in Chapter 4, most social psychologists accept the idea that competition over scarce economic or social resources heightens intergroup discrimination and hostility. Experimental studies in the laboratory confirm Sherif's findings that placing groups in competition increases ingroup bias and discrimination (Brewer 1979) as well as anxiety and negative affect toward the outgroup (Wilder and Shapiro 1989b). In real life, perceived incompatibility of goals is clearly a component of conflict between labour and management in industry, between political groups within nations, and between nations in the global scene (see Chapter 6).

Although objective conflicts of interest certainly play an important role in intergroup relations, some social psychologists argue that competition is not the sole basis for conflict between groups. In some instances, in fact, competition may be the consequence of ingroup–outgroup differentiation rather than its cause (Tajfel 1978; Tajfel and Turner 1986). The minimal intergroup experiments described in Chapter 3 clearly demonstrate that ingroup favouritism and discrimination against outgroup members occur as soon as individuals are classified into distinct categories, in the absence of pre-existing conflict of interests. According to social identity theory, this happens because positive ingroup identity is attained through comparisons with the outgroup. As Tajfel (1981: 258) put it, 'the characteristics of one's group as a whole . . . achieve most of their significance in relation to perceived differences from other groups and the value connotations of these differences'. Thus, the need for positive identity creates a kind of 'social competition' between groups that is the product (rather than the cause) of ingroup–outgroup categorization.

Social categorization and intergroup contact

Social categorization theory emphasizes the role of cognitive representations of the contact situation as a critical factor determining the outcome of intergroup interactions. When a particular social category distinction is highly salient in a given situation, individuals will respond to the situation in accord with the relevant social identities, acting towards others in the setting in terms of their corresponding group memberships rather than their personal identities (Brewer and Miller 1984; Worchel 1986; Brewer et al. 1995). How the interaction is experienced will, in turn, determine the perceptions and attitudes that are expressed during contact and the changes in attitudes that might result from those experiences.

Based on this general idea, three different models of intergroup contact have been developed. These three models are represented schematically in Figure 5.2. Each makes somewhat different predictions of what will be the optimal conditions for effective contact experiences. The rationale and relevant evidence for each of the models will be discussed in turn.

Decategorization: the personalization model

The first model (**decategorization**) is based on the idea that contact will be most effective if interactions are person based rather than category based (Brewer and Miller 1984). A primary consequence of categorization is the depersonalization of members of the outgroup. Social behaviour in category-based interactions is characterized by a tendency to treat individual members of the outgroup as undifferentiated representatives of a unified social category, independent of individual differences that may exist within groups. In situations where visual cues or status differences make participants continually aware of category membership, contact is not likely to break down prior prejudices or stereotypes (Brewer and Miller 1984; Worchel 1986). When category identity is salient, all of the

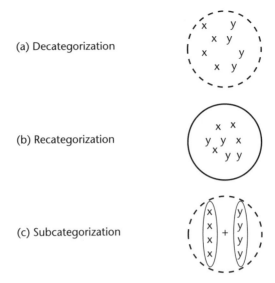

(a) Decategorization

(b) Recategorization

(c) Subcategorization

Figure 5.2   Alternative models of cooperative intergroup contact

cognitive biases we discuss in other chapters conspire to preserve and maintain category differences and negative expectations about the outgroup.

Categorization, accompanied by the need for positive distinctiveness (see Chapter 3), leads participants in the contact situation to be selectively attentive to information that differentiates members of the ingroup from members of the outgroup along dimensions that are favourable to the ingroup. Intergroup contact under such conditions should reinforce, rather than reduce, ingroup biases and favouritism. Even if the contact itself is pleasant and free of conflict, it is not likely to have any lasting effects on intergroup attitudes.

This perspective on the contact situation suggests that intergroup interactions should be structured so as to reduce the salience of category distinctions and to promote opportunities to get to know outgroup members as individuals. Attending to personal characteristics of group members not only provides the opportunity to disconfirm category stereotypes, it also breaks down the monolithic perception of the outgroup as a homogeneous unit (Wilder 1978). The resulting cognitive representation of the contact situation is that depicted in Figure 5.2a. In this scheme, the contact situation encourages attention to information at the individual level that replaces category identity as the most useful basis for classifying participants. Brewer and Miller (1984) assume that such contact experiences effectively break down stereotyping and prejudice because they undermine the availability and usefulness of ingroup–outgroup categorization in interactions with group members.

Evidence for the effectiveness of personalized interactions with outgroup members is provided by results of laboratory experiments with artificially created social categories (Miller et al. 1985). In one such experiment, participants first established ingroup identities as 'overestimators' or 'underestimators' based on their performance in a dot estimation task. Then four-person teams were composed of two members of the overestimator category and two underestimators. The teams engaged in a cooperative problem-solving task in which they had to discuss an issue until they reached consensus on a common solution.

During the cooperative interaction phase of the experiment, some groups were encouraged to be highly task oriented, to focus their attention on the quality of their solution to the problem. In other groups, participants were encouraged to socialize and get to know each other as individuals. Following the cooperative experience, participants in the task-focused teams still exhibited ingroup bias in their evaluations of ingroup and outgroup members, but those in the more personalized groups showed significantly less ingroup bias (Bettencourt et al. 1992). Outside of the laboratory, the effectiveness of personalization in reducing prejudice is supported by studies indicating that contact in the form of outgroup friendships has greater positive effects than other forms of contact (Pettigrew 1997; Pettigrew and Tropp 2000).

Although intergroup friendships may be important, highly personalized relationships do not always reduce prejudice toward the outgroup as a whole. Critics of the decategorization model point out that positive inter-personal experiences do not necessarily generalize to attitudes toward the group (Rothbart and John 1985; Hewstone and Brown 1986). As Wilder (1986b) points out, two elements have to be established for intergroup contact to be considered a success. First, the individual has to establish positive connections to individual members of the outgroup *and* those associations have to be extended to the outgroup category itself.

Experimental studies have demonstrated that positive experiences with a single outgroup member do not readily generalize to the group as a whole unless the individual is viewed as a 'typical' category member (Wilder 1984; Desforges et al. 1991; Johnston and Hewstone 1992). It is all too easy to define one's friend as an 'exception to the rule', and dissociate them from the outgroup category (Rothbart and John 1985). As a consequence, personalized interactions may create pleasant contact experiences but do not ultimately change category stereotypes or intergroup prejudice.

Brewer and Miller (1988) acknowledge that highly personalized contact with members of an outgroup may not directly alter outgroup stereotypes. They argue, however, that frequent exposure to the outgroup under personalizing conditions will reduce the salience of category boundaries and increase the complexity and variability of representations of the outgroup as a whole. A review of contact effects by Hamburger (1994) confirms the idea that contact even with atypical outgroup members can alter group stereotypes. Experiences with atypical category members may not directly change the central tendency of the group stereotype but it is likely to change the perceived variability with the category. Such changes in complexity and variability of the category stereotype reduce the likelihood of applying the stereotype to individual group members in the future. Ultimately, then, personalized contact can be expected to alter intergroup attitudes in the long run, especially when it involves multiple group members and many occasions of interaction.

Recategorization: the common ingroup identity model

The second model (**recategorization**) of intergroup contact (Figure 5.2b) is also based on the premise that ingroup bias is most difficult to overcome when ingroup–outgroup distinctions are highly salient. This model, however, proposes an opposite solution to the reduction of category salience than that represented by the decategorization model. Instead of focusing attention on individuating information in the contact situation, the Common Ingroup Identity Model (Gaertner et al. 1993; Gaertner and Dovidio 2000) suggests structuring the contact situation so as to focus attention on superordinate category identification that encompasses both ingroup and outgroup in a single social group representation.

According to the common ingroup identity model, one reason that superordinate goals are effective in reducing intergroup hostility is that they minimize attention to category differences by creating a new inclusive group identity. When such a superordinate category is made salient, group members are more likely to think of themselves as 'one unit', rather than two separate groups. Original ingroup–outgroup distinctions become less salient when both groups are included in a new ingroup that encompasses previously separate groups. When this form of recategorization is successful, ingroup loyalties and concern for collective welfare are transferred from the original subgroups to the new social category as a whole.

The model has been tested in a series of experimental studies to assess the conditions under which two previously segregated workgroups can be successfully merged in a superordinate unit. The experimental manipulations in these studies have focused on situational variables that enhance or reduce the perceptual salience of subgroup identities during the combined work team experience. Symbolic features such as group names and colours, or seating patterns that influence proximity and who interacts with whom, have been varied to control relative salience. Consistently, conditions that enhance the salience of the common team identity and reduce the salience of subcategory identities are found to diminish or eliminate ingroup bias in evaluation of fellow team members (Gaertner et al. 1989, 1990). To the extent that participants perceive the combined team as a single entity, rather than an aggregate of two separate groups, evaluations of former outgroup members become more positive. Such a merger of group identities would be represented in organizational settings when two departments are successfully merged into a new functional unit, or when previously segregated male and female workgroups are integrated in a single working unit.

Subcategorization: the mutual differentiation model

A very different approach to promoting effective intergroup contact is that represented in Figure 5.2c. This **subcategorization** model is based on the idea that the need for positive social identity should be capitalized upon in the intergroup contact situation. When intergroup contact experiences are cooperative and pleasant, the effects are more likely to generalize to attitudes toward the outgroup as a whole when contact is experienced as an intergroup interaction rather than an interpersonal one (Hewstone and Brown 1986; van Oudenhoven et al. 1996). An intergroup orientation is maintained when category identities remain salient in the contact setting.

In order to promote positive intergroup contact, Hewstone and Brown (1986) recommend that the contact situation be structured so that members of the respective groups have distinct but complementary roles to contribute toward achieving common goals. In this way, both groups can maintain positive distinctiveness within a cooperative framework. Some evidence in support of this approach comes from the results of an experiment by Deschamps and Brown (1983). Work teams composed of students from two different faculties engaged in a cooperative effort to produce a two-page magazine article. When the representatives of the two groups were assigned separate roles in the team task (one group working on figures and layout, the other working on text), the contact experience had a more positive effect on intergroup attitudes than when the two groups were not provided with distinctive roles.

The subgroup differentiation strategy for effective intergroup contact produces something of a dilemma. On the one hand, if the contact provides positive experiences that disconfirm negative stereotypes about the outgroup, there is reason to expect that attitudes toward the group as a whole will become more positive. On the other hand, such contact also reinforces perceptions that the two groups are distinctly different and thus perpetuates ingroup–outgroup categorization. Associated negative beliefs about the outgroup may also be strengthened, even if the interaction context is a positive one. Salient intergroup boundaries are associated with mutual distrust (Brown and Gardham 2001) which reduces the potential for mutual cooperation. Thus, the effectiveness of the differentiated social identity strategy depends on the presence of a strong common goal that creates positive interdependence between the groups and overrides other forms of social competition.

Integrating theoretical perspectives

Both experimental and field studies demonstrate that all three models of intergroup contact discussed above can be effective, under appropriate conditions, in reducing intergroup prejudice and discrimination. Yet there is also reason to believe that all three models represent unstable solutions to the problems of intergroup conflict in the long run. Personalized contact may effectively break down category-based interactions in the contact situation, but category boundaries may easily be re-established when the context changes. Both the common ingroup and subgroup differentiation models rely heavily on the salience of superordinate categorizations and goals, which may also be highly situation specific. As contexts change, the salience of superordinate category membership may diminish while subgroup identities remain available as a primary basis for group loyalties and attachment. This is particularly likely when the superordinate category is a large collective, the psychological 'presence' of which is difficult to maintain.

Unfortunately for all three models, cognitive and motivational forces conspire to re-establish subgroup differentiation and ingroup–outgroup distinctions in most social contexts. Brewer's (1991) optimal distinctiveness theory (discussed in Chapter 2) provides one explanation for why this might be so. This theory postulates that social identity is driven by two opposing social motives – the need for inclusion and the need for differentiation. Human beings strive to belong to groups that transcend their own personal identity, but at the same time, they need to feel special and distinct from others. In order to satisfy both of these motives simultaneously, individuals seek inclusion in distinctive social groups where the boundaries between those who are members of the social category and those who are excluded can be clearly drawn.

Large, diverse social categories are not likely to have the properties necessary to engage strong social identification and ingroup loyalties. Within such contexts, individuation fails to meet group members' need for inclusion and belonging, but inclusion in the superordinate category fails to meet the need for differentiation and distinctiveness. Within that context, subgroup identities are more likely to satisfy members' needs for optimal group identification. In effect, superordinate category identity and awareness of common goals may be necessary conditions for effective intergroup contact, but they may not be sufficient to produce enduring changes in ingroup–outgroup relationships.

One solution to the dilemmas of intergroup contact may lie in structuring contact situations in ways that contain elements of all three models (Hewstone 1996; Brewer and Gaertner 2001). A number of lines of research suggest that various combinations of decategorization, recategorization and mutual differentiation within the contact setting prove to be more effective in the long run than any one strategy alone (Gaertner et al. 2000).

Personalization and differentiation

As mentioned earlier, the primary criticism of decategorization as a mechanism for reducing intergroup prejudice is the possibility that highly personalized relationships may not generalize to the outgroup category. Individual outgroup friends may be disassociated from their category membership as atypical exceptions. Personalized contact is more likely to have generalized effects on prejudice if category memberships are also salient (and frequently mentioned) during contact (Brown et al. 1999; Hewstone et al. 2000; Brown et al. 2001). Effective contact should involve high interpersonal *and* high intergroup experiences (Hewstone 1996).

Dual identities

In the common ingroup identity model, superordinate social identities are created through the merger of subgroups into a single, common category that replaces the original category differentiation. An alternative route to superordinate group identity involves making salient an inclusive categorization in which both groups have common membership. Two competing departments, for instance, might be reminded of their common interest in the success of the organization as a whole, or heterogeneous work teams may be created with accountability to the larger organization. This **dual identity** model does not require eliminating subgroup distinctions but relies instead on enhancing the relative salience of common group membership over differentiated categories (Brewer and Schneider 1990). Both common identity and differentiated subgroup identities may be salient simultaneously.

A field study in a multi-ethnic high school (Gaertner et al. 1994) found that intergroup bias was lowest when students identified themselves at both subgroup (that is, ethnic group) and superordinate (that is, American) levels and perceived their school as different ethnic groups 'all playing on the same team'. Experimental studies have also shown that a dual identity can lead to more positive outgroup attitudes than a superordinate identity alone (Hornsey and Hogg 2000), especially if the superordinate category is too inclusive and undifferentiated (Hornsey and Hogg 1999).

The dual identity approach runs into problems when the different subgroups vary in size and status within the superordinate category. When one subgroup is a dominant majority, the superordinate group may be seen as having the characteristics of that dominant group, rather than an all-inclusive common ingroup (Mummendey and Wenzel 1999). Thus, dual identity may have little effect on reducing ingroup bias for the majority subgroup (Zagefka and Brown 2002).

Cross-categorization

Multiple social identities may be more effective in reducing intergroup bias when group memberships are cross-cutting rather than hierarchically organized. This approach relies on extending the cross-categorization effects discussed in Chapter 1, where others can be simultaneously categorized as ingroup or outgroup members on different dimensions.

One possible source of multiple identity in an intergroup setting is category memberships and roles. Within a cooperative group, individuals can be differentiated not only in terms of the different social category identities they represent but also in terms of the different roles or functions they serve in achieving the group's goals. In a sports team, for instance, players take different positions or perform specialized functions. In most work groups, individuals bring different expertise or specializations to the task at hand. In many cases, roles are associated with particular social categories; men are expected to perform different functions than women in the workplace and in the household; and labour and management positions are often divided on the basis of demographic categories.

When roles and category distinctions converge (as in the experimental work teams created by Deschamps and Brown (1983) discussed earlier), they are essentially redundant. There is no need to individuate the characteristics or contributions of category members because they are functionally equivalent or interchangeable in terms of the roles or contributions they make to the collective effort. As a consequence, the experience of interdependent cooperative interaction within such a work group may ultimately reinforce category distinctions and associated category stereotypes. In contrast to this convergence of category and role would be task structures in which functional roles were systematically (or randomly) crossed with category membership. Under these conditions, the job of getting the task done would require group members to differentiate among members of the respective social categories according to their role or contribution to the team goal. Even if subgroup category identities were highly salient, this categorization would not be sufficient to identify the team member's functional position in the cooperative group. Instead, each individual's contribution would necessarily be separately evaluated in relation to the collective goal.

The comparative effects of convergent and cross-cutting role assignments were tested in a laboratory experiment by Marcus-Newhall et al. (1993). The purpose of the experiment was to assess the effectiveness of cross-cutting categories and roles in cooperative work teams for reducing ingroup bias in how the performance and contribution of fellow team members are perceived and evaluated. Members of two artificially created social categories ('overestimators' and 'underestimators') were assigned to a four-person work team to complete a problem-solving task. The team consisted of two overestimators and two underestimators whose category identity was clearly visibly salient throughout the session by the use of coloured labels and identity tags.

The team task was structured in such a way that it required the input from two specialized roles or sources of expertise to achieve. The problem given to the teams was to identify the seven most important traits or characteristics that should be used to select potential astronauts for the National Aeronautics and Space Administration (NASA). The job requirements of an astronaut include both technical competencies and social emotional skills. At the initial stages of the team task, individual team members were given one of two scripts to read. Two received a script describing the social-emotional demands placed on an astronaut during a typical space flight, while the other two received a script describing the cognitive and technical demands of being part of a space flight crew. Thus, two of the team members acquired expertise in one aspect (social-emotional) of the astronaut job while the others had expertise in the complementary aspects of the job.

Assignment of team members to the respective roles constituted the primary experimental manipulation. For half of the teams, roles and category membership were convergent in that the two overestimators read one script (social or technical) while the two underestimators read the other prior to team discussion. For the remaining half, the scripts were systematically assigned to one overestimator and one underestimator prior to interaction.

Once the differential role assignments had been established, the four members of the team worked together to reach consensus on a single list of seven traits to be submitted as their team product. Teams expected their products to be evaluated against a standard developed by NASA, as a measure of the quality of their performance. (No such evaluation was actually made.) While the results were ostensibly being 'scored', team members individually completed a series of questionnaires assessing their ratings of the group experience, evaluations of fellow team members, perceived similarity among members of the team, and trait ratings of overestimators and underestimators in general. The perceived contribution of each team member to the group product was assessed by a reward allocation measure in which each team member distributed 'chips' to each of the other team members from a set of chips of up to 100 for each participant.

Of particular interest was the presence of biased evaluations of fellow team members who were members of the subject's own subgroup (ingroup) compared to those who were outgroup members. Indices of ingroup bias on the evaluative and allocation measures were obtained by subtracting mean evaluations (or reward allocations) of ingroup team members from mean evaluations of outgroup members for each individual subject. In addition, the researchers were interested in the effect of team role assignment structure on the perception of differences between ingroup and outgroup members. When ingroup–outgroup differentiation is salient, members of the same group are perceived to be more similar in personality and values than members of different groups. From ratings of interpersonal similarity following team interaction, a similarity index was computed that represented the perceived similarity of team members across category identities relative to within category similarity.

The direction of results on each of the dependent variables supported the hypothesis that cross-cutting role assignments would result in less intergroup differentiation and less ingroup bias following contact in a cooperative team experience. These effects were particularly pronounced on measures of reward allocation and intergroup differentiation/similarity. In general, the cross-cutting of categories and task assignment succeeded in reducing intergroup discrimination even under conditions where ingroup–outgroup categorization was salient and meaningful. These effects of cross-cutting role and category memberships have since been replicated in a number of experiments, even when the two subgroups differ in size (Bettencourt and Dorr 1998) and status (Rust 1996). In general, research from both laboratory and field settings indicates that crossing two or more social categories reduces intergroup bias in comparison to a single ingroup–outgroup categorization (Crisp et al. 2001; Mullen et al. 2001). Of course, these effects can only be realized when multiple social identities and group memberships are simultaneously salient and meaningful. The effectiveness of cross-categorization is limited when one category distinction becomes functionally dominant (Pepels 1999; Crisp and Hewstone 2001).

Assimilation versus cultural pluralism: is multiculturalism possible?

The three models depicted in Figure 5.2 have parallels in political ideologies and policies represented by different multi-ethnic nations. Models 5.2a and 5.2b represent variations of assimilationist philosophies, in which ethnic distinctions are submerged in a larger societal identity. Model 5.2c, on the other hand, represents a version of cultural pluralism, in which separate identities are maintained or enhanced.

Much of the debate in the political arena is over the question of whether multicultural societies must choose between assimilationism or separatism. Proponents of multiculturalism assert that alternative models are possible

Table 5.1 Alternative forms of ethnic identification in pluralistic societies

		Value of superordinate culture	
Value of subculture		*High*	*Low*
	High	Integration	Assimilation
	Low	Separatism	Deculturation

Source: Adapted from Berry (1984).

in which respect for ethnic subgroup distinctiveness and loyalties to a common superordinate group are both achieveable. Berry (1984), for instance, has argued that four different forms of ethnic identification are possible in a pluralistic society, depending on how members of distinct ethnic groups relate to their own ethnic identity and to the society at large. Berry's classification system is depicted in Table 5.1. Integration is the form of intercultural relations in which identification with ethnic subgroups and with the larger society are engaged simultaneously.

Research by Tyler and his colleagues (Tyler 1994; Huo et al. 1996) supports Berry's distinction between assimilation, separatism and integration in how individuals view issues of social justice. Members of ethnic minorities in the USA who expressed high social identification with their own ethnic group but not with the superordinate culture defined fairness primarily in terms of distributive justice. Fairness for these individuals was judged by the relative outcomes to their own group compared to others. Individuals who scored high on social identification with both their own ethnic group and with the superordinate culture, on the other hand, exhibited more concern with procedural justice. They judged fairness in terms of the fairness of the rules and procedures applied to their group, independent of the distribution of outcomes.

The results of experimental studies of intergroup cooperation reviewed above suggest that there are structural arrangements in which the salience of superordinate identities can be achieved without sacrificing identification with distinctive subgroups. Conditions in which subgroups are highly interdependent with complementary roles, or in which roles and category identities are independent, appear to be arrangements that optimize intergroup cooperation. If such arrangements can be generalized to the social policies, they may be critical to multicultural societies.

Some important caveats

The results of social psychological experiments on intergroup contact are promising in suggesting how contact can be structured to optimize the positive effects of cooperative interaction between groups. However, there are a number of reasons why the translation of findings from basic research to application in real-world settings still requires additional research and theory.

For one thing, there is reason to believe that the structural arrangements that lead ultimately to better intergroup relations also elicit initial resistance to team formation and negative attitudes toward the cooperative task. When social identification with subgroup categories is high, the prospect of cooperative interdependence between the ingroup and outgroup raises a threat to group identity (Hewstone and Brown 1986). As a consequence, individual group members approach cooperative settings with (at best) mixed motives. On the one hand there are personal and collective incentives to reach common goals, but there is also a strong reluctance to rely on outgroup contributions to achieve group goals, or to share the benefits of successful achievements with outgroup members. The cross-cutting of role assignments (which reduces the contribution to the team product that can be clearly attributable to the ingroup) may well exacerbate these sources of resistance to cooperative team efforts.

A second potentially important limitation of many social psychology experiments is the lack of attention to status relationships between social groups. The creation of arbitrary social identities in the laboratory setting precludes any history of status differentials between the categories under study. Although the processes of ingroup bias and favouritism may lead members of each group to perceive that their group is better than the outgroup, these biases are symmetric in the absence of any objective status hierarchy. Further, the cooperative structure of laboratory tasks is carefully designed to bring the groups together under equal-status conditions, even when differentiated roles are involved. In real-world societies, by contrast, intergroup relationships are often played out in the context of well established status differences among social groups. Further, the nature of the status hierarchy is often such that category identity, functional roles, and position within the society are largely convergent. Such pre-existing status relationships can be expected to moderate the effects of intergroup contact under any structural arrangements and, at a minimum, cannot be ignored within the contact setting (Cohen 1984).

CONCLUSION

In retrospect, then, the 'contact hypothesis' has come a long way since it was discussed by Allport (1954). Experimental and field research indicate that the effectiveness of intergroup contact experiences as a method of reducing intergroup prejudice depends on a complex interaction of the structure and quality of the contact experience, the context in which it takes place, and the frequency and extensiveness of contact relationships. Nonetheless, in the long run, cooperative contact does seem to be the key to improving intergroup relations and changing the social psychological processes that underlie prejudice and discrimination. In the next chapter we turn to the implications of this research for understanding the causes and reduction of large-scale intergroup conflict.

FURTHER READINGS

Brewer, M.B. and Miller, N. (1984) Beyond the contact hypothesis: theoretical perspectives on desegregation, in N. Miller and M.B. Brewer (eds) *Groups in Contact: The Psychology of Desegregation*. New York: Academic Press. A chapter integrating research on the contact hypothesis within the framework of the authors' decategorization model.

Cook, S.W. (1984) The 1954 Social Science statement and school desegregation: a reply to Gerard, *American Psychologist*, 39: 819–32. A review of the outcomes of school desegregation research and implications for social psychological theory.

Gaertner, S.L. and Dovidio, J. (2000) *Reducing Intergroup Bias: The Common Ingroup Identity Model*. Phildelphia, PA: Psychology Press. A review of the authors' theories of aversive racism and recategorization and related experimental research.

Hewstone, M. and Brown, R. (1986) Contact is not enough: an intergroup perspective on the 'contact hypothesis', in M. Hewstone and R. Brown (eds) *Contact and Conflict in Intergroup Encounters*. Oxford: Blackwell. An introductory overview of research on the contact hypothesis from the perspective of social identity theory.

Sherif, M., Harvey, O.J., White, B.J., Hood, W.R. and Sherif, C.W. (1961) *Intergroup Conflict and Cooperation: The Robbers Cave Experiment*. Norman, OK: University of Oklahoma Book Exchange. The original report of the Sherifs' classic field experiment on manipulating intergroup behaviour in a boys' summer camp in Oklahoma.

SIX

INTERNATIONAL CONFLICT: WHAT MAKES WAR POSSIBLE?

Key concepts: misperception, prospect theory, image theory, groupthink

Much of the content of the previous chapters in this book has been devoted to explaining why intergroup relations are more often characterized by conflict and competition than by cooperative coexistence. Indeed, the psychology of intergroup relations is often equated with the study of conflict and aggression. But when we consider group conflict at the international level, we move from the realm of social psychology into the realms of political science and history. In seeking to explain the causes of war and global conflict, social scientists most often look to political and economic determinants rather than the psychology of individuals. Warfare appears to be driven by institutional forces that transcend individual rationality. Yet, ultimately, wars are entered into, fought and ended by the decisions and behaviours of individual human beings. Whatever the institutional factors that precipitate and sustain intergroup conflict, it is psychological factors that make war possible in the first place.

From a social psychological perspective, warfare and terrorism represent extreme forms of intergroup hostility and discrimination, directed toward the outgroup as a whole. However, unlike the individual acts of hostility and aggression reviewed in Chapter 4, war represents aggression at the collective level – where acts of aggression are carried out collectively, supported by collective resources and collective beliefs and sentiments. Thus, in this chapter we shall not be focusing on the psychology of the individual soldier in the battlefield but on the shared psychological forces that make war seem necessary and sustain its legitimacy within a group.

The study of the psychological underpinnings of international conflict draws extensively from research on the cognitive and motivational processes underlying ingroup identification, outgroup hostility and intergroup behaviour. Understanding the psychology of warfare provides an opportunity for review and application of basic social psychological research on intergroup relations covered throughout this book.

THEORIES OF HUMAN NATURE: THE BIOLOGICAL PERSPECTIVE

One approach to the psychology of intergroup conflict attributes the propensity for war to features inherent in 'human nature' – possibly characteristics unique to human beings as a biological species (Goodall 1990). Psychoanalytic and sociobiological explanations for intergroup conflict associate warfare with biological drives of aggression and dominance at the individual level.

'Macho pride': a motivational basis for war

One of the more interesting psychoanalytic theories of conflict is that proposed by psychiatrist Jerome Frank (1967), who brings together the psychoanalytic concept of 'narcissism' at the individual level and national power at the group level. Frank proposes that group power is valued because it compensates for personal feelings of insignificance and helplessness experienced as individuals. By transferring needs for achievement and pride to the group or nation, individuals can achieve a sense of effectance on a much grander scale than otherwise possible. Ralph White (1984) provided evidence for the operation of such 'macho pride' in the history of US–Soviet relations during the Cold War era.

A closely related motivational account of intergroup conflict is represented by social dominance theory (Sidanius 1993; Sidanius and Pratto 1999). Like Frank's theory, the social dominance perspective emphasizes the importance of achieving power and dominance at the level of intergroup (rather than interpersonal) relations. The need for social dominance at the group level is postulated to be an inherent human characteristic that functions to maintain stable status hierarchies in social systems. It is also of interest to note that Sidanius speculates that the need for social dominance is more characteristic of human males than of the female of the species.

The genetic imperative

Sociobiological models of human evolution (see Chapter 2) rely on the concept of 'inclusive fitness' to account for collective social behaviour such as group warfare. In this view, group identity is based on genetic relatedness among members of ethnic groups. The higher the proportion of genes that individuals share, the more likely they are to cooperate according to the genetic imperative of kin selection (van den Berghe 1981).

Just as the likelihood of cooperation increases with genetic similarity, the likelihood of conflict increases as the proportion of shared genes among individuals decreases. Ethnic groups evolve to define the boundaries of genetic relatedness, with such groups characterized by ingroup cooperation and outgroup conflict. Like earlier ethologists (for example, Eibl-Eibesfeldt 1979), many sociobiologists assume that humans are particularly prone to aggressive violence, but directed towards ethnic outgroups (Shaw and Wong 1989). The predisposition to war is an extension of competition for survival between kin groups competing for scarce resources.

Biological theories of group identification and intergroup conflict have received renewed attention in light of the rise of ethnonationalism in international affairs (Horowitz 1985; A.D. Smith 1993; Connor 1994; Gurr 1994). Since the collapse of the Soviet Union and the end of the Cold War era in international relations, intergroup conflict seems to have shifted from conflict among nation-states to conflicts over demands for separation and autonomy by ethnic groups throughout the world. A survey in the late 1980s identified 233 politically significant ethnic groups in the world, and during 1993–94 these groups were involved in 50 serious ethnopolitical conflicts or open warfare (Gurr 1994). The apparent virulence of ethnic identification has led some theorists to assume that ethnic identities are primordial, intrinsically more fundamental and stable than other social identities such as superordinate states. Because ethnic groups are characterized not only by shared culture but also by beliefs in shared history and common ancestry, they come closest to the extended kinship groups emphasized by sociobiological theory.

The leap from intergroup relations among small ethnic bands to modern international and interethnic warfare is a rather large one, and the basic assumptions of the sociobiological model of intergroup conflict have been criticized on a number of grounds (for example, Ross 1991). For one thing, the idea that ingroup cooperation characterizes small ethnic bands is not universally supported. In many small-scale societies internal conflict and violence among closely related individuals are very high, even in the absence of resource scarcities (Ross 1986). In the modern international system, both the size and diversity of nation-states and the pattern of alliances in warfare belie the close correspondence between genetic relatedness and war versus peace. Although in recent times the importance of ethnic identification and interethnic conflict would be difficult to deny, most social scientists believe that such identities are socially rather than biologically transmitted (Anderson 1991).

PERCEPTION AND MISPERCEPTION: THE COGNITIVE PERSPECTIVE

Whereas sociobiologists and psychodynamic theorists place the psychological foundations of warfare in the system of human needs and motivations, political psychologists tend to focus on the cognitive system as the basis for international conflict. In this view, warfare is made possible by cognitive biases and belief systems that limit our capacity for international trust and cooperation. Many of these cognitive biases are rooted in the ingroup favouritism and ethnocentric affect that were discussed at length in previous chapters.

The image of the enemy

The competitive atmosphere that characterizes intergroup relations is a breeding ground for mistrust and misperception. The relationship between competitiveness and social perception was cleverly demonstrated in a laboratory experiment reported by Cooper and Fazio (1986). Participants, who were in groups of three to six individuals, viewed a videotape of a team of two people engaging in a communication task. In one condition, participants believed that they were taking part in a person perception experiment and were instructed merely to observe the dyad. In another condition, participants were told that they themselves would be assigned to pairs who would later compete against the team in the videotape for a cash prize.

During the course of the videotape, the members of the team requested a 'time out', which was responded to reluctantly by the experimenter since time outs were not part of the rules of the task. At this point the members of the dyad in the video had a brief discussion and then resumed the task. Thus the nature and purpose of their request for a time out was left ambiguous. After viewing this videotape, participants in the person perception condition tended to interpret the request for time out in a neutral way, assuming it was for the purpose of asking clarifying questions or going to the bathroom. For observers in the future competition condition, however, the request took on more sinister implications. Most participants in this condition assumed that the purpose was to cheat or gain some unfair advantage in the task. When they evaluated the video team at the end of the experiment, these judges rated them as significantly less honest than did participants in the person perception condition. Apparently, the same ambiguous behaviour was deemed to be more suspicious and dishonest when the team on the videotape was a competing outgroup.

Distrust and misattributions of intent are also characteristic of social perception at the international level (White 1970, 1977; Jervis 1976; Silverstein 1989). Nations in conflict tend to perceive each other in remarkably predictable ways. When psychologist Uri Bronfenbrenner returned to the USA from a trip to the former Soviet Union in 1960 he reported his observations drawn from conversations with Russian citizens (Bronfenbrenner 1961). As he talked with people about US–Soviet relations he found that 'the Russian's distorted picture of us was curiously similar to our view of them – a mirror image' (Bronfenbrenner 1961: 46). The view of the enemy's aggressive intent is mirrored in each group's image of the other. The substance of this mutual **enemy image** has been verified in many contexts of intergroup conflict (Silverstein 1989).

One aspect of the perceptual distortion that characterizes the mutual images that groups in conflict hold of each other is a tendency for each group to exaggerate the hostile intent and threat posed by the other group while minimizing the threat posed by their own group toward the other. In other words, members of each group view themselves as less threatening than they are perceived by the outgroup. In an interesting demonstration of this perceptual bias, Kemmelmeier and Winter (2000) had US college students read the text of speeches given by Bill Clinton and by Saddam

Hussein during a 1996 confrontation in the Persian Gulf. After they had had a chance to read through both speeches, participants were instructed to highlight phrases and sentences in each speech that they considered most important and representative of the substance of the speech as a whole. The highlighted portions were then content coded for power imagery associated with the USA or with Iraq. As expected, the proportion of power imagery referring to the USA was significantly lower among the highlighted materials than the proportion of power imagery referring to Iraq.

Although mutual enemy images are characteristic of the perceptions of groups under conflict, it is not clear whether such images are a cause or consequence of conflict itself. Some would argue that perceptions of an outgroup as evil and malintended is the product of realistic conflict brought on by competition over scarce resources or ideological disputes. Nonetheless, the readiness with which group members embrace such images of the outgroup is clearly a factor in sustaining intergroup conflict once initiated.

Attributional biases

In previous chapters we have described various forms of ethnocentric biases in the attributions that are made about the causes of ingroup and outgroup behaviours. Such biases are prevalent in the arena of international relations as well. For instance, Burn and Oskamp (1989) reported the results of a 1986 survey of community college adults in the USA that demonstrated how citizens interpret government actions in ways that preserved positive views of the United States and negative views of the Soviet Union. Causal explanations for similar actions were different depending on whether the action had been initiated by the USA or USSR governments. Potentially positive or negative actions by the Soviets (for example, the 1985 moratorium on underground nuclear testing or the invasion of Afghanistan) were most often attributed to negative causes (for example, false propaganda, expansionistic motives), whereas ambiguous actions by the USA (for example, invasion of Grenada, bombing of Libya) were attributed to more positive motives or justifications.

In a similar series of studies, Sande et al. (1989) had students review newspaper articles describing either benevolent actions (for example, a whale-saving mission) or negative actions (for example, arms dealing) attributed either to Americans, Soviets, or French. For US respondents, Soviet actions were interpreted as more self-serving than the same actions by Americans or French, and US actions were seen as most altruistic. Canadian respondents, however, attributed US and Soviet actions to the same motives, suggesting that attributional biases depend on the nature of ingroup–outgroup relations.

The arms race and the psychology of escalating conflict

One problem with the attribution of competitive intent to others is that such expectations tend to be self-fulfilling. When we act to defend ourselves against the expected aggression, our competitive actions confirm the outgroup's expectations of our own intent and elicit competition in return (Kelley and Stahelski 1970). Thus each side behaves in a way that reinforces the other's misperceptions.

Missiles versus factories

Mutual distrust is particularly disastrous in situations involving inherent conflict between motives to cooperate and compete. In Chapter 2 we discussed the prisoner's dilemma paradigm as a classic situation in which individual self-interest is served by acting competitively, but everyone's interests are better served by mutual cooperation. Intergroup behaviour is particularly likely to be dominated by competitive choices in such dilemma situations.

The arms race between the USA and the USSR from 1950 to 1990 has been characterized as a prisoner's dilemma game on a large scale. To study the way people make decisions in such dilemmas, social psychologists have devised experimental games that simulate the arms race in the laboratory (Pilisuk 1984). In one such game, two players each begin with five 'missiles'. Over the course of five moves, they each have the opportunity to convert any of these missiles into factories (that is, to disarm). These decisions are made secretly, but at the end of five trials, the payoffs to each of the players are determined by the number of missiles each has at that point, according to the payoff matrix illustrated in Figure 6.1.

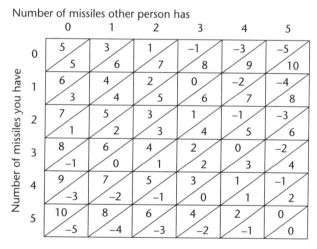

+1 unit for each factory
+2 units for each missile more than other person
−2 units for each missile less than other person

Figure 6.1 The 'arms race' game
Note: number to left of diagonal is payoff to subject: number to right of diagonal is payoff to other player.
Source: Pilisuk (1984: 299). *Journal of Conflict Resolution*, 28: 296–315, copyright © 1984 by Sage. Reprinted with permission.

The nature of this payoff structure is such that each player is better off if they finish with more missiles than the other player. For instance, if the 'other person' ends with two missiles, you are better off if you have three missiles rather than two (even though you also have fewer factories). However, if both players pursue this competitive strategy, they both finish with nothing (the lower right cell of the matrix), whereas they each could have won five points if they had both disarmed completely (no missiles each). In studies using this experimental game, Pilisuk found that players finished with an average of three missiles at the end of the series of five moves. As a result, they both won far fewer points (two points each) than they could have had with a mutual disarmament strategy (five points each). Further, Pilisuk found that if players were given the opportunity to initiate a 'surprise attack' after one five-trial sequence, fully one-third of the time at least one player took the attack option even if there was virtually no chance of success from such an attack. Apparently out of fear of the opponent, many players chose a pre-emptive attack rather than risk falling behind in the arms race.

Risk and the security dilemma

Choices in intergroup dilemma situations involve risk-taking decisions. In order to achieve mutual benefits, decision makers must determine how much they risk losing if the other players act malevolently, and whether the potential benefits are worth that risk. Kahneman and Tversky's (1979) **prospect theory** provides an interesting account of the psychology behind such risk-taking judgements, with implications for intergroup decision making.

According to prospect theory, the most important factor in risk decisions is whether the decision maker faces the decision in terms of potential losses or potential gains. When individuals make choices between possible positive outcomes, they tend to prefer options that give them a small gain with certainty over more risky (uncertain) higher gains (for example, most individuals will choose to accept a $100 prize rather than forgo that prize in order to have a 10 per cent chance of winning $1000 instead). On the other hand, when individuals are contemplating possible losses, they are more likely to risk a large potential loss in order to avoid a smaller, certain loss (for example if individuals have to choose between giving up $100 versus risking a 10 per cent chance of losing $1000 instead, most choose the risk-taking option).

Applying prospect theory to the realm of international politics, political scientist Robert Jervis (1992) suggests that political decision making is characterized by a 'loss aversion' mentality. Conditions of international competition or tension place decision makers in a state of anticipating losses (rather than gains). It is when political leaders believe that they are facing certain loss that they are willing to risk even greater losses in order to have a chance at recovering the status quo. According to Jervis, reckless behaviour in the international arena is more likely to be undertaken with the aim of recouping losses, or saving a bad situation, than by seeking gains. Situations in which both sides see themselves as operating in the range of losses are particularly dangerous and likely to escalate into war.

Jervis's analysis of international decision making is supported by results of a series of laboratory experiments conducted by Kramer (1989). In a choice situation similar to that used by Pilisuk (1984), participants had to make a series of decisions regarding investing their available resources in 'security' or in a monetary account. Although the security account was worth no monetary value, investment in the monetary account alone left a player vulnerable to a possible 'takeover' by other players with a larger security account.

The participants in Kramer's experiments made their investment choices under one of two different decision 'frames'. For some players, at the beginning of each trial, ten resource points were added to their monetary account and they then had to decide how much to leave in that account and how much to move to the security account. For other players, each trial began with the addition of ten points to the security account followed by a decision as to how much to move into the monetary account. From an economics perspective, these two decision frames are equivalent – in either case the individual is deciding how to allocate ten points between two accounts. But the starting point of the decision made a significant difference in the allocations that were actually made. Those who started out with points in the monetary account wound up investing much more into security than those who started each trial with security points. According to Kramer's interpretation, the former players saw themselves as faced with a security deficit, potentially vulnerable to loss of their monetary funds. Players in the other condition saw themselves as having a surfeit in the security account and focused on the potential gains associated with investment in the alternative monetary account. As predicted by Jervis, those who were oriented toward loss aversion were more likely to escalate the race for security and sacrifice actual gains in the process.

Deterrence beliefs

In addition to perceived vulnerability to loss, investment in preparations for war is fed by beliefs that such preparations will deter other groups from undertaking war. The potentially paradoxical consequences of the deterrence philosophy is well illustrated in this description from Sherif's summer camp experiment (described fully in Chapter 5):

> one group adopted a strategy to deter the other from future raids on its cabin. They collected green apples 'just in case,' to be prepared. The other group promptly began collecting apples themselves, and these also were hoarded against eventuality of attack. Although expressly forbidden by the research staff and actually prevented on one occasion, the upper crust of one group succeeded in carrying out a raid when both groups had what they considered ample supplies of apples.
>
> (Sherif 1966a: 119)

Whether military build-up does deter war in the international arena is still a matter of much debate among political analysts. But a study by Wallace (1979) suggests that history provides little support for the deterrence notion. Wallace identified 99 serious international disputes in the period between 1816 and 1965. Each dispute involved some movement of troops, withdrawal of diplomatic relations, and other actions bordering on direct conflict. Wallace then classifed each incident on two dimensions: first, whether or not the dispute had been preceded by arms build-up on both sides, and second, whether or not the dispute erupted into overt warfare. The results indicated a strong association between the presence of an arms race and war. Of those cases characterized by arms build-up, 82 per cent of the disputes escalated to war. Without a prior arms race, only 4 per cent of incidents resulted in warfare.

With so little empirical base, why does the belief in deterrence persist so strongly? White (1984) suggests that part of the reason is that a few specific historic incidents (for example, Munich and the absence of deterrence of Hitler, the avoidance of nuclear war between the USA and the USSR) are particularly vivid and memorable. When policy makers think about deterrence theory, these incidents are most likely to come to mind. Because of the availability heuristic (Tversky and Kahneman 1973), the frequency of such events is overestimated (compared to many other historical events that contradict deterrence assumptions) and are overweighted in making judgements.

One particularly interesting form of ethnocentric bias may also be a contributing factor to belief in deterrence. Rothbart and Hallmark (1988) hypothesized that people's judgements about the effectiveness of coercion as a social influence strategy differ depending on whether the target is an ingroup or an outgroup. Participants in their study were given descriptions of a hypothetical conflict situation between two nations, one of which was their 'own' country and the other an outgroup. After reading the description, participants were asked to make ratings of the potential effectiveness of various methods for getting one of the countries to reduce the buildup of new weapons. When the intended target was the outgroup nation, various coercive strategies (for example, threat to build up one's own weapon stocks) were given high effectiveness ratings. But when the ingroup was the target, those same strategies were rated as likely to be ineffective and more conciliatory strategies were given higher ratings. In other words, people seem to think that 'we' will not be influenced by coercion, but 'they' will. When both sides of a dispute hold this ethnocentric perception, the possibilities for escalation of conflict are high.

Beyond rational cognition: images and emotions

Many of the ideas concerning the cognitive factors underlying intergroup conflict were formulated during the Cold War era of international relations. The basic conceptualization prevailing during that period was that of nations as 'rational actors', behaving in accord with their perceptions about the intent and motives of other nation-actors. The demise of the Soviet Union marked the end of the Cold War, and with it, changes in perspective on the nature of intergroup conflict. For one thing, the arena of international relations changed from a focus on conflict between two 'superpowers' to a multi-group context in which local conflicts and their ramifications predominate. Further, it has become apparent that conflict between groups is as much a product of emotions and symbolic identities as it is of cold cognition (Horowitz 1985; Mercer 1995). In this new climate, social psychological perspectives on ingroup identification and the affective components of intergroup attitudes have become especially relevant.

Image theory

One theoretical perspective that links perceptions and emotions in intergroup contexts is represented by 'image theories' of international relations as developed by Cottam (1977) and Herrmann (1985). These theorists argue that images form as a *consequence* of strategic relationships between nations, and serve a functional purpose. Working from Heider's (1958) balance theory, Herrmann (1985) suggested that images in international relations serve to balance a positive self-image and behavioural inclinations toward another nation. Herrmann argued that the nature of relationships between nations is represented in terms of perceived threats and perceived opportunities that give rise to emotions and associated behavioural implications. The cognitive system is balanced when the evaluative and behavioural implications of the image of the other nation match the behavioural inclination generated from the threat or opportunity in a way that maintains consistency with a positive, moral self-image (see also Sande et al. 1989). Thus, appraisals of the nature of the relationship between ingroup and outgroup (threat versus opportunity) give rise to specific images of the outgroup nation that *serve to account for and justify affective and behavioural orientations toward that group*.

Herrmann (1985) identified three critical dimensions of intergroup relationships that give rise to sentiments and subsequent images of the other. These appraisal dimensions are

- evaluations of competitive versus cooperative goal interdependence
- assessments of relative power
- evaluations of relative cultural status.

Together, these three assessments are the primary determinants of perceived threat and opportunity in intergroup relationships. When relationships are perceived to be characterized by extreme values on these three dimensions, emotions are aroused that determine both specific behavioural orientations toward the outgroup and specific content of the cognitive image of that group. Among the generic images that can arise from different configurations of intergroup relationship appraisals, five were identified as particularly relevant to international relations. These were labelled the 'ally' image, the 'enemy' image, the 'barbarian' image, the 'dependent (colonial)' image and the 'imperialist' image (Herrmann and Fischerkeller 1995).

The **enemy image** arises when the relationship between a person's ingroup and an outgroup is characterized by intense competition between two groups that are similar in cultural status and in power or strength. These relationship characteristics generate a sentiment of threat associated with arousal of affect and a behavioural inclination to eliminate the threat by attack. The enemy stereotype is generated to balance the tension between this behavioural inclination and moral constraints. It portrays the adversary as hostile, strategically manipulative and untrustworthy so that destroying it, even by the pre-emptive use of force, is justified. Although the enemy image represents the outgroup as monolithic in decision making and intent, the leaders are perceived to be capable and persistent in pursuing their group's interests. Hence, the enemy image is that of a 'worthy adversary'.

If the enemy image facilitates behaviour in a threatening situation with a co-equal other, then the **ally image** serves a comparable function in facilitating the pursuit of cooperation when the relationship is appraised as non-threatening. The ally image is associated with intergroup relationships characterized by positive goal interdependence, similar capabilities and equal status. This is expected to produce an image of the outgroup nation that is dominated by positive attributes. The partner's motives will be seen as benign and, in the ideal form, mostly altruistic. The stereotypical image eliminates reservations that might inhibit full cooperation or cast any moral doubt on the partnership. By describing the outgroup in entirely positive terms, the ally image, like its enemy image counterpart, constructs a picture where acting upon the behavioural inclination induced by the relationship is not just acceptable but a moral duty.

Other relationship configurations that have received substantial attention in image theory are those generated by mutually incompatible goal interdependence between groups that differ in power and status. One asymmetric relationship image theorists have examined is the case in which the ingroup nation perceives itself as having high cultural status but as weaker than an outgroup which is viewed as a potential invader. Because the outgroup is appraised as culturally inferior, their strength (and unpredictability) severely threatens the ingroup's position and resources. This relationship pattern is expected to produce a behavioural inclination that involves insulating the ingroup from the outgroup's invasive threat. In order to avoid any self-perception as cowardly in this situation, the ingroup constructs a picture in which insularity is not only the prudent course but also the normatively correct choice. The **barbarian image** does this by picturing the outgroup as evil and as enjoying wanton destruction for its own sake. The barbarian outgroup is also seen as immune from deterrence because they do not process costs and benefits in a rational way and is led by highly emotional and not terribly intelligent leaders who will destroy at the slightest provocation.

At the other extreme, a second asymmetric relationship pattern is one in which the ingroup nation also sees itself as having higher cultural status but as much stronger than the target outgroup. In this relationship there is opportunity for ingroup members to eliminate goal incompatibility by exploiting the asymmetries in their favour. Thus this pattern of intergroup relationships generates a behavioural inclination to seize the opportunity, assert control over the outgroup, and exploit the situation in order to maximize the likelihood of achieving the ingroup's own goals. Exploitation, however, is typically constrained by moral norms that do not equate might with right. This tension generates a cognitive representation of the outgroup which permits exploitative behaviour to be reinterpreted as helping. In the resulting **dependent image**, the target group is described as generally inept and vulnerable, deeply divided between moderate but incompetent good leaders and radical agitating bad ones. This image of a divided and vulnerable nation justifies using asymmetries in power and status to take control of the target outgroup, which can now be construed as a moral duty. It is not exploiting the group, but protecting it from their own ineptitude. In the nineteenth century, metaphors like 'white man's burden' captured the essence of the stereotype as it was applied to Asians and Africans by Europeans. Like the other images, it allowed people to seize the opportunity and act on the behavioural inclination without creating doubts about self-image. In the extreme case, perceivers expect gratitude and thanks from the target group. They are mystified and offended by complaints and resistance from the target group, especially if these complaints suggest the ingroup is simply advancing its own self-interest.

Complementary to the dependent image is the image generated when the ingroup nation is the one that is weaker and lower in status and perceives threat from an outgroup nation that is more powerful and culturally superior. Given that the outgroup is perceived as having vastly superior capability and strength, directly attacking the outgroup is not a viable option, but more indirect resistance, sabotage and acts of revolt or rebellion are elicited. The **imperialist image** of the outgroup functions to justify and sustain this behaviour orientation. An imperialist outgroup is perceived as exploitative, controlling, and motivated by the desire to dominate the ingroup. The image also includes the belief that some members of one's own ingroup have sold out to the outgroup and have allowed themselves to be used as agents or pawns of the imperialists. This image of a controlling, exploitative outgroup nation validates reactance against the imperialist regime in forms ranging from passive resistance to open revolt.

In a series of laboratory experiments, Alexander et al. (1999) sought to test the viability of image theory as a generalized model of intergroup perceptions. For this purpose, four specific intergroup contexts were constructed that were expected to give rise to the ally, the enemy, the dependent, or the barbarian image respectively. In three separate experiments, participants were asked to imagine themselves in scenarios in which they were part of an ingroup team in a context involving one other group. The description of the intergroup situation was varied across conditions by providing information about the nature of the relationship between the two groups. Goal compatibility was varied by creating a situation in which the two teams would either compete or cooperate to achieve a desired outcome. Relative power was manipulated by information about the amount of resources available to the ingroup and outgroup to reach their goal, and status was manipulated by describing the outgroup as similar to the ingroup or as inferior to the ingroup on status relevant dimensions.

Consistent with predictions derived from image theory, the various configurations of the intergroup situation did have a significant effect on behavioural orientations and on which specific images were formed of the outgroup team. Participants endorsed descriptions of the outgroup and response strategies that were consistent with the manipulated information. When the two groups were in competition but equal in power and status, participants were most likely to prefer an attack strategy against the outgroup and endorsement of items related to the enemy image was increased. When goals were incompatible and the outgroup was stronger but lower in status, a defensive appeasement strategy was preferred and components of the barbarian image were more likely to be endorsed. Finally, when the outgroup was both weaker and lower in status than the ingroup, an exploitative strategy was preferred and a dependent image was endorsed.

The influence of specific perceptions of the intergroup situation to create images and reactions is consistent with appraisal theories of intergroup emotions discussed in Chapters 1 and 4. In fact, the mediating role of emotions is implicit in the premises of image theory. First, the theory holds that appraisals of the pattern of intergroup relationships give rise to 'sentiments' (Herrmann 1985) that drive the behavioural orientations and consequent image activation. While the sentiments were not identified in terms of specific emotions, the idea that emotions correspond to specific action tendencies is integral to appraisal theories of emotion.

Based on this, a case can be made for incorporating an appraisal theory of emotions into image theory more formally (Brewer and Alexander 2002). Information about the goals, status and power relationships between ingroup and outgroup gives rise to appraisals along the dimensions of goal congruence, coping (relative ingroup strength and resources) and legitimacy (status evaluations). The resulting appraisal configuration elicits specific emotions (for example, fear, anger, resentment) that are associated with specific action tendencies (for example, retreating, attacking, resisting). In the context of intergroup relations, these emotional responses and associated action orientations are translated into cognitive representations of the outgroup (images) and preferences for behaviour and policies toward that group. Table 6.1 summarizes this emotion appraisal model

Table 6.1 Image theory of intergroup emotions

Relationship pattern	Intergroup emotion	Outgroup image	Action tendency

Goal compatibility
    Status equal
    Power equal
	Admiration
	Trust
		Ally	Cooperation

Goal incompatibility
    Status equal
    Power equal
	Anger	Enemy	Containment
			Competition

Goal independent
    Status lower
    Power lower
	Disgust
	Contempt
		Dependent	Exploit or
			protect

Goal incompatibility
    Status lower
    Power higher
	Fear
	Intimidation
		Barbarian	Defence

Goal independent
    Status higher
    Power higher
	Jealousy
	Resentment
		Imperialist	Seize

Source: Adapted from Brewer and Alexander (2002) with permission.

with respect to five specific intergroup configurations that have been drawn from image theory in international relations. By combining political theory with recent advances in the social psychology of intergroup emotions, we have a much more nuanced picture of the cognitive and affective under-pinnings of different forms of intergroup behaviour.

FAULTY DECISION MAKING: THE GROUP DYNAMICS PERSPECTIVE

Biological, cognitive and emotional perspectives on international conflict emphasize the role of intra-individual processes as factors contributing to war. A more uniquely social psychological perspective places emphasis on factors related to the way in which individuals and groups go about making collective decisions. In Chapter 2 we described research demon-strating the propensity for group discussion to result in polarization of opinions and decisions, and that such polarization is closely related to the formation of strong ingroup identification. We now consider the implica-tions of group polarization for those situations in which groups are mak-ing decisions about relations with an outgroup.

The psychology of groupthink

Based on evidence from psychological research and political history, political scientist Ole Holsti (1972) compiled a compelling case for the idea that political decision making under crisis conditions is analogous to individual decision making under stress. Emotional stress and crisis impair rational, realistic thinking in both individuals and groups. Two char-acteristics typical of crisis situations – time pressure and information overload – are particularly inimical to complex thought and evaluation of alternative options. As a consequence, crisis politics is subject to the dangers of tunnel vision and premature cognitive closure (Lebow 1981).

Following Holsti's analysis, Irving Janis conducted what is probably the most comprehensive review of the forces that interfere with high-quality decision making in groups (Janis 1972, 1982, 1989). Janis first became intrigued by this problem when he read historical accounts of the Bay of Pigs fiasco – a major US foreign policy blunder that occurred during John F. Kennedy's presidency. In April 1961, a small band of Cuban exiles, under the sponsorship of the USA, launched an invasion of their homeland at the Bay of Pigs. The plan, developed by the Central Intelli-gence Agency (CIA), was to train a squad of commandos and give them the means to launch an amphibious assault on Cuba. The expectation was that once these troops established a beach head, they would serve as the nucleus for a popular uprising by which the Cuban people would over-throw the Communist regime of Fidel Castro.

As it turned out, events did not unfold as expected. The Cuban military forces easily repelled the invasion, the Cuban people did not rise up against their leader, and the attempt was an embarrassing failure. In retrospect, it

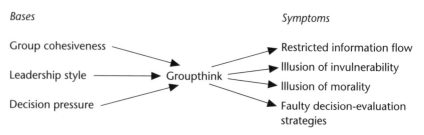

Figure 6.2   The elements of 'groupthink'

was easy to see why the invasion was likely to fail. Why, then, did President Kennedy and his cadre of high-powered advisers not see the major flaws in the plan (for example, underestimating Castro's popular appeal; thinking that a small band of troops could successfully overcome massive, well-trained armed forces; and so forth)?

Janis studied the details of the group decision processes that led to this, and other government blunders (for example, Watergate; escalation of the Vietnam War), as well as group decisions on a less grand scale (for example, those made by airline crews). From his examination of these situations, Janis developed ideas about a destructive psychological force that he termed **groupthink**.

Janis (1972, 1982) concluded that faulty decision making occurs primarily as a consequence of a distorted cognitive style ('groupthink') that prevents group members from evaluating evidence, supporting ideas and making decisions in a careful, rational manner. In Janis's view, groupthink is generated by specific conditions and is expressed in specific symptoms that are similar to the characteristics of decision making under stress (see Figure 6.2).

Bases of groupthink

Janis identified a number of group dynamics that he thought were the likely determinants of groupthink. He hypothesized that strong cohesiveness is one important contributing factor. Cohesiveness involves a sense of camaraderie and the belief that the group is special and worthwhile. Strong cohesiveness can create an atmosphere in which harmony and good feeling take precedence over critical thinking and expressions of dissent. Similarly, Janis saw the isolation of the decision-making group as a potential problem. When a group has limited input from outside sources, the information and options it considers are likely to be incomplete and biased. He also speculated that a closed leadership style, in which the leader tends to be autocratic and forceful in presenting her or his preferences, leads to groupthink. Finally, Janis believed that decision pressure also contributes to faulty group process. A sense of urgency to come to a decision (partly to leave time for bolstering and rationalizing the choice that is made) minimizes time spent in important orientation and discussion activities.

Symptoms of groupthink

Janis speculated that groupthink is manifested in a variety of symptoms. First, there are a number of factors that operate to restrict the flow of information and ideas among members:

- pressure from others to maintain the 'party line'
- self-censorship (avoiding expression of deviant opinions) as a consequence of concerns with maintaining a positive image in the minds of fellow group members
- the presence of mindguards – members who take it on themselves to prevent the intrusion into group discussions of ideas and information that they think would be disruptive.

All three factors limit the information that members have available to consider, with the consequence that a group decision is based on incomplete information and inadequate review of potential options. They also lead members to perceive more unanimity of views than actually exists; thus, the faulty option that becomes the group's choice benefits from support in (illusory) social reality. These are the same forces that operate to produce extremitization of group norms in many settings.

Second, members engaging in groupthink harbour certain illusions about their group, and about relevant outside groups and entities. Group members often believe that their group is highly competent, infallible, powerful and effective – that is, they share an illusion of invulnerability. Similarly, they also view their cause as just, guided by the highest ideals, on God's side and so forth, all expressions of the illusion of morality. In contrast, members can share a perception of relevant outsiders as weak, evil and easily beaten, thus contributing to the belief that one's own side will prevail. In other words, group discussion tends to exaggerate the components of ethnocentric bias as originally described by Sumner (1906) (see also Chapter 2 in this volume).

Finally, groups whose members are affected by groupthink manifest many signs of faulty decision-making strategies. For instance, groups can become so involved in the details of a plan that they overlook the basic goals they are seeking to accomplish. As a result, a series of smaller decisions are made without consideration of their overall consequences. Bad decisions often escalate, as groups seek to justify their past behaviour rather than abandon poor investments (Turner et al. 1992).

Research evidence for groupthink

Research conducted to assess the validity of Janis's ideas about the dynamics of small, cohesive decision-making groups has been generally supportive of his perspective. Herek et al. (1987), for example, examined a variety of international problems that the US government faced, and analysed the content of the group deliberations that preceded relevant policy decisions. Results showed that the larger the number of groupthink symptoms observed in the predecision deliberations, the lower the quality the decisions were judged to be.

Discussion groups studied in the social psychological laboratory have also been found to exhibit symptoms of groupthink, particularly when

the groups have high cohesion and share a sense of common social identity (Turner et al. 1992). Cohesive groups sometimes make poor decisions
because they are more concerned with protecting a positive image of their
group than with the validity of the ideas they are relying on. As we
discussed in Chapter 2, social identity is a powerful force for conformity
to group norms.

Based on a systematic review of results of groupthink research, McCauley
(1989) concluded that Janis may have overestimated the importance of
distorted thinking and cognitive biases as the basis of groupthink, and
underestimated the importance of compliance in generating flawed collective decisions. Conforming to a group decision does not always mean
that the individual agrees with that judgement. Compliance is going along
with the group even when one is not personally convinced. Some members might really know better, but do not express their contrary views;
instead, they merely acquiesce to the group's choice. Such self-censorship
of dissenting opinions appears to be a particularly important ingredient
of groupthink. As McCauley suggests, it may not be impaired reasoning
but the processes of group decision making itself that produce faulty
decisions.

CONCLUDING PERSPECTIVES: PUTTING THE BUILDING BLOCKS TOGETHER

In many respects, the social psychological study of intergroup relations
involves decomposing the phenomena into constituent cognitive and
motivational elements. As we said at the outset of this book, understanding the mechanisms underlying prejudice and intergroup conflict engages
virtually all areas of social psychological inquiry, including the study
of attribution and impression formation, social attitudes, aggression, self-
esteem, social comparison, cooperation and competition, and conformity
and compliance. These are the 'building blocks' of a social psychological
theory of intergroup relations discussed in Chapter 1.

But building blocks are just that – components that do not of themselves comprise an integrated theory. From various areas of research we
have a wealth of information that is relevant to the understanding of
intergroup behaviour, but this has yet to be integrated into a single comprehensive model. The study of ingroup bias, stereotyping, interpersonal
discrimination and intergroup contact constitute essentially different lines
of research that exist largely in isolation from each other. Certainly, there
is justification for studying each of these in their own right. But prejudice
and intergroup hate are complex phenomena that are more than the sum
of the parts (Brewer 1994).

An integrated theory will also necessarily take into account the socio-
political context in which intergroup relations are embedded. In particular,
social psychological theories need to be expanded to reflect three important elements of most real-world settings. First, most intergroup relations
are embedded in a multi-group context, not just the classic two-category
situation that has dominated most research on prejudice and discrimination. Second, most multi-group settings involve some kind of power or

dominance hierarchy in which groups differ in access to economic resources, education and political control. Although social psychological research on intergroup discrimination has looked at the influence of intergroup status differentials (see Chapter 3), the real impact of power differentials has yet to be fully explored. Finally, social psychologists have largely ignored the influence of group leadership on intergroup relations. Research on groupthink does acknowledge the influence of leader style on intragroup processes, but this is only one way in which influential leaders or group representatives may play a crucial role in mobilizing ingroup identity and defining the perception of relevant outgroups.

As we discussed in Chapter 1, social psychology is unique in its emphasis on linking structural aspects of groups at the societal level with psychological processes at the individual level. These linkages are yet to be completely mapped, but the cumulative research on ingroup identity, intergroup comparison and outgroup hostility provides many of the elements of a truly integrated theory of intergroup behaviour that now defines the agenda for this crucial area of research.

FURTHER READINGS

Bronfenbrenner, U. (1961) The mirror image in Soviet–American relations: a social psychologist's report, *Journal of Social Issues*, 17(3): 45–56. Bronfenbrenner's autobiographical analysis of his experience of mutual intergroup perceptions between the USA and the USSR during the Cold War.

Herrmann, R.K. (1985) *Perceptions and Behaviour in Soviet Foreign Policy*. Pittsburgh, PA: University of Pittsburgh Press. A review of image theory in international relations.

Horowitz, D. (1985) *Ethnic Groups in Conflict*. Berkeley, CA: University of California Press. Analysis of ethnonationalism and ethnic warfare by a political psychologist.

Janis, I.L. (1972) *Victims of Groupthink*. Boston, MA: Houghton Mifflin. The original book describing Janis's model of 'groupthink', drawing on illustrations from historical political decisions.

GLOSSARY

Affective priming: also known as mood-congruency effects. Positive mood states facilitate thoughts and memories that are positive in valence and inhibit negative thoughts; conversely, negative mood states facilitate negative and inhibit positive thoughts and memories.

Ally image: the perceptions associated with outgroups that are viewed as cooperative partners with the ingroup. The ally image is dominated by positive attributes.

Ambivalence/amplification: emotional ambivalence associated with arousal of negative affect in situations where positive attitudes are desirable. The theory of ambivalence amplification refers to a complex motivational state that applies particularly to the relation between a dominant, politically powerful group (such as whites in the USA) and a less powerful or disadvantaged minority group (such as blacks). The conflict between egalitarian values and antipathy toward the outgroup creates ambivalent feelings and motivates exaggerated evaluations of blacks, leading whites to evaluate blacks more extremely – either more extremely positive or more extremely negative, depending on the situation.

Ambivalent discrimination: differential treatment of an outgroup that is inconsistent with explicit norms of equality and fairness but rationalized by beliefs and stereotypes so as to be justified.

Appraisal: the assessment that an object or event has some significant positive or negative implications for the perceiver's goals or values.

Attribution theory: that branch of social cognition research that deals with how people perceive the causes of social events and of their own and others' behaviour.

Automatic categorization: category distinctions that are so familiar and frequently utilized that they are activated whenever relevant cues are present.

Automatic evaluation (automatic affect): the capacity of a salient outgroup to elicit negative affect or evaluations without conscious intent or awareness.

Aversive racism: the ambivalence associated with internal conflicts between egalitarian values and negative affect toward outgroups; in particular, the tendency of white respondents in the USA to mask overt expression of prejudice toward black Americans.

Barbarian image: perceptions and stereotypes of an outgroup that depict the group as evil and as enjoying wanton destruction for its own sake.

Category accentuation: the tendency for perceivers to exaggerate the extent of differences between members of one category and another. This category accentuation is a consequence of processes of assimilation and contrast whereby we judge items within the same category as more similar (assimilation) and items from different categories as more dissimilar (contrast) than they actually are.

Category accessibility: the likelihood that a particular category distinction will be salient, based on the frequency or importance of that categorization to the perceiver.

Collective self-esteem: self-esteem derived from the value of one's group memberships.

Common fate: the perception that members of a social category are likely to experience similar treatment and similar outcomes.

Comparative fit: the extent to which differences within categories are less than differences between categories among the persons in a particular context.

Contact hypothesis: the idea that opportunities for personal contact between members of opposing groups should reduce hostility by increasing mutual knowledge and acquaintance.

Crossed categorization: the result of categorizing people on more than one dimension at the same time, such that some individuals are ingroup members on one category dimension and outgroup members on another dimension.

Decategorization: intergroup contact situations in which interactions are highly personalized so that category salience is reduced.

Dependent image: perceptions and stereotypes of an outgroup that depict the group as generally inept and vulnerable.

Discontinuity effect: the finding that people are consistently more competitive in intergroup contexts than in interpersonal exchanges.

Displaced aggression: an act of harm directed at a target other than the original source of provocation.

Dual identities: holding social identities with a superordinate category and a subgroup category at the same time.

Enemy image: perceptions and stereotypes of an adversary outgroup which depicts the group as hostile, strategically manipulative and untrustworthy.

Equality: seeking to minimize the difference between one's own and others' outcomes. This is the social motive that is opposite to that associated with competition. With this orientation, goals of fairness and equal distribution of outcomes are primary.

Equity: the norm of fairness that individuals should receive outcomes proportional to their inputs.

Ethnocentrism: the view that one's own ingroup is the centre, and all others are scaled and rated with reference to it; the tendency to perceive the ingroup as defining what is positive, correct and good.

Fraternal deprivation: resentment that arises from comparisons between the outcomes of one's ingroup as a whole and those of other groups, particularly more advantaged outgroups.

Group polarization: the finding that positions on issues following a period of group discussion and consensus formation tend to be significantly more extreme than the average positions advocated when individuals express their personal opinions prior to group discussion.

Group status: the relative value or prestige accorded to a group in an intergroup context.

Groupthink: faulty group decision making that occurs as a consequence of a distorted cognitive style promoting conformity and consensus, which prevents group members from evaluating evidence, generating ideas and making decisions in a careful, rational manner.

Imperialist image: perceptions and stereotypes of an outgroup that depicts the group as exploitative, controlling and motivated by the desire to dominate the ingroup.

Implicit attitudes: positive or negative evaluations of objects or social groups that are held without awareness.

Incidental affect: emotions or moods that are caused by factors external to the immediate social situation or object of attention.

Ingroup: a social category to which the perceiver belongs.

Ingroup bias: see **ingroup favouritism.**

Ingroup favouritism (ingroup bias): distributing rewards and evaluations in a way that favours ingroup members over outgroup members.

Integral affect: affective reactions that arise directly from responses to the immediate social situation, person or event.

Intentional discrimination: deliberate differential treatment (usually negative toward an outgroup) that is perceived to be normative and deserved.

Intergroup anxiety: feelings of anxiety or concern that are elicited in anticipation of, or during, intergroup contact.

Intergroup discrimination: differential treatment based on group membership; usually, favourable treatment of ingroups compared to less favourable treatment of outgroups.

Intergroup emotions: emotions that are experienced on behalf of the groups to which a person belongs and feels identified, usually in intergroup contexts.

Intergroup power: the degree of control that one group has over its own fate and that of outgroups.

Intergroup social comparison: evaluating group outcomes and value relative to that of other groups.

Joint gain: seeking to maximize the total outcomes for self and others combined. This is the motivational orientation of pure cooperation.

Mindless ingroup favouritism: discriminatory bias that arises from automatic positive evaluations of the ingroup, without much thought or attempt to justify the differential benefits.

Minimal intergroup situation: an experimental paradigm in which participants are classified arbitrarily into separate categories that have no prior meaning. Category members are unknown to each other; there is no group interaction, no history of intergroup conflict and participants have no self-interest tied to the ingroup.

Mood-congruency effects: see **affective priming.**

Mutual differentiation: see **subcategorization.**

Narcissism of minor differences: an apparent preoccupation of group members with small or trivial distinctions that maintain differentiation between groups.

Normative fit: the match between behaviour by members of different social categories and category expectations.

Optimal distinctiveness: the theory that human beings have two opposing social motives – a need for inclusion which is satisfied by assimilation of the self into larger collectives, and an opposing need for differentiation which is satisfied by distinguishing the self from others. Social group identities are optimal if they meet both needs simultaneously through intragroup inclusion and intergroup distinctiveness.

Outgroup: a social category to which the perceiver does not belong.

Outgroup bias: see **reverse discrimination**.

Permeability: the extent to which group members can expect to be able to move from one group to another, or shift their social identity.

Positive distinctiveness: seeking positive advantage for the ingroup over the outgroup, thus enhancing the ingroup's value in comparison to that of the outgroup.

Positive-negative asymmetry: the finding that when the outcomes to be distributed are negative or harmful, ingroup favouritism is reduced (compared to distribution of positive outcomes), or may disappear all together.

Prejudice: broadly, any positive or negative evaluation of others based on group membership; more specifically, negative affect and evaluations directed toward specific outgroups.

Prisoner's dilemma game: a situation in which players are faced with a decision in which choosing one response (C) provides the best possible outcomes for both players combined, but choosing a different response (D) gives each player a chance to win while the other loses. However, if both choose D, both come out worse than if they had both chosen C.

Prospect theory: a theory of decision making framed in terms of potential losses or potential gains. When individuals make choices between possible positive outcomes (gains), they tend to be 'risk averse' (that is, prefer options that give them a small gain with certainty over more uncertain higher gains). On the other hand, when individuals are contemplating possible losses, they are more likely to be 'risk seeking' (that is, prefer a large potential loss in order to avoid a smaller, certain loss).

Realistic group conflict theory: a theory which holds that the nature of group relations is determined by the actual or perceived relationship between ingroup and outgroup interests. When one group can attain its goals (for resources, status or power) only at the expense of another group, intergroup conflict is the inevitable consequence.

Recategorization: intergroup contact situations in which members of different groups come together and form a superordinate, common ingroup identity.

Relative deprivation: feelings of resentment and the sense of injustice that arises from perceiving that one has less than is deserved compared to others or to one's expectations.

Relative gain: seeking to maximize the difference between outcomes to oneself compared to others. This is the motivational orientation associated with pure competition, where the value associated with one's own outcomes is determined by how much they exceed another's outcomes.

Reverse discrimination: behaviour that favours an outgroup over the ingroup; also known as outgroup bias.

Schema-based distrust: the learned belief or expectation that intergroup relations are competitive and therefore the outgroup is not to be trusted and the ingroup's welfare must be protected.

Self-categorization theory: a theory that personal and social identity differ in that they represent different levels of abstraction (inclusiveness) for self-categorization. Which level of categorization predominates in self-perception is a function of the situation or frame of reference at a given time.

Self-stereotyping: ascribing to oneself the traits and characteristics that are prototypic of one's ingroup.

Self-verification: the drive or motive to establish and maintain a consistent, coherent self-image.

Social attraction: preferential liking for ingroup members to the extent that a particular group member exemplifies the characteristics that are distinctive or important to that group.

Social categorization: classifying persons into discrete subsets based on similarities within groups and differences between groups. As a theory of intergroup relations, social categorization means that when a particular social category distinction is highly salient in a given situation, individuals will respond to the situation in accord with the relevant social identities, acting towards others in the setting in terms of their corresponding group memberships.

Social comparison: evaluating one's own traits, abilities and attitudes relative to those of other persons.

Social competition: responding to intergroup differences in power and status by seeking to change the structure of intergroup dominance to the ingroup's advantage.

Social creativity: achieving positive ingroup distinctiveness by redefining the bases of intergroup comparison, choosing new dimensions on which the ingroup can be assigned higher values than relevant outgroups, or changing the valuation attached to existing comparisons.

Social dilemmas: choice situations in which individuals acting in their own self-interest make decisions that conflict with collective welfare; the prisoner's dilemma generalized to groups of more than two people.

Social dominance: a theory of intergroup relations that emphasizes the importance of achieving power and dominance between groups. The need for social dominance at the group level is postulated to be an inherent human characteristic that functions to maintain stable status hierarchies in social systems.

Social identity: representation of the self as an integral part of a more inclusive social group or social category; emotional attachment to ingroup memberships.

Social reality: beliefs are seen as valid when they are shared by similar others, that is, by members of appropriate reference groups.

Subcategorization (mutual differentiation): an intergroup contact situation in which separate category identities remain salient in the contact setting.

Superordinate goals: important needs shared by members of different groups that can be met only by mutual cooperation.

Terror management theory: a theory of human nature based on the idea that when human beings evolved the capacity for self-awareness, this included awareness of mortality and the inevitability of one's own death. This awareness creates a high level of anxiety which could lead to paralysing fear if not sufficiently suppressed. As a consequence, human societies have evolved shared world-views and cultural values as an adaptation to cope with this anxiety over death.

Ultimate attribution error: a self-serving bias extended to intergroup contexts whereby good outcomes (or behaviours) for the ingroup are explained by, internal attributions, while bad outcomes are explained by situational factors, or unstable internal attributes. By contrast, good outcomes for the outgroup are explained by situational factors, or by unstable internal factors (such as effort or luck), and bad outcomes for the outgroup are explained by stable, internal factors.

Universal stereotype: traits attributed to all ingroups vis-à-vis outgroups, such that ingroups are believed to be trustworthy, cooperative, peaceful and honest, while outgroups are perceived to be untrustworthy, competitive, quarrelsome and dishonest.

Zero-sum situation: a competitive situation in which one group's win is always the other group's loss.

REFERENCES

Aberson, C.L., Healy, M. and Romero, V. (2000) Ingroup bias and self-esteem: a meta-analysis, *Personality and Social Psychology Review*, 4: 157–73.

Abrams, D. (1985) Focus of attention in minimal intergroup discrimination, *British Journal of Social Psychology*, 24: 65–7.

Abrams, D. and Hogg, M.A. (1988) Comments on the motivational significance of self-esteem in social identity and intergroup discrimination, *European Journal of Social Psychology*, 18: 317–34.

Albert, S. (1977) Temporal comparison theory, *Psychological Review*, 6: 485–503.

Alexander, M.G., Brewer, M.B. and Herrmann, R.K. (1999) Images and affect: a functional analysis of out-group stereotypes, *Journal of Personality and Social Psychology*, 77: 78–93.

Allen, V.L., Wilder, D.A. and Atkinson, M.L. (1983) Multiple group membership and social identity, in T. Sarbin and K. Scheibe (eds) *Studies in Social Identity*. New York: Praeger.

Allport, G.W. (1954) *The Nature of Prejudice*. Cambridge, MA: Addison-Wesley.

Amir, Y. (1969) Contact hypothesis in ethnic relations, *Psychological Bulletin*, 71: 319–42.

Ancok, D. and Chertkoff, J.M. (1983) Effects of group membership, relative performance and self-interest on the division of outcomes, *Journal of Personality and Social Psychology*, 45: 1256–62.

Anderson, B. (1991) *Imagined Communities: Reflections on the Origin and Spread of Nationalism*. New York: Verso.

Archer, J. (1991) Human sociobiology: basic concepts and limitations, *Journal of Social Issues*, 47(3): 11–26.

Aronson, E. and Gonzalez, A. (1988) Desegregation, jigsaw and the Mexican–American experience, in P. Katz and D. Taylor (eds) *Eliminating Racism: Profiles in Controversy*. New York: Plenum.

Aronson, E., Blaney, N., Stephan, C., Sikes, J. and Snapp, M. (1978) *The Jigsaw Classroom*. Beverly Hills, CA: Sage.

Ashbach, C. and Schermer, V. (eds) (1987) *Object Relations, the Self and the Group*. London: Routledge & Kegan Paul.

Azzi, A.E. (1992) Procedural justice and the allocation of power in intergroup relations: studies in the United States and South Africa, *Personality and Social Psychology Bulletin*, 18: 736–47.

Bagby, J.W. (1957) A cross-cultural study of perceptual predominance in binocular rivalry, *Journal of Abnormal and Social Psychology*, 54: 331–4.

Bargh, J. (1989) Conditional automaticity: varieties of automatic influence on social perception and cognition, in J. Uleman and J. Barth (eds) *Unintended Thought*. New York: Guilford.

Barnes-Nacoste, R. (1992) About the psychology of affirmative action: putting the science back in. Presentation at the annual meeting of the American Psychological Society, San Diego, CA.

Baron, R.A. (1972) Reducing the influence of an aggressive model: the restraining effects of peer censure, *Journal of Experimental Social Psychology*, 8: 266–75.

Baron, R.A. (1979) Effects of victim's pain cues, victim's race and level of prior instigations upon physical aggression, *Journal of Applied Social Psychology*, 9: 10–114.

Berg, J.H. and Wright-Buckley, C. (1988) Effects of racial similarity and interviewer intimacy in a peer-counseling analogue, *Journal of Counseling Psychology*, 35: 377–84.

Berry, J.W. (1984) Cultural relations in plural societies: alternatives to segregation and their sociopsychological implications, in N. Miller and M.B. Brewer (eds) *Groups in Contact: The Psychology of Desegregation*. New York: Academic Press.

Betancourt, H. and Blair, I. (1992) A cognitive (attribution)-emotion model of violence in conflict situations, *Personality and Social Psychology Bulletin*, 18: 343–50.

Bettencourt, B.A. and Dorr, N. (1998) Cooperative interaction and intergroup bias: effects of numerical representation and cross-cut role assignment, *Personality and Social Psychology Bulletin*, 24: 1276–93.

Bettencourt, B.A., Brewer, M.B., Croak, M.R. and Miller, N. (1992) Cooperation and reduction of intergroup bias: the role of reward structure and social orientation, *Journal of Experimental Social Psychology*, 28: 301–19.

Bettencourt, B.A., Dorr, N., Charlton, K. and Hume, D. (2001) Status differences and ingroup bias: a meta-analytic examination of the effects of status stability, status legitimacy and group permeability, *Psychological Bulletin*, 127: 520–42.

Biernat, M., Manis, M. and Nelson, T. (1991) Stereotypes and standards of judgment, *Journal of Personality and Social Psychology*, 60: 485–99.

Blake, R.R. and Mouton, J.S. (1986) From theory to practice in interface problem solving, in S. Worchel and W. Austin (eds) *Psychology of Intergroup Relations*. Chicago: Nelson-Hall.

Blanz, M., Mummendey, A. and Otten, S. (1997) Normative evaluations and frequency expectations regarding positive and negative outcome allocations between groups, *European Journal of Social Psychology*, 27: 165–76.

Bodenhausen, G.V. (1993) Emotions, arousal and stereotypic judgments: a heuristic model of affect and stereotyping, in D.M. Mackie and D.L. Hamilton (eds) *Affect, Cognition and Stereotyping: Interactive Processes in Group Perception*. New York: Academic Press.

Bourhis, R., Giles, H. and Lambert, W.E. (1975) Social consequences of accommodating one's style of speech: a cross-national investigation, *International Journal of the Sociology of Language*, 6: 53–71.

Bourhis, R., Giles, H., Leyens, J-P. and Tajfel, H. (1979) Psycholinguistic distinctiveness: language divergence in Belgium, in H. Giles and R. St Clair (eds) *Language and Social Psychology*. Oxford: Blackwell.

Bower, G.H. (1981) Mood and memory, *American Psychologist*, 36: 129–48.

Bower, G.H. (1991) Mood congruity of social judgments, in J.P. Forgas (ed.) *Emotion and Social Judgments*. Oxford: Pergamon.

Braddock, J.H. (1985) School desegregation and black assimilation, *Journal of Social Issues*, 41(3): 9–22.

Brewer, M.B. (1979) In-group bias in the minimal intergroup situation: a cognitive-motivational analysis, *Psychological Bulletin*, 86: 307–24.

Brewer, M.B. (1991) The social self: on being the same and different at the same time, *Personality and Social Psychology Bulletin*, 17: 475–82.

Brewer, M.B. (1994) The social psychology of prejudice: getting it all together, in M. Zanna and J. Olson (eds) *The Psychology of Prejudice: The Ontario Symposium*, Vol. 7. Hillsdale, NJ: Erlbaum.

Brewer, M.B. (1999) The psychology of prejudice: ingroup love or outgroup hate?, *Journal of Social Issues*, 55: 429–44.

Brewer, M.B. (2001) Ingroup identity and intergroup conflict: when does ingroup love become outgroup hate?, in R. Ashmore, L. Jussim and D. Wilder (eds) *Social Identity, Intergroup Conflict and Conflict Reduction*. New York: Oxford University Press.

Brewer, M.B. and Alexander, M.G. (2002) Intergroup emotions and images, in D.M. Mackie and E.R. Smith (eds) *From Prejudice to Intergroup Emotions*. Philadelphia, PA: Psychology Press.

Brewer, M.B. and Campbell, D.T. (1976) *Ethnocentrism and Intergroup Attitudes: East African Evidence*. New York: Halstead.

Brewer, M.B. and Gaertner, S.L. (2001) Toward reduction of prejudice: intergroup contact and social categorization, in R. Brown and S. Gaertner (eds) *Blackwell Handbook of Social Psychology: Intergroup Relations*. Oxford: Blackwell.

Brewer, M.B. and Kramer, R.M. (1986) Choice behavior in social dilemmas: effects of social identity, group size and decision framing, *Journal of Personality and Social Psychology*, 50: 543–9.

Brewer, M.B. and Miller, N. (1984) Beyond the contact hypothesis: theoretical perspectives on desegregation, in N. Miller and M.B. Brewer (eds) *Groups in Contact: The Psychology of Desegregation*. New York: Academic Press.

Brewer, M.B. and Miller, N. (1988) Contact and cooperation: when do they work?, in P. Katz and D. Taylor (eds) *Eliminating Racism: Profiles in Controversy*. New York: Plenum.

Brewer, M.B. and Schneider, S. (1990) Social identity and social dilemmas: a double-edged sword, in D. Abrams and M. Hogg (eds) *Social Identity Theory: Constructive and Critical Advances*. London: Harvester Wheatsheaf.

Brewer, M.B., Ho, H-K., Lee, J-Y. and Miller, N. (1987) Social identity and social distance among Hong Kong school children, *Personality and Social Psychology Bulletin*, 13: 156–65.

Brewer, M.B., Manzi, J. and Shaw, J. (1993) In-group identification as a function of depersonalization, distinctiveness and status, *Psychological Science*, 4: 88–92.

Brewer, M.B., Weber, J.G. and Carini, B. (1995) Person memory in intergroup contexts: categorization versus individuation, *Journal of Personality and Social Psychology*, 69: 29–40.

Bronfenbrenner, U. (1961) The mirror image in Soviet–American relations: a social psychologist's report, *Journal of Social Issues*, 17(3): 45–56.

Brown, J.D., Collins, R.L. and Schmidt, G.W. (1988) Self-esteem and direct versus indirect forms of self-enhancement, *Journal of Personality and Social Psychology*, 55: 445–53.

Brown, R.J. and Gardham, K. (2001) Two forms of intergroup discrimination with positive and negative outcomes: explaining the positive–negative asymmetry effects, *Personality and Social Psychology Bulletin*, 40: 23–34.

Brown, R.J. and Middendorf, J. (1996) The underestimated role of temporal comparison: a test of the life-span model, *Journal of Social Psychology*, 136: 325–31.

Brown, R.J. and Turner, J.C. (1979) The criss-cross categorisation effect in intergroup discrimination, *British Journal of Social and Clinical Psychology*, 18: 371–83.

Brown, R.J., Vivian, J. and Hewstone, M. (1999) Changing attitudes through intergroup contact: the effects of group membership salience, *European Journal of Social Psychology*, 29: 741–64.

Brown, R.J., Maras, P., Masser, B., Vivian, J. and Hewstone, M. (2001) Life on the ocean wave: testing some intergroup hypotheses in a naturalistic setting, *Group Processes and Intergroup Relations*, 4: 81–98.

Brown v. Board of Education of Topeka (1953) The effect of segregation and the consequences of desegregation: a social science statement. Appendix to appellants' briefs, *Minnesota Law Review*, 37: 427–39.

Brown v. Board of Education of Topeka (1954) 347 US 483.

Bruins, J., Platow, M. and Ng, S.H. (1995) Distributive and procedural justice in interpersonal and intergroup situations, *Social Justice Research*, 8: 103–21.

Bruner, J.S. (1957) On perceptual readiness, *Psychological Review*, 64: 123–52.

Burn, S.M. and Oskamp, S. (1989) Ingroup biases and US–Soviet conflict, *Journal of Social Issues*, 45(2): 73–89.

Buss, D.M. (1990) Evolutionary social psychology: prospects and pitfalls, *Motivation and Emotion*, 14: 265–86.

Buss, D.M. (1991) Evolutionary personality psychology, *Annual Review of Psychology*, 45: 459–91.

Byrne, D. (1971) *The Attraction Paradigm*. New York: Academic Press.

Byrne, D., Clore, G. and Smeaton, G. (1986) The attraction hypothesis: do similar attitudes affect anything?, *Journal of Personality and Social Psychology*, 51: 1167–70.

Cacioppo, J. and Berntson, G. (1994) Relationships between attitudes and evaluative space: a critical review, with emphasis on the separability of positive and negative substrates, *Psychological Bulletin*, 115: 401–23.

Caddick, B. (1982) Perceived illegitimacy and intergroup relations, in H. Tajfel (ed.) *Social Identity and Intergroup Relations*. Cambridge: Cambridge University Press.

Campbell, D.T. (1956) Enhancement of contrast as composite habit, *Journal of Abnormal and Social Psychology*, 53: 350–5.

Campbell, D.T. (1967) Stereotypes and the perception of outgroup differences, *American Psychologist*, 22: 812–29.

Caporael, L.R. and Brewer, M.B. (1991) Reviving evolutionary psychology: biology meets society, *Journal of Social Issues*, 47(3): 187–95.

Carlson, M. and Miller, N. (1988) The differential effects of social and nonsocial negative events on aggressiveness, *Sociology and Social Research*, 72: 155–8.

Cheng, P. and Holyoak, K. (1985) Pragmatic reasoning schemas, *Cognitive Psychology*, 17: 391–416.

Cialdini, R.B. and Richardson, K.D. (1980) Two indirect tactics of image management: basking and blasting, *Journal of Personality and Social Psychology*, 39: 406–15.

Cialdini, R.B., Borden, R., Thorne, A. et al. (1976) Basking in reflected glory: three (football) field studies, *Journal of Personality and Social Psychology*, 34: 366–75.

Coates, D. and Winston, T. (1983) Counteracting the deviance of depression: peer support groups for victims, *Journal of Social Issues*, 39: 169–94.

Cohen, E.G. (1982) Expectation states and interracial interaction in school settings, *Annual Review of Sociology*, 8: 209–35.

Cohen, E.G. (1984) The desegregated school: problems in status power and interethnic climate, in N. Miller and M.B. Brewer (eds) *Groups in Contact: The Psychology of Desegregation*. New York: Academic Press.

Cole, R. and Bourhis, R.Y. (1990) Power differentials between the sexes: two intergroup studies. Paper presented at the annual meeting of the Canadian Psychological Association, Ottawa, Ontario.

Connor, W. (1994) *Ethnonationalism: The Quest for Understanding*. Princeton, NJ: Princeton University Press.

Cook, S.W. (1984) The 1954 Social Science statement and school desegregation: a reply to Gerard, *American Psychologist*, 39: 819–32.

Cook, S.W. (1985) Experimenting on social issues: the case of school desegregation, *American Psychologist*, 40: 452–60.

Cooper, J. and Fazio, R.H. (1986) The formation and persistence of attitudes that support intergroup conflict, in S. Worchel and W. Austin (eds) *Psychology of Intergroup Relations*. Chicago: Nelson-Hall.

Cottam, R. (1977) *Foreign Policy Motivation: A General Theory and a Case Study*. Pittsburgh, PA: University of Pittsburgh Press.

Crisp, R.J. and Hewstone, M. (2001) Multiple categorization and implicit intergroup bias: differential category dominance and the positive–negative asymmetry effect, *European Journal of Social Psychology*, 31: 45–62.

Crisp, R.J., Hewstone, M. and Rubin, M. (2001) Does multiple categorization reduce intergroup bias?, *Personality and Social Psychology Bulletin*, 27: 76–89.

Crocker, J. and Luhtanen, R. (1990) Collective self-esteem and ingroup bias, *Journal of Personality and Social Psychology*, 58: 60–7.

Crocker, J. and Major, B. (1989) Social stigma and self-esteem: the self-protective properties of stigma, *Psychological Review*, 96: 608–30.

Crocker, J. and Schwartz, I. (1985) Prejudice and ingroup favoritism in a minimal intergroup situation: effects of self-esteem, *Personality and Social Psychology Bulletin*, 11: 379–86.

Crocker, J., Thomson, L., McGraw, K. and Ingerman, C. (1987) Downward comparison, prejudice and evaluations of others: effects of self-esteem and threat, *Journal of Personality and Social Psychology*, 52: 907–16.

Crocker, J., Voelkl, K., Testa, M. and Major, B. (1991) Social stigma: the affective consequences of attributional ambiguity, *Journal of Personality and Social Psychology*, 60: 218–28.

Crocker, J., Blaine, B. and Luhtanen, R. (1993) Prejudice, intergroup behaviour and self-esteem: enhancement and protection motives, in M. Hogg and D. Abrams (eds) *Group Motivation: Social Psychological Perspectives*. London: Harvester Wheatsheaf.

Crocker, J., Luhtanen, R., Blaine, B. and Broadnax, S. (1994) Collective self-esteem and psychological well-being among White, Black and Asian college students, *Personality and Social Psychology Bulletin*, 20: 503–13.

Crosby, F. (1982) *Relative Deprivation and Working Women*. New York: Oxford University Press.

Crosby, F., Bromley, S. and Saxe, L. (1980) Recent unobtrusive studies of black and white discrimination and prejudice: a literature review, *Psychological Bulletin*, 87: 546–63.

Crosby, F.J., Ferdman, B.M. and Wingate, B.R. (2001) Addressing and redressing discrimination: affirmative action in social psychological perspective, in R. Brown and S. Gaertner (eds) *Blackwell Handbook of Social Psychology: Intergroup Relations*. Oxford: Blackwell.

Cross, W.E. (1985) Black identity: rediscovering the distinction between personal identity and reference group orientation, in M. Spencer, G. Brookins and W. Allen (eds) *Beginnings: The Social and Affective Development of Black Children*. Hillsdale, NJ: Erlbaum.

Darley, J.M. (1966) Fear and social comparison as determinants of conformity behavior, *Journal of Personality and Social Psychology*, 4: 73–8.

Darwin, C. ([1872] 1955) *The Expression of Emotions in Man and Animals*. New York: Greenwood.

Davis, J.A. (1959) A formal interpretation of the theory of relative deprivation, *Sociometry*, 22: 280–96.

DeCremer, D. and Van Vugt, M. (1999) Social identification effects in social dilemmas: a transformation of motives, *European Journal of Social Psychology*, 29: 871–93.

Deschamps, J-C. and Brown, R.J. (1983) Superordinate goals and intergroup conflict, *British Journal of Social Psychology*, 22: 189–95.

Deschamps, J-C. and Doise, W. (1978) Crossed category memberships in intergroup relations, in H. Tajfel (ed.) *Differentiation between Social Groups*. Cambridge: Cambridge University Press.

Desforges, D., Lord, C., Ramsey, S., Mason, J., Van Leeuwen, M., West, S. and Lepper, M. (1991) Effects of structured cooperative contact on changing negative attitudes toward stigmatized social groups, *Journal of Personality and Social Psychology*, 60: 531–44.

Deutsch, M. and Collins, M.E. (1951) *Interracial Housing: A Psychological Evaluation of a Social Experiment*. Minneapolis, MN: University of Minnesota Press.

Devine, P.G. (1989) Stereotypes and prejudice: their automatic and controlled components, *Journal of Personality and Social Psychology*, 56: 5–18.

Devine, P.G., Hamilton, D.L. and Ostrom, T.M. (1994) *Social Cognition: Impact on Social Psychology*. New York: Academic Press.

Diehl, M. (1988) Social identity and minimal groups: the effects of interpersonal and intergroup attitudinal similarity on intergroup discrimination, *British Journal of Social Psychology*, 27: 289–300.

Diehl, M. (1989) Justice and discrimination between minimal groups: the limits of equity, *British Journal of Social Psychology*, 28: 227–38.

Diehl, M. (1990) The minimal group paradigm: theoretical explanations and empirical findings, in W. Stroebe and M. Hewstone (eds) *European Review of Social Psychology*, Vol. 1. Chichester: Wiley.

Dijker, A.J.M. (1987) Emotional reaction to ethnic minorities, *European Journal of Social Psychology*, 17: 305–25.

Dijker, A.J.M. (1989) Ethnic attitudes and emotions, in J.P. van Oudenhoven and T.M. Willemsen (eds) *Ethnic Minorities: Social Psychology Perspectives*. Amsterdam: Swets and Zeitlinger.

Dion, K.L. (1973) Cohesiveness as a determinant of ingroup–outgroup bias, *Journal of Personality and Social Psychology*, 28: 163–71.

Dollard, J., Doob, L.W., Miller, N.E., Mowrer, O.H. and Sears, R.R. (1939) *Frustration and Aggression*. New Haven, CT: Yale University Press.

Donnerstein, M. and Donnerstein, E. (1973) Variables in interracial aggression: potential ingroup censure, *Journal of Personality and Social Psychology*, 27: 143–50.

Donnerstein, M. and Donnerstein, E. (1975) The effects of attitudinal similarity on interracial aggression, *Journal of Personality*, 43: 485–502.

Donnerstein, M. and Donnerstein, E. (1978) Direct and vicarious censure in the control of interracial aggression, *Journal of Personality*, 48: 162–75.

Donnerstein, M., Donnerstein, E., Simon, S. and Ditrichs, R. (1972) Variables in interracial aggression: anonymity, expected retaliation and a riot, *Journal of Personality and Social Psychology*, 22: 236–45.

Doosje, B., Ellemers, N. and Spears, R. (1995) Perceived intragroup variability as a function of group status and identification, *Journal of Experimental and Social Psychology*, 31: 410–36.

Dovidio, J.F., Evans, N. and Tyler, R.B. (1986) Racial stereotypes: the contents of their cognitive representations, *Journal of Experimental Social Psychology*, 22: 22–37.

Dovidio, J.F., Kawakami, K. and Beach, K.R. (2001) Implicit and explicit attitudes: examination of the relationship between measures of intergroup bias, in R. Brown and S. Gaertner (eds) *Blackwell Handbook of Social Psychology: Intergroup Relations*. Oxford: Blackwell.

Dutton, D.G. (1973) Reverse discrimination: the relationship of amount of perceived discrimination toward a minority group on the behavior of majority group members, *Canadian Journal of Behavioural Sciences*, 5: 34–45.

Dutton, D.G. and Lake, R.A. (1973) Threat of own prejudice and reverse discrimination in interracial situations, *Journal of Personality and Social Psychology*, 28: 94–100.

Eakins, B.W. and Eakins, R.G. (1978) *Sex Differences in Human Communication*. Boston, MA: Houghton Mifflin.

Easterbrook, J.A. (1959) The effect of emotion on cue utilization and the organization of behavior, *Psychological Review*, 66: 183–201.

Edwards, J. (1985) *Language, Society and Identity*. Oxford: Blackwell.

Eibl-Eibesfeldt, I. (1979) *The Biology of Peace and War: Men, Animals and Aggression*. New York: Viking.

Ellemers, N. (1993) The influence of socio-structural variables on identity management strategies, in W. Stroebe and M. Hewstone (eds) *European Review of Social Psychology*, Vol. 4. Chichester: Wiley.

Ellemers, N. and Barreto, M. (2001) The impact of relative group status: affective, perceptual and behavioral consequences, in R. Brown and S. Gaertner (eds) *Blackwell Handbook of Social Psychology: Intergroup Relations*. Oxford: Blackwell.

Ellemers, N., van Knippenberg, A., de Vries, N. and Wilke, H. (1988) Social identification and permeability of group boundaries, *European Journal of Social Psychology*, 18: 497–513.

Ellemers, N., van Knippenberg, A. and Wilke, H. (1990) The influence of permeability of group boundaries and stability of group status on strategies of individual mobility and social change, *British Journal of Social Psychology*, 29: 233–46.

Ellemers, N., Doosje, B., van Knippenberg, A. and Wilke, H. (1992) Status protection in high status minority groups, *European Journal of Social Psychology*, 22: 123–40.

Ellemers, N., Wilke, H. and van Knippenberg, A. (1993) Effects of the legitimacy of low group or individual status on individual and collective identity enhancement strategies, *Journal of Personality and Social Psychology*, 64: 766–78.

Ellemers, N., Barreto, M. and Spears, R. (1999) Commitment and strategic responses to social context, in N. Ellemers, R. Spears and B. Doosje (eds) *Social Identity: Context, Commitment, Content*. Oxford: Blackwell.

Epstein, J.L. (1985) After the bus arrives: resegregation in desegregated schools, *Journal of Social Issues*, 41(3): 23–43.

Esses, V.M., Haddock, G. and Zanna, M.A. (1993) Values, stereotypes and emotions as determinants of intergroup attitudes, in D.M. Mackie and D.L. Hamilton (eds) *Affect, Cognition and Stereotyping*. San Diego, CA: Academic Press.

Esses, V.M., Haddock, G. and Zanna, M.A. (1994) The role of mood in the expression of intergroup stereotypes, in M. Zanna and J. Olson (eds) *The Psychology of Prejudice: The Ontario Symposium*, Vol. 7. Hillsdale, NJ: Erlbaum.

Eurich-Fulcer, R. and Schofield, J.W. (1995) Correlated versus uncorrelated social categorizations: the effect on intergroup bias, *Personality and Social Psychology Bulletin*, 21: 149–59.

Farnham, S.D., Greenwald, A.G. and Banaji, M.R. (1999) Implicit self-esteem, in D. Abrams and M. Hogg (eds) *Social Identity and Social Cognition*. Oxford: Blackwell.

Fazio, R.H., Jackson, J.R., Dunton, B.C. and Williams, C.J. (1995) Variability in automatic activation as an unobtrusive measure of racial attitudes: a bona fide pipeline?, *Journal of Personality and Social Psychology*, 69: 1013–27.

Feagin, J.R. (1992) The continuing significance of racism: discrimination against Black students in White colleges, *Journal of Black Studies*, 22: 546–78.

Feinman, S. (1980) Infant responses to race, size, proximity and movement of strangers, *Infant Behavior and Child Development*, 3: 187–204.

Festinger, L. (1950) Informal social communication, *Psychological Review*, 57: 271–82.

Festinger, L. (1954) A theory of social comparison processes, *Human Relations*, 7: 117–40.

Festinger, L. (1957) *A Theory of Cognitive Dissonance*. Stanford, CA: Stanford University Press.

Forgas, J.P. (1990) Affective influences on individual and group judgments, *European Journal of Social Psychology*, 41: 197–214.

Forgas, J.P. and Fiedler, K. (1996) Us and them: mood effects on intergroup discrimination, *Journal of Personality and Social Psychology*, 70: 28–40.

Frank, J.D. (1967) *Sanity and Survival: Psychological Aspects of War and Peace*. New York: Vintage.

Freud, S. ([1912] 1957) *Totem and Taboo*, in *The Standard Edition of the Complete Psychological Works of Sigmund Freud*, Vol. 13. London: Hogarth Press.

Freud, S. ([1921] 1960) *Group Psychology and the Analysis of the Ego*. New York: Bantam.

Frey, D. and Gaertner, S.L. (1986) Helping and avoidance of inappropriate interracial behavior: a strategy which perpetuates a non-prejudiced self-image, *Journal of Personality and Social Psychology*, 50: 1083–90.

Fridlund, A.J. (1994) *Human Facial Expression: An Evolutionary View*. San Diego, CA: Academic Press.

Gaertner, L., Sedikides, C. and Graetz, K. (1999) In search of self-definition: motivational primacy of the individual self, motivational primacy of the collective self, or contextual primacy?, *Journal of Personality and Social Psychology*, 76: 5–18.

Gaertner, S.L. and Dovidio, J.F. (1986) The aversive form of racism, in J.F. Dovidio and S.L. Gaertner (eds) *Prejudice, Discrimination and Racism*. Orlando, FL: Academic Press.

Gaertner, S.L. and Dovidio, J.F. (2000) *Reducing Intergroup Bias: The Common Ingroup Identity Model*. Philadelphia, PA: Psychology Press.

Gaertner, S.L., Mann, J., Murrell, A. and Dovidio, J. (1989) Reducing intergroup bias: the benefits of recategorization, *Journal of Personality and Social Psychology*, 57: 239–49.

Gaertner, S.L., Mann, J., Dovidio, J., Murrell, A. and Pomare, M. (1990) How does cooperation reduce intergroup bias?, *Journal of Personality and Social Psychology*, 59: 692–704.

Gaertner, S.L., Dovidio, J., Anastasio, P., Bachman, B. and Rust, M. (1993) The Common Ingroup Identity Model: recategorization and the reduction of intergroup bias, in W. Stroebe and M. Hewstone (eds) *European Review of Social Psychology*, Vol. 4. London: Wiley.

Gaertner, S.L., Rust, M., Dovidio, J.F., Bachman, B. and Anastasio, P. (1994) The contact hypothesis: the role of a common ingroup identity on reducing intergroup bias, *Small Groups Research*, 25: 224–9.

Gaertner, S.L., Dovidio, J.F., Banker, B. et al. (2000) Reducing intergroup conflict: from superordinate goals to decategorization, recategorization and mutual differentiation, *Group Dynamics*, 4: 98–114.

Garza, R.T. and Santos, S.J. (1991) Ingroup/outgroup balance and interdependent interethnic behavior, *Journal of Experimental Social Psychology*, 27: 124–37.

Gelman, S.A. (1988) The development of induction within natural kind and artifact categories, *Cognitive Psychology*, 20: 65–91.

Gelman, S.A. and Wellman, H.M. (1991) Insides and essence: early understandings of the non-obvious, *Cognition*, 38: 213–44.

Gerard, H.B. (1983) School desegregation: the social science role, *American Psychologist*, 38: 869–87.

Gerard, H.B. and Miller, N. (1975) *School Desegregation: A Long-term Study*. New York: Plenum.

Gerard, H.B. and Orive, R. (1987) The dynamics of opinion formation, in L. Berkowitz (eds) *Advances in Experimental Social Psychology*, Vol. 20. San Diego, CA: Academic Press.

Gibbons, F.X. (1985) Social stigma perception: social comparison among mentally retarded persons, *American Journal of Mental Deficiency*, 90: 98–106.

Gibbons, F.X., Gerrard, M., Lando, H. and McGovern, P. (1991) Social comparison and smoking cessation: the role of the 'typical smoker', *Journal of Experimental Social Psychology*, 27: 239–58.

Giles, H. (1978) Linguistic differentiation in ethnic groups, in H. Tajfel (ed.) *Differentiation between Social Groups*. London: Academic Press.

Giles, H. and Byrne, J.L. (1982) The intergroup model of second language acquisition, *Journal of Multilingual and Multicultural Development*, 3: 17–40.

Giles, H. and Johnson, P. (1981) The role of language in ethnic group relations, in J. Turner and H. Giles (eds) *Intergroup Behaviour*. Oxford: Blackwell.

Giles, H. and Smith, P.M. (1979) Accommodation theory: optimal levels of convergence, in H. Giles and R. St Clair (eds) *Language and Social Psychology*. Oxford: Pergamon.

Giles, H., Bourhis, R. and Taylor, D.M. (1977) Towards a theory of language in ethnic group relations, in H. Giles (ed.) *Language, Ethnicity and Inter-group Relations*. London: Academic Press.

Giles, H., Robinson, W.P. and Smith, P.M. (eds) (1980) *Language: Social Psychological Perspectives*. Oxford: Pergamon.

Goodall, J. (1990) *Through a Window: My Thirty Years with the Chimpanzees of Gombe*. Boston, MA: Houghton Mifflin.

Gorenflo, D.W. and Crano, W.D. (1989) Judgmental subjectivity/objectivity and locus of choice in social comparison, *Journal of Personality and Social Psychology*, 57: 605–14.

Gouaux, C. (1971) Induced affective states and interpersonal attraction, *Journal of Personality and Social Psychology*, 20: 37–43.

Greenberg, J., Simon, L., Pyszczynski, T., Solomon, S. and Chatel, D. (1992) Terror management and tolerance: does mortality salience always intensify negative reactions to others who threaten one's worldview?, *Journal of Personality and Social Psychology*, 63: 212–20.

Greenwald, A.G. (1980) The totalitarian ego: fabrication and revision of personal history, *American Psychologist*, 35: 603–18.

Greenwald, A.G., McGhee, D. and Schwartz, J. (1998) Measuring individual differences in implicit cognition: the implicit association test, *Journal of Personality and Social Psychology*, 74: 1464–80.

Griffitt, W.B. (1970) Environmental effects on interpersonal affective behavior: ambient effective temperature and attraction, *Journal of Personality and Social Psychology*, 15: 240–4.

Guimond, S. and Dubé-Simard, L. (1983) Relative deprivation theory and the Quebec Nationalist Movement: the cognition-emotion distinction and the personal-group deprivation issue, *Journal of Personality and Social Psychology*, 44: 526–35.

Gurin, P. and Townsend, A. (1986) Properties of gender identity and their implications for gender consciousness, *British Journal of Social Psychology*, 25: 139–48.

Gurin, P., Miller, A. and Gurin, G. (1980) Stratum identification and group consciousness, *Social Psychology Quarterly*, 43: 30–47.

Gurr, T.R. (1994) Peoples against states: ethnopolitical conflict and the changing world system, *International Studies Quarterly*, 38: 347–77.

Hagendoorn, L. (1995) Intergroup biases in multiple group systems: the perception of ethnic hierarchies, in W. Stroebe and M. Hewstone (eds) *European Review of Social Psychology*, Vol. 6. London: Wiley.

Hagendoorn, L. and Henke, R. (1991) The effect of multiple category membership on intergroup evaluations in a North Indian context: class, caste and religion, *British Journal of Social Psychology*, 30: 247–60.

Hamburger, Y. (1994) The contact hypothesis reconsidered: effects of the atypical outgroup member on the outgroup stereotype, *Basic and Applied Social Psychology*, 15: 339–58.

Hamilton, D.L. and Mackie, D.M. (1993) Cognitive and affective process in intergroup perception: the developing interface, in D.M. Mackie and D.L. Hamilton (eds) *Affect, Cognition and Stereotyping: Interactive Processes in Group Perception*. New York: Academic Press.

Hamilton, D.L. and Trolier, T. (1986) Stereotypes and stereotyping: an overview of the cognitive approach, in J.F. Dovidio and S.L. Gaertner (eds) *Prejudice, Discrimination and Racism*. Orlando, FL: Academic Press.

Harmon-Jones, E., Greenberg, J., Solomon, S. and Simon, L. (1996) The effects of mortality salience on intergroup bias between minimal groups, *European Journal of Social Psychology*, 26: 677–81.

Haslam, N. and Rothschild, L. (2000) Essentialist beliefs about human social categories, *British Journal of Social Psychology*, 39: 113–27.

Hass, R.G., Katz, I., Rizzo, N., Bailey, J. and Eisenstadt, D. (1991) Cross-racial appraisal as related to attitude ambivalence and cognitive complexity, *Personality and Social Psychology Bulletin*, 17: 83–92.

Heider, F. (1944) Social perception and phenomenal causality, *Psychological Review*, 51: 358–74.

Heider, F. (1958) *The Psychology of Interpersonal Relations*. New York: Wiley.

Helson, H. (1964) *Adaptation-level Theory: An Experimental and Systematic Approach to Behavior*. New York: Harper & Row.

Henley, N. (1977) *Body Politics*. Englewood Cliffs, NJ: Prentice-Hall.

Herek, G., Janis, I.L. and Huth, P. (1987) Decisionmaking during international crises: is quality of process related to outcome?, *Journal of Conflict Resolution*, 31: 203–26.

Herrmann, R.K. (1985) *Perceptions and Behavior in Soviet Foreign Policy*. Pittsburgh, PA: University of Pittsburgh Press.

Herrmann, R.K. and Fischerkeller, M. (1995) Beyond the enemy image and spiral model: cognitive-strategic research after the cold war, *International Organization*, 49: 415–50.

Hewstone, M. (1990) The 'ultimate attribution error'? A review of the literature on intergroup causal attribution, *European Journal of Social Psychology*, 20: 311–35.

Hewstone, M. (1996) Contact and categorization: social psychological interventions to change intergroup relations, in C.N. Macrae, C. Stangor and M. Hewstone (eds) *Stereotypes and Stereotyping*. New York: Guilford.

Hewstone, M. and Brown, R. (1986) Contact is not enough: an intergroup perspective on the 'contact hypothesis', in M. Hewstone and R. Brown (eds) *Contact and Conflict in Intergroup Encounters*. Oxford: Blackwell.

Hewstone, M., Fincham, F. and Jaspars, J. (1981) Social categorization and similarity in intergroup behaviour: a replication with 'penalties', *European Journal of Social Psychology*, 11: 101–7.

Hewstone, M., Hantzi, A. and Johnston, L. (1991) Social categorization and person memory: the pervasiveness of race as an organizing principle, *European Journal of Social Psychology*, 21: 517–28.

Hewstone, M., Islam, M.R. and Judd, C.M. (1993) Models of crossed categorization and intergroup relations, *Journal of Personality and Social Psychology*, 64: 779–93.

Hewstone, M., Cairns, E., Judd, C., Voci, A. and McLernon, F. (2000) Intergroup contact in Northern Ireland: mediational and moderational hypotheses. Paper presented at the annual meeting of the Society of Experimental Social Psychology, Atlanta, GA, October.

Higgins, E.T. and King, G. (1981) Accessibility of social constructs: information processing consequences of individual and contextual variability, in N. Cantor and J. Kihlstrom (eds) *Personality, Cognition and Social Interaction*. Hillsdale, NJ: Erlbaum.

Hinkle, S. and Brown, R. (1990) Intergroup comparisons and social identity: some links and lacunae, in D. Abrams and H. Hogg (eds) *Social Identity Theory: Constructive and Critical Advances*. London: Harvester Wheatsheaf.

Hirschfield, L. (1988) On cognizing social categories: cognitive development and anthropological wisdom, *Man*, 23: 611–38.

Hirt, E., Zillmann, D., Erickson, G. and Kennedy, C. (1992) Costs and benefits of allegiance: changes in fans' self-ascribed competencies after team victory versus defeat, *Journal of Personality and Social Psychology*, 63: 724–38.

Hogg, M.A. (1992) *The Social Psychology of Group Cohesiveness: From Attraction to Social Identity*. London: Harvester Wheatsheaf.

Hogg, M.A. (1993) Group cohesiveness: a critical review and some new directions, in W. Stroebe and M. Hewstone (eds) *European Review of Social Psychology*, Vol. 4. London: Wiley.

Hogg, M.A. (2000) Subjective uncertainty reduction through self-categorization: a motivational theory of social identity processes and group phenomena, in W. Stroebe and M. Hewstone (eds) *European Review of Social Psychology*, Vol. 11. Chichester: Wiley.

Hogg, M.A. and Abrams, D. (1988) *Social Identifications*. London: Routledge.

Hogg, M.A. and Abrams, D. (1990) Social motivation, self-esteem and social identity, in D. Abrams and M. Hogg (eds) *Social Identity Theory: Constructive and Critical Advances*. London: Harvester Wheatsheaf.

Hogg, M.A. and Abrams, D. (1993) Towards a single-process uncertainty-reduction model of social motivation in groups, in M. Hogg and D. Abrams (eds) *Group Motivation: Social Psychological Perspectives*. London: Harvester Wheatsheaf.

Hogg, M.A. and Hardie, E.A. (1991) Social attraction, personal attraction and self-categorization: a field study, *Personality and Social Psychology Bulletin*, 17: 175–80.

Hogg, M.A. and Turner, J.C. (1985) Interpersonal attraction, social identification and psychological group formation, *European Journal of Social Psychology*, 15: 51–66.

Hogg, M.A. and Turner, J.C. (1987) Intergroup behaviour, self-stereotyping and the salience of social categories, *British Journal of Social Psychology*, 26: 325–40.

Holsti, O. (1972) *Crisis Escalation War*. Montreal: McGill-Queen's University Press.

Hornsey, M.J. and Hogg, M.A. (1999) Subgroup differentiation as a response to an overly-inclusive group: a test of optimal distinctiveness theory, *European Journal of Social Psychology*, 29: 543–50.

Hornsey, M.J. and Hogg, M.A. (2000) Subgroup relations: two experiments comparing subgroup differentiation and common ingroup identity models of prejudice reduction, *Personality and Social Psychology Bulletin*, 26: 242–56.

Horowitz, D. (1985) *Ethnic Groups in Conflict*. Berkeley, CA: University of California Press.

Huo, Y., Smith, H., Tyler, T.R. and Lind, E.A. (1996) Superordinate identification, subgroup identification and justice concerns, *Psychological Science*, 7: 40–5.

Hymes, D. (1967) Models of the interaction of language and social setting, *Journal of Social Issues*, 23: 8–28.

Ickes, W. (1984) Compositions in Black and White: determinants of interaction in interracial dyads, *Journal of Personality and Social Psychology*, 7: 330–41.

Insko, C.A. and Schopler, J. (1987) Categorization, competition and collectivity, in C. Hendrick (ed.) *Group Processes*, Vol. 8. Beverly Hills, CA: Sage.

Insko, C.A., Pinkley, R., Hoyle, R. et al. (1987) Individual versus group discontinuity: the role of intergroup contact, *Journal of Experimental Social Psychology*, 23: 250–67.

Insko, C.A., Schopler, J., Hoyle, R., Dardis, G. and Graetz, K. (1990) Individual–group discontinuity as a function of fear and greed, *Journal of Personality and Social Psychology*, 58: 68–79.

Insko, C.A., Schopler, J., Kennedy, J. et al. (1992) Individual–group discontinuity from the differing perspectives of Campbell's realistic group conflict theory and Tajfel and Turner's social identity theory, *Social Psychology Quarterly*, 55: 272–91.

Insko, C.A., Schopler, J. and Sedikides, C. (1998) Personal control, entitativity and evolution, in C. Sedikides, J. Schopler and C. Insko (eds) *Intergroup Cognition and Intergroup Behavior*. Mahwah, NJ: Erlbaum.

Isen, A.M. and Daubman, K.A. (1984) The influence of affect on categorization, *Journal of Personality and Social Psychology*, 47: 1206–17.

Isenberg, D.J. (1986) Group polarization: a critical review and meta-analysis, *Journal of Personality and Social Psychology*, 50: 1141–51.

Islam, M.R. and Hewstone, M. (1993) Dimensions of contact as predictors of intergroup anxiety, perceived out-group variability and out-group attitude: an integrative model, *Personality and Social Psychology Bulletin*, 19: 700–10.

Jackson, L.A., Sullivan, L.A. and Hodge, C.N. (1993) Stereotype effects on attributions, predictions and evaluations: no two judgments are quite alike, *Journal of Personality and Social Psychology*, 65: 69–84.

Janis, I.L. (1972) *Victims of Groupthink*. Boston, MA: Houghton Mifflin.

Janis, I.L. (1982) *Groupthink: Psychological Studies of Policy Decisions and Fiascos*. Boston, MA: Houghton Mifflin.

Janis, I.L. (1989) *Crucial Decisions: Leadership in Policymaking and Crisis Management*. New York: Free Press.

Jaynes, G.D. and Williams, R.M., Jr (1989) *A Common Destiny: Blacks and American Society*. Washington, DC: National Academy Press.

Jervis, R. (1976) *Perception and Misperception in International Politics*. Princeton, NJ: Princeton University Press.

Jervis, R. (1992) Political implications of loss aversion, *Political Psychology*, 13: 187–205.

Jetten, J., Spears, R. and Manstead, A.S.R. (1996) Intergroup norms and intergroup discrimination: distinctive self-categorization and social identity effects, *Journal of Personality and Social Psychology*, 71: 1222–33.

Jetten, J., Spears, R. and Manstead, A.S.R. (1997) Distinctiveness threat and prototypicality: combined effects on intergroup discrimination and collective self-esteem, *European Journal of Social Psychology*, 27: 635–57.

Jetten, J., Spears, R. and Manstead, A.S.R. (1998) Dimensions of distinctiveness: group variability makes a difference to differentiation, *Journal of Personality and Social Psychology*, 74: 1481–92.

Johnson, D.W. and Johnson, R.T. (1981) Effects of cooperative and individualistic learning experiences on interethnic interaction, *Journal of Educational Psychology*, 73: 444–9.

Johnson, G.R. (1986) Kin selection, socialization and patriotism: an integrating theory, *Politics and the Life Sciences*, 4: 127–40.

Johnson, G.R. (1989) The role of kin recognition mechanisms in patriotic socialization: further reflections, *Politics and the Life Sciences*, 8: 62–9.

Johnston, L. and Hewstone, M. (1992) Cognitive models of stereotype change (3): subtyping and the perceived typicality of disconfirming group members, *Journal of Experimental Social Psychology*, 28: 360–86.

Jones, E.E. (1979) The rocky road from acts to dispositions, *American Psychologist*, 34: 107–17.

Jones, J.M. (1972) *Prejudice and Racism*. Reading, MA: Addison-Wesley.

Jussim, L., Coleman, M. and Lerch, L. (1987) The nature of stereotypes: a comparison and integration of three theories, *Journal of Personality and Social Psychology*, 52: 536–46.

Kahneman, D. and Tversky, A. (1979) Prospect theory: an analysis of decision under risk, *Econometrica*, 47: 263–91.

Katz, I. and Hass, R.G. (1988) Racial ambivalence and American value conflict: correlational and priming studies of dual cognitive structures, *Journal of Personality and Social Psychology*, 55: 893–905.

Katz, P.A. and Zalk, S.R. (1978) Modification of children's racial attitudes, *Developmental Psychology*, 14: 447–61.

Kawakami, K. and Dion, K. (1993) The impact of salient self-identities on relative deprivation and action intentions, *European Journal of Social Psychology*, 23: 525–40.

Kawakami, K. and Dovidio, J.F. (2001) The reliability of implicit stereotyping, *Personality and Social Psychology Bulletin*, 27: 212–25.

Kelley, H.H. and Stahelski, A.J. (1970) The social interaction basis of cooperators' and competitors' beliefs about others, *Journal of Personality and Social Psychology*, 16: 66–91.

Kelly, C. and Breinlinger, S. (1996) *The Social Psychology of Collective Action: Identity, Injustice and Gender*. Washington, DC: Taylor & Francis.

Kemmelmeier, M. and Winter, D.G. (2000) Putting threat into perspective: experimental studies on perceptual distortion in international conflict, *Personality and Social Psychology Bulletin*, 26: 795–809.

Kim, H-S. and Baron, R.S. (1988) Exercise and illusory correlation: does arousal heighten stereotypic processing?, *Journal of Experimental Social Psychology*, 24: 366–80.

Klein, M. (1975) *Love, Guilt and Reparation and Other Works: 1921–1945*. New York: Delta.

Kovel, J. (1970) *White Racism: A Psychohistory*. New York: Pantheon.

Kramer, R.M. (1989) Windows of vulnerability or cognitive illusions? Cognitive processes and the nuclear arms race, *Journal of Experimental Social Psychology*, 25: 79–100.

Kramer, R.M. and Brewer, M.B. (1984) Effects of group identity on resource utilization in a simulated commons dilemma, *Journal of Personality and Social Psychology*, 46: 1044–57.

Krueger, J., Rothbart, M. and Sriram, N. (1989) Category learning and change: differences in sensitivity to information that enhances or reduces intercategory distinctions, *Journal of Personality and Social Psychology*, 56: 866–75.

Larson, R.J. and Diener, E. (1992) Promises and problems with the circumplex model of emotion, in M. Clark (ed.) *Emotion*, Vol. 13. Newbury Park, CA: Sage.

Lazarus, R.S. (1966) *Psychological Stress and the Coping Process*. New York: McGraw-Hill.

Lebow, R.N. (1981) *Between Peace and War: The Nature of International Crisis*. Baltimore, MD: Johns Hopkins University Press.

Leippe, M.R. and Eisenstadt, D. (1994) Generalization of dissonance reduction: decreasing prejudice through induced compliance, *Journal of Personality and Social Psychology*, 67: 395–413.

Lemyre, L. and Smith, P.M. (1985) Intergroup discrimination and self-esteem in the minimal group paradigm, *Journal of Personality and Social Psychology*, 29: 660–70.

Lenk, H. (1969) Top performance despite internal conflict: an antithesis to a functional proposition, in J. Loy and G. Kenyon (eds) *Sport, Culture and Society*. New York: Macmillan.

Leonardelli, G.J. and Brewer, M.B. (2001) Minority and majority discrimination: when and why, *Journal of Experimental Social Psychology*, 37: 468–85.

Lerner, M.L. and Grant, P.R. (1990) The influences of commitment to justice and ethnocentrism on children's allocations of pay, *Social Psychology Quarterly*, 53: 229–38.

Levin, S., Federico, C., Sidanius, J. and Rabinowitz, J. (2002) Social dominance orientation and intergroup bias: the legimation of favoritism for high-status groups, *Personality and Social Psychology Bulletin*, 28: 144–57.

LeVine, R.A. and Campbell, D.T. (1972) *Ethnocentrism: Theories of Conflict, Ethnic Attitudes and Group Behavior*. New York: Wiley.

Luhtanen, R. and Crocker, J. (1991) Self-esteem and intergroup comparisons: toward a theory of collective self-esteem, in J. Suls and T. Wills (eds) *Social Comparison: Contemporary Theory and Research*. Hillsdale, NJ: Erlbaum.

Luhtanen, R. and Crocker, J. (1992) A collective self-esteem scale: self-evaluation of one's social identity, *Personality and Social Psychology Bulletin*, 18: 302–18.

McCallum, D., Harring, K., Gilmore, R. et al. (1985) Competition between groups and between individuals, *Journal of Experimental Social Psychology*, 21: 301–20.

McCauley, C. (1989) The nature of social influence in groupthink: compliance and internalization, *Journal of Personality and Social Psychology*, 57: 250–60.

McClintock, C.G. (1972) Social motivation: a set of propositions, *Behavioral Science*, 17: 438–54.

McClintock, C.G. and Liebrand, W.B.G. (1988) Role of interdependence structure, individual value orientation and another's strategy in social decision making: a transformational analysis, *Journal of Personality and Social Psychology*, 55: 396–409.

McConahay, J.B. (1986) Modern racism, ambivalence and the modern racism scale, in J.F. Dovidio and S.L. Gaertner (eds) *Prejudice, Discrimination and Racism*. Orlando, FL: Academic Press.

McConahay, J.B. and Hough, J.C., Jr (1976) Symbolic racism, *Journal of Social Issues*, 32: 23–45.

MacCrimmon, K.R. and Messick, D.M. (1976) A framework for social motives, *Behavioral Science*, 21: 86–100.

Mackie, D.M. (1986) Social identification effects in group polarization, *Journal of Personality and Social Psychology*, 50: 720–8.

Mackie, D.M. and Cooper, J. (1984) Attitude polarization: effects of group membership, *Journal of Personality and Social Psychology*, 46: 575–85.

Mackie, D.M. and Smith, E.R. (eds) (2002) *From Prejudice to Intergroup Emotions*. Philadelphia, PA: Psychology Press.

Mackie, D.M., Hamilton, D.L., Schroth, H.A. et al. (1989) The effects of induced mood on expectancy-based illusory correlations, *Journal of Personality and Social Psychology*, 25: 524–44.

Mackie, D.M., Devos, T. and Smith, E.R. (2000) Intergroup emotions: explaining offensive action tendencies in intergroup contexts, *Journal of Personality and Social Psychology*, 79: 602–16.

Major, B. (1994) From social inequality to personal entitlement: the role of social comparisons, legitimacy appraisals and group membership, in M. Zanna (ed.) *Advances in Experimental Social Psychology*, Vol. 26. New York: Academic Press.

Marcus-Newhall, A., Miller, N., Holtz, R. and Brewer, M.B. (1993) Cross-cutting category membership with role assignment: a means of reducing intergroup bias, *British Journal of Social Psychology*, 32: 125–46.

Marcus-Newhall, A., Pedersen, W.C., Carlson, M. and Miller, N. (2000) Displaced aggression is alive and well: a meta-analytic review, *Journal of Personality and Social Psychology*, 78: 670–89.

Marks, G. (1984) Thinking one's abilities are unique and one's opinions are common, *Personality and Social Psychology Bulletin*, 10: 203–8.

Medin, D. (1989) Concepts and conceptual structure, *American Psychologist*, 44: 1469–81.

Meindl, J. and Lerner, M.J. (1984) Exacerbation of extreme responses to an out-group, *Journal of Personality and Social Psychology*, 47: 71–84.

Mercer, J. (1995) Anarchy and identity, *International Organization*, 49: 229–52.

Messé, L., Hymes, R. and MacCoun, R. (1986) Group categorization and distributive justice decisions, in H.W. Bierhoff, R.L. Cohen and J. Greenberg (eds) *Justice in Social Relations*. New York: Plenum.

Messick, D.M. and Brewer, M.B. (1983) Solving social dilemmas: a review, in L. Wheeler and P. Shaver (eds) *Review of Personality and Social Psychology*, Vol. 4. Beverly Hills, CA: Sage.

Messick, D.M. and Mackie, D. (1989) Intergroup relations, *Annual Review of Psychology*, 40: 45–81.

Messick, D.M., Bloom, S., Boldizar, J. and Samuelson, C. (1985) Why we are fairer than others, *Journal of Experimental Social Psychology*, 21: 480–500.

Miller, N. and Brewer, M.B. (eds) (1984) *Groups in Contact: The Psychology of Desegregation*. New York: Academic Press.

Miller, N., Brewer, M.B. and Edwards, K. (1985) Cooperative interaction in desegregated settings: a laboratory analogue, *Journal of Social Issues*, 41(3): 63–79.

Miller, N.E. and Dollard, J. (1941) *Social Learning and Imitation*. New Haven, CT: Yale University Press.

Mullen, B., Brown, R. and Smith, C. (1992) Ingroup bias as a function of salience, relevance and status: an integration, *European Journal of Social Psychology*, 22: 103–22.

Mullen, B., Migdal, M. and Hewstone, M. (2001) Crossed categorization vs simple categorization and intergroup evaluations: a meta-analysis, *European Journal of Social Psychology*, 31: 721–36.

Mummendey, A. and Otten, S. (1998) Positive–negative asymmetry in social discrimination, in W. Stroebe and M. Hewstone (eds) *European Review of Social Psychology*, Vol. 9. Chichester: Wiley.

Mummendey, A. and Schreiber, H. (1983) Better or just different? Positive social identity by discrimination against or by differentiation from out-groups, *European Journal of Social Psychology*, 13: 389–97.

Mummendey, A. and Schreiber, H. (1984) 'Different' just means 'better': some obvious and some hidden pathways to in-group favouritism, *British Journal of Social Psychology*, 23: 363–8.

Mummendey, A. and Simon, B. (1989) Better or different? III: the impact of importance of comparison dimension and relative ingroup size upon intergroup discrimination, *British Journal of Social Psychology*, 21: 1–16.

Mummendey, A. and Wenzel, M. (1999) Social discrimination and tolerance in intergroup relations: reactions to intergroup difference, *Personality and Social Psychology Review*, 3: 158–74.

Mummendey, A., Simon, B., Dietze, C. et al. (1992) Categorization is not enough: intergroup discrimination in negative outcome allocations, *Journal of Experimental Social Psychology*, 28: 125–44.

Myers, D. and Lamm, H. (1976) The group polarization phenomenon, *Psychological Bulletin*, 83: 602–27.

Nacoste, R.B. (1990) Sources of stigma: analyzing the psychology of affirmative action, *Law and Policy*, 12: 175–95.

Nelson, L.J., Moore, D.L., Olivetti, J. and Scott, T. (1997) General and personal mortality salience and nationalistic bias, *Personality and Social Psychology Bulletin*, 23: 884–92.

Newcomb, T.M. (1947) Autistic hostility and social reality, *Human Relations*, 1: 69–86.

Ng, S.H. (1981) Equity theory and the allocation of rewards between groups, *European Journal of Social Psychology*, 11: 439–44.

Ng, S.H. (1982a) Power and intergroup discrimination, in H. Tajfel (ed.) *Social Identity and Intergroup Relations*. Cambridge: Cambridge University Press.

Ng, S.H. (1982b) Power and appeasement in intergroup discrimination, *Australian Journal of Psychology*, 34: 37–44.

Ng, S.H. (1984) Equity and social categorization effects on intergroup allocation of rewards, *British Journal of Social Psychology*, 23: 165–72.

Ng, S.H. (1989) Intergroup behaviour and the self, *New Zealand Journal of Psychology*, 18: 1–12.

Ng, S.H. and Wilson, S. (1989) Self-categorization theory and belief polarization among Christian believers and atheists, *British Journal of Social Psychology*, 28: 47–56.

Norvell, N. and Worchel, S. (1981) A re-examination of the relation between equal status contact and intergroup attraction, *Journal of Personality and Social Psychology*, 41: 902–8.

Oakes, P.J. and Turner, J.C. (1980) Social categorization and intergroup behaviour: does minimal intergroup discrimination make social identity more positive?, *European Journal of Social Psychology*, 10: 295–301.

Oakes, P.J., Turner, J.C. and Haslam, S.A. (1991) Perceiving people as group members: the role of fit in the salience of social categorization, *British Journal of Social Psychology*, 30: 125–44.

Oakes, P.J., Haslam, S.A. and Turner, J.C. (1994) *Stereotyping and Social Reality*. Oxford: Blackwell.

Orive, R. (1988) Social projection and social comparison of opinions, *Journal of Personality and Social Psychology*, 54: 953–64.

Oskamp, S. and Perlman, D. (1965) Factors affecting cooperation in the Prisoner's Dilemma game, *Journal of Conflict Resolution*, 9: 359–74.

Otten, S. and Moskowitz, G.B. (2000) Evidence for implicit evaluative ingroup bias: affect-biased spontaneous trait inference in a minimal group paradigm, *Journal of Experimental Social Psychology*, 36: 77–89.

Otten, S. and Wentura, D. (1999) About the impact of automaticity in the minimal group paradigm: evidence from affective priming tasks, *European Journal of Social Psychology*, 29: 1049–71.

Otten, S., Mummendey, A. and Wenzel, M. (1995) Evaluation of aggressive interactions in interpersonal and intergroup contexts, *Aggressive Behavior*, 21: 205–24.

Pepels, J. (1999) *The Myth of the Positive Crossed Categorization Effect*. Amsterdam: European Centre on Migration and Ethnic Relations.

Perdue, C., Dovidio, J., Gurtman, M. and Tyler, R. (1990) Us and them: social categorization and the process of intergroup bias, *Journal of Personality and Social Psychology*, 59: 475–86.

Petta, G. and Walker, I. (1992) Relative deprivation and ethnic identity, *British Journal of Social Psychology*, 31: 285–93.

Pettigrew, T.F. (1975) Preface, in T.F. Pettigrew (ed.) *Racial Discrimination in the United States*. New York: Harper & Row.

Pettigrew, T.F. (1979) The ultimate attribution error: extending Allport's cognitive analysis of prejudice, *Personality and Social Psychology Bulletin*, 5: 461–76.

Pettigrew, T.F. (1997) Generalized intergroup contact effects on prejudice, *Personality and Social Psychology Bulletin*, 23: 173–85.

Pettigrew, T.F. (1998) Intergroup contact theory, *Annual Review of Psychology*, 49: 65–85.

Pettigrew, T.F. and Meertens, R.W. (1995) Subtle and blatant prejudice in Western Europe, *European Journal of Social Psychology*, 25: 57–75.

Pettigrew, T.F. and Tropp, L.R. (2000) Does intergroup contact reduce prejudice? Recent meta-analytic findings, in S. Oskamp (ed.) *Reducing Prejudice and Discrimination*. Mahwah, NJ: Erlbaum.

Pettigrew, T.F., Jackson, J.S., Ben Brika, J. et al. (1998) Outgroup prejudice in Western Europe, in W. Stroebe and M. Hewstone (eds) *European Review of Social Psychology*, Vol. 8. Chichester: Wiley.

Pickett, C.L., Bonner, B.L. and Coleman, J.M. (2002a) Motivated self-stereotyping: heightened assimilation and differentiation needs result in increased levels of positive and negative self-stereotyping, *Journal of Personality and Social Psychology*, 82: 543–62.

Pickett, C.L., Silver, M. and Brewer, M.B. (2002b) The impact of assimilation and differentiation needs on perceived group importance and judgments of ingroup size, *Personality and Social Psychology Bulletin*, 28: 546–58.

Pilisuk, M. (1984) Experimenting with the arms race, *Journal of Conflict Resolution*, 28: 296–315.

Platow, M.J., McClintock, C.G. and Liebrand, W.G. (1990) Predicting intergroup fairness and ingroup bias in the minimal group paradigm, *European Journal of Social Psychology*, 20: 221–39.

Platow, M., O'Connell, A., Shave, R. and Hanning, P. (1995) Social evaluations of fair and unfair allocations in interpersonal and intergroup situations, *British Journal of Social Psychology*, 34: 363–81.

Platow, M., Hoar, S., Reid, S., Harley, K. and Morrison, D. (1997) Endorsement of distributively fair and unfair leaders in interpersonal and intergroup situations, *European Journal of Social Psychology*, 27: 465–94.

Prentice, D.A. and Miller, D.T. (1992) The psychology of ingroup attachment. Paper presented at Conference on The Self and the Collective, Princeton University, Princeton, NJ.

Prentice, D.A., Miller, D.T. and Lightdale, J.R. (1994) Asymmetries in attachments to groups and to their members: distinguishing between common-identity and common-bond groups, *Personality and Social Psychology Bulletin*, 20: 484–93.

Rabbie, J.M. and Horwitz, M. (1969) The arousal of ingroup–outgroup bias by a chance win or loss, *Journal of Personality and Social Psychology*, 69: 223–8.

Rabbie, J.M. and Horwitz, M. (1988) Categories versus groups as explanatory concepts in intergroup relations, *European Journal of Social Psychology*, 18: 117–23.

Rabbie, J.M., Schot, J.C. and Visser, L. (1989) Social identity theory: a conceptual and empirical critique from the perspective of a behavioural interaction model, *European Journal of Social Psychology*, 19: 171–202.

Rapoport, A. and Chammah, A. (1965) *Prisoner's Dilemma*. Ann Arbor, MI: University of Michigan Press.

Reynolds, V., Falger, V. and Vine, I. (eds) (1987) *The Sociobiology of Ethnocentrism*. London: Croom Helm.

Richardson, D.R., Hammock, G., Smith, S., Gardner. W. and Signo, M. (1994) Empathy as a cognitive inhibitor of interpersonal aggression, *Aggressive Behavior*, 20: 275–89.

Roccas, S. and Schwartz, S.H. (1993) Effects of intergroup similarity on intergroup relations, *European Journal of Social Psychology*, 23: 581–95.

Rogers, R.W. and Prentice-Dunn, S. (1981) Deindividuation and anger-mediated interracial aggression: unmasking regressive racism, *Journal of Personality and Social Psychology*, 41: 63–73.

Roseman, I.J. (1984) Cognitive determinants of emotion: a structural theory, in P. Shaver (ed.) *Review of Personality and Social Psychology*. Beverly Hills, CA: Sage.

Rosenberg, M. (1979) *Conceiving the Self*. New York: Basic Books.

Ross, L. (1977) The intuitive psychologist and his shortcomings: distortions in the attribution process, in L. Berkowitz (ed.) *Advances in Experimental Social Psychology*, Vol. 10. New York: Academic Press.

Ross, M.H. (1986) A cross-cultural theory of political conflict and violence, *Political Psychology*, 7: 427–69.

Ross, M.H. (1991) The role of evolution in ethnocentric conflict and its management, *Journal of Social Issues*, 47(3): 167–85.

Rothbart, M. and Hallmark, W. (1988) Ingroup–outgroup differences in the perceived efficacy of coercion and conciliation in resolving social conflict, *Journal of Personality and Social Psychology*, 55: 248–57.

Rothbart, M. and John, O.P. (1985) Social categorization and behavioral episodes: a cognitive analysis of the effects of intergroup contact, *Journal of Social Issues*, 41(3): 81–104.

Rothbart, M. and Taylor, M. (1992) Category labels and social reality: do we view social categories as natural kinds?, in G. Semin and K. Fiedler (eds) *Language, Interaction and Social Cognition*. London: Sage.

Rubin, M. and Hewstone, M. (1998) Social identity theory's self-esteem hypothesis: a review and some suggestions for clarification, *Personality and Social Psychology Review*, 2: 40–62.

Runciman, W.C. (1966) *Relative Deprivation and Social Justice: A Study of Attitudes to Social Inequality in Twentieth Century England*. Berkeley, CA: University of California Press.

Rust, M.C. (1996) Social identity and social categorization. Unpublished dissertation, University of Delaware.

Ryan, E., Hewstone, M. and Giles, H. (1984) Language and intergroup attitudes, in J. Eiser (ed.) *Attitudinal Judgements*. New York: Springer-Verlag.

Sachdev, I. and Bourhis, R.Y. (1985) Social categorization and power differentials in group relations, *European Journal of Social Psychology*, 15: 415–34.

Sachdev, I. and Bourhis, R.Y. (1987) Status differentials and intergroup behaviour, *European Journal of Social Psychology*, 17: 277–92.

Sachdev, I. and Bourhis, R.Y. (1990) Language and social identification, in D.
Abrams and M. Hogg (eds) *Social Identity Theory: Constructive and Critical
Advances*. London: Harvester Wheatsheaf.

Sachdev, I. and Bourhis, R.Y. (1991) Power and status differentials in minority
and majority group relations, *European Journal of Social Psychology*, 21: 1–
24.

Sande, G., Goethals, G., Ferrari, L. and Worth, L. (1989) Value-guided attributions: maintaining the moral self-image and the diabolical enemy-image,
Journal of Social Issues, 45(2): 91–118.

Schachter, S. (1959) *The Psychology of Affiliation*. Stanford, CA: Stanford University Press.

Scherer, K.R. (1988) Criteria for emotion-antecedent appraisal: a review, in V.
Hamilton, G. Bower and N. Frijda (eds) *Cognitive Perspectives on Emotion
and Motivation*. Norwell, MA: Kluwer Academic.

Schofield, J.W. (1979) The impact of positively structured contact on intergroup
behavior: does it last under adverse conditions?, *Social Psychology Quarterly*, 42: 280–4.

Schofield, J.W. and Eurich-Fulcer, R. (2001) When and how school desegrega-
tion improves intergroup relations, in R. Brown and S. Gaertner (eds)
Blackwell Handbook of Social Psychology: Intergroup Relations. Oxford:
Blackwell.

Schofield, J.W. and Sagar, H.A. (1977) Peer interaction patterns in an integrated middle school, *Sociometry*, 40: 130–8.

Schopler, J.W. and Insko, C.A. (1992) The discontinuity effect in interpersonal
and intergroup relations: generality and mediation, in W. Stroebe and
M. Hewstone (eds) *European Review of Social Psychology*, Vol. 3. Chichester:
Wiley.

Schuman, H., Steeh, C., Bobo, L. and Krysan, M. (1997) *Racial Attitudes in
America: Trends and Interpretations*. Cambridge, MA: Harvard University
Press.

Schwarzwald, J. and Cohen, S. (1982) Relationship between academic tracking
and the degree of interethnic acceptance, *Journal of Educational Psychology*,
74: 588–97.

Sears, D.O. (1988) Symbolic racism, in P.A. Katz and D.A. Taylor (eds) *Eliminating Racism: Profiles in Controversy*. New York: Plenum.

Sears, D.O. and Funk, C.L. (1991) The role of self-interest in social and political attitudes, in M.P. Zanna (ed.) *Advances in Experimental Psychology*, Vol.
24. New York: Academic Press.

Sharan, S. (1980) Cooperative learning in small groups: recent methods and
effects on achievement, attitudes and ethnic relations, *Review of Educational Research*, 50: 241–71.

Shaw, R.P. and Wong, Y. (1989) *The Genetic Seeds of Warfare: Evolution, Nationalism and Patriotism*. Boston, MA: Unwin & Hyman.

Sherif, M. (1966a) *In Common Predicament: Social Psychology of Intergroup Conflict and Cooperation*. New York: Houghton Mifflin.

Sherif, M. (1966b) *Groups in Harmony and Tension: An Integration of Studies on
Intergroup Relations*. New York: Octagon.

Sherif, M., Harvey, O.J., White, B.J., Hood, W.R. and Sherif, C.W. (1961)
Intergroup Conflict and Cooperation: The Robbers Cave Experiment. Norman,
OK: University of Oklahoma Book Exchange.

Sidanius, J. (1993) The psychology of group conflict and the dynamics of oppression: a social dominance perspective, in S. Iyengar and W. McGuire (eds) *Explorations in Political Psychology*. Durham, NC: Duke University Press.

Sidanius, J. and Pratto, F. (1999) *Social Dominance: An Intergroup Theory of Social Hierarchy and Oppression*. New York: Cambridge University Press.

Silverstein, B. (1989) Enemy images: the psychology of US attitudes and cognitions regarding the Soviet Union, *American Psychologist*, 44: 903–13.

Simon, B. and Hamilton, D.H. (1994) Social identity and self-stereotyping: the effects of relative group size and group status, *Journal of Personality and Social Psychology*, 66: 699–711.

Simon, B., Aufderheide, B. and Kampmeier, C. (2001) The social psychology of minority–majority relations, in R. Brown and S. Gaertner (eds) *Blackwell Handbook of Social Psychology: Intergroup Relations*. Oxford: Blackwell.

Slavin, R.E. (1985) Cooperative learning: applying contact theory in desegregated schools, *Journal of Social Issues*, 41(3): 45–62.

Smith, A.D. (1993) The ethnic sources of nationalism, in M. Brown (ed.) *Ethnic Conflict and International Security*. Princeton, NJ: Princeton University Press.

Smith, C.A. and Ellsworth, P.C. (1985) Patterns of cognitive appraisal in emotion, *Journal of Personality and Social Psychology*, 48: 813–38.

Smith, C.A. and Lazarus, R.S. (1990) Emotion and adaptation, in L. Pervin (ed.) *Handbook of Personality: Theory and Research*. New York: Guilford Press.

Smith, E.R. (1993) Social identity and social emotions: toward new conceptualizations of prejudice, in D.M. Mackie and D.L. Hamilton (eds) *Affect, Cognition and Stereotyping*. San Diego, CA: Academic Press.

Solomon, S., Greenberg, J. and Pyszczynski, T. (1991) A terror management theory of social behavior: the psychological functions of self-esteem and cultural worldviews, in M. Zanna (ed.) *Advances in Experimental Social Psychology*, Vol. 24. San Diego, CA: Academic Press.

Spears, R. and Manstead, A.S.R. (1989) The social context of stereotyping and differentiation, *European Journal of Social Psychology*, 19: 101–21.

Spears, R. and Manstead, A.S.R. (1990) Consensus estimation in social context, in W. Stroebe and M. Hewstone (eds) *European Review of Social Psychology*, Vol. 1. London: Wiley.

Stangor, C. and Ford, T.E. (1992) Accuracy and expectancy-confirming processing orientations and the development of stereotypes and prejudice, in W. Stroebe and M. Hewstone (eds) *European Review of Social Psychology*, Vol. 3. London: Wiley.

Stangor, C., Sullivan, L. and Ford, T.E. (1991) Affective and cognitive determinants of prejudice, *Social Cognition*, 9: 359–80.

Steele, C.M. (1992) Race and the schooling of black Americans, *Atlantic Monthly*, April: 68–78.

Stephan, C.W. (1992) Intergroup anxiety and intergroup interaction, in J. Lynch, D. Modgil and S. Modgil (eds) *Cultural Diversity and the Schools: Prejudice, Polemic or Progress?* London: Falmer.

Stephan, W.G. (1986) The effects of school desegregation: an evaluation 30 years after *Brown*, in M. Saks and L. Saxe (eds) *Advances in Applied Social Psychology*, Vol. 3. Hillsdale, NJ: Erlbaum.

Stephan, W.G. and Stephan, C.W. (1985) Intergroup anxiety, *Journal of Social Issues*, 41(3): 157–75.

Stephan, W.G. and Stephan, C.W. (1993) Cognition and affect in stereotyping: parallel interactive networks, in D.M. Mackie and D.L. Hamilton (eds) *Affect, Cognition and Stereotyping*. San Diego, CA: Academic Press.

Stouffer, S., Suchman, E., DeVinney, L., Stat, S. and Williams, R. (1949) *The American Soldier: Adjustments during Army Life*, Vol. 1. Princeton, NJ: Princeton University Press.

Stroessner, S.J. and Mackie, D.M. (1993) Affect and perceived group variability: implications for stereotyping and prejudice, in D.M. Mackie and D.L. Hamilton (eds) *Affect, Cognition and Stereotyping*. San Diego, CA: Academic Press.

Struch, N. and Schwartz, S.H. (1989) Intergroup aggression: its predictors and distinctness from in-group bias, *Journal of Personality and Social Psychology*, 56: 364–73.

Sumner, W.G. (1906) *Folkways*. New York: Ginn.

Swann, W.B. (1987) Identity negotiation: where two roads meet, *Journal of Personality and Social Psychology*, 53: 1038–51.

Tajfel, H. (1969) Cognitive aspects of prejudice, *Journal of Social Issues*, 25: 79–97.

Tajfel, H. (1970) Experiments in intergroup discrimination, *Scientific American*, 223(2): 96–102.

Tajfel, H. (1978) *Differentiation between Social Groups: Studies in the Social Psychology of Intergroup Relations*. London: Academic Press.

Tajfel, H. (1979) Individuals and groups in social psychology, *British Journal of Social and Clinical Psychology*, 18: 183–90.

Tajfel, H. (1981) *Human Groups and Social Categories*. Cambridge: Cambridge University Press.

Tajfel, H. and Forgas, J.P. (1981) Social categorization: cognitions, values and groups, in J. Forgas (ed.) *Social Cognition*. London: Academic Press.

Tajfel, H. and Turner, J.C. (1986) The social identity theory of intergroup behavior, in S. Worchel and W. Austin (eds) *Psychology of Intergroup Relations*. Chicago: Nelson-Hall.

Tajfel, H. and Wilkes, A. (1963) Classification and quantitative judgement, *British Journal of Psychology*, 54: 101–13.

Tajfel, H., Nemeth, C., Jahoda, G., Campbell, J. and Johnson, N. (1970) The development of children's preference for their own country: a cross-national study, *International Journal of Psychology*, 5: 245–53.

Tajfel, H., Billig, M., Bundy, R. and Flament, C. (1971) Social categorization and intergroup behaviour, *European Journal of Social Psychology*, 1: 149–78.

Taylor, D.M. and McKirnan, D.J. (1984) A five-stage model of intergroup relations, *British Journal of Social Psychology*, 23: 291–300.

Taylor, D.M. and Moghaddam, F.M. (1994) *Theories of Intergroup Relations: International Social Psychological Perspectives*, 2nd edn. Westport, CT: Praeger.

Taylor, D.M., Moghaddam, F.M., Gamble, I. and Zellerer, E. (1987) Disadvantaged group responses to perceived inequality: from passive acceptance to collective action, *Journal of Social Psychology*, 127: 259–72.

Taylor, D.M., Wright, S., Moghaddam, F. and Lalonde, R. (1990) The personal/group discrimination discrepancy: perceiving my group but not myself to be a target for discrimination, *Personality and Social Psychology Bulletin*, 16: 254–62.

Taylor, S.E. and Brown, J.D. (1988) Illusion and well-being: a social psychological perspective on mental health, *Psychological Bulletin*, 103: 193–210.

Trafimow, D., Triandis, H.C. and Goto, S.G. (1991) Some tests of the distinction between the private self and the collective self, *Journal of Personality and Social Psychology*, 60: 649–55.

Triandis, H.C. (1989) The self and social behavior in differing cultural contexts, *Psychological Review*, 96: 506–20.

Turner, J.C. (1975) Social comparison and social identity: some prospects for intergroup behaviour, *European Journal of Social Psychology*, 5: 5–34.

Turner, J.C. (1978) Social categorization and social discrimination in the minimal group paradigm, in H. Tajfel (ed.) *Differentiation between Social Groups*. London: Academic Press.

Turner, J.C. (1981) The experimental social psychology of intergroup behaviour, in J. Turner and H. Giles (eds) *Intergroup Behaviour*. Oxford: Blackwell.

Turner, J.C. (1982) Towards a cognitive redefinition of the social group, in H. Tajfel (ed.) *Social Identity and Intergroup Relations*. Cambridge: Cambridge University Press.

Turner, J.C. (1984) Social identification and psychological group formation, in H. Tajfel (ed.) *The Social Dimension: European Developments in Social Psychology*, Vol. 2. Cambridge: Cambridge University Press.

Turner, J.C. (1985) Social categorization and the self-concept: a social cognitive theory of group behavior, in E. Lawler (ed.) *Advances in Group Processes*, Vol. 2. Greenwich, CT: JAI Press.

Turner, J.C. (1991) *Social Influence*. Buckingham: Open University Press.

Turner, J.C. and Brown, R. (1978) Social status, cognitive alternatives and intergroup relations, in H. Tajfel (ed.) *Differentiation between Social Groups*. London: Academic Press.

Turner, J.C., Hogg, M., Turner, P. and Smith, P. (1984) Failure and defeat as determinants of group cohesiveness, *British Journal of Social Psychology*, 23: 97–111.

Turner, J.C., Hogg, M., Oakes, P., Reicher, S. and Wetherell, M. (1987) *Rediscovering the Social Group: A Self-categorization Theory*. Oxford: Blackwell.

Turner, J.C., Wetherell, M.S. and Hogg, M.A. (1989) Referent informational influence and group polarization, *British Journal of Social Psychology*, 28: 135–47.

Turner, M., Pratkanis, A., Probasco, P. and Leve, C. (1992) Threat, cohesion and group effectiveness: testing a social identity maintenance perspective on groupthink, *Journal of Personality and Social Psychology*, 63: 781–96.

Tversky, A. and Kahneman, D. (1973) Availability: a heuristic for judging frequency and probability, *Cognitive Psychology*, 5: 207–32.

Tyler, T.R. (1994) Psychological models of the justice motive: the antecedents of distributive justice and procedural justice, *Journal of Personality and Social Psychology*, 67: 850–63.

Tyler, T.R. (2001) Social justice, in R. Brown and S. Gaertner (eds) *Blackwell Handbook of Social Psychology: Intergroup Relations*. Oxford: Blackwell.

Tyler, T.R., Degoey, P. and Smith, H. (1996) Understanding why the justice of group procedures matters: a test of the psychological dynamics of the group-value model, *Journal of Personality and Social Psychology*, 70: 913–30.

Vanbeselaere, N. (1987) The effects of dichotomous and crossed social categorizations upon intergroup discrimination, *European Journal of Social Psychology*, 17: 143–56.

van den Berghe, P.L. (1981) *The Ethnic Phenomenon*. New York: Elsevier.

van Knippenberg, A. and Ellemers, N. (1990) Social identity and intergroup differentiation processes, in W. Stroebe and M. Hewstone (eds) *European Review of Social Psychology*, Vol. 1. Chichester: Wiley.

van Knippenberg, A. and Ellemers, N. (1993) Strategies in intergroup relations, in M. Hogg and D. Abrams (eds) *Group Motivation: Social Psychological Perspectives*. London: Harvester Wheatsheaf.

van Knippenberg, A. and van Oers, H. (1984) Social identity and equity concerns in intergroup perceptions, *British Journal of Social Psychology*, 23: 351–61.

van Knippenberg, A., van Twuyver, M. and Pepels, J. (1994) Factors affecting social categorization processes in memory, *British Journal of Social Psychology*, 33: 419–31.

Vanneman, R.D. and Pettigrew, T.F. (1972) Race and relative deprivation in the urban United States, *Race*, 13: 461–86.

van Oudenhoven, J.P., Groenewoud, J.T. and Hewstone, M. (1996) Cooperation, ethnic salience and generalization of interethnic attitudes, *European Journal of Social Psychology*, 26: 649–61.

Veitch, R. and Griffitt, W.B. (1976) Good news, bad news: affective and interpersonal effects. *Journal of Applied Social Psychology*, 6: 69–95.

Volkan, V.D. (1988) *The Need to have Enemies and Allies*. Northvale, NJ: Aronson.

Wagner, U. and Ward, P.I. (1993) Variation of out-group presence and evaluation of the in-group, *British Journal of Social Psychology*, 32: 241–51.

Walker, I. and Pettigrew, T.F. (1984) Relative deprivation theory: an overview and conceptual critique, *British Journal of Social Psychology*, 23: 301–10.

Wallace, M.D. (1979) Arms races and escalation: some new evidence, in J. Singer (ed.) *Explaining War: Selected Papers from the Correlates of War Project*. Beverly Hills, CA: Sage.

Walster, E., Walster, G. and Berscheid, E. (1978) *Equity: Theory and Research*. Boston, MA: Allyn & Bacon.

Weber, J.G. (1994) The nature of ethnocentric attribution bias: ingroup protection or enhancement?, *Journal of Experimental Social Psychology*, 30: 482–504.

Weber, R. and Crocker, J.C. (1983) Cognitive processes in the revision of stereotypic beliefs, *Journal of Personality and Social Psychology*, 45: 961–67.

Wegener, D.T. and Petty, R.E. (1994) Mood management across affective states: the hedonic contingency hypothesis, *Journal of Personality and Social Psychology*, 66: 1034–48.

Weiner, B. (1985) An attributional theory of motivation and emotion, *Psychological Review*, 92: 548–73.

Weiner, B. (1986) *An Attributional Theory of Motivation and Emotion*. New York: Springer-Verlag.

Weiner, B., Amirkhan, J., Folkes, V. and Verette, J. (1987) An attributional analysis of excuse giving: studies of a naive theory of emotion, *Journal of Personality and Social Psychology*, 52: 316–24.

Wenzel, M. (2000) Justice and identity: the significance of inclusion for perceptions of entitlement and the justice motive, *Personality and Social Psychology Bulletin*, 26: 157–76.

Wetherell, M.S. (1987) Social identity and group polarization, in J.C. Turner, M. Hogg, P. Oakes, S. Reicher and M. Wetherell, *Rediscovering the Social Group: A Self-categorization Theory*. Oxford: Blackwell.

White, R.K. (1970) *Nobody Wanted War: Misperceptions in Vietnam and Other Wars*. Garden City, NY: Doubleday.

White, R.K. (1977) Misperception in the Arab–Israeli conflict, *Journal of Social Issues*, 33(1): 190–221.

White, R.K. (1984) *Fearful Warriors: A Psychological Profile of US–Soviet Relations.* New York: Free Press.

Wilder, D.A. (1978) Reduction of intergroup discrimination through individuation of the outgroup, *Journal of Personality and Social Psychology,* 36: 1361–74.

Wilder, D.A. (1981) Perceiving persons as a group: categorization and intergroup relations, in D. Hamilton (ed.) *Cognitive Processes in Stereotyping and Intergroup Behavior.* Hillsdale, NJ: Erlbaum.

Wilder, D.A. (1984) Intergroup contact: the typical member and the exception to the rule, *Journal of Experimental Social Psychology,* 20: 177–94.

Wilder, D.A. (1986a) Social categorization: implications for creation and reduction of intergroup bias, in L. Berkowitz (ed.) *Advances in Experimental Social Psychology,* Vol. 19. New York: Academic Press.

Wilder, D.A. (1986b) Cognitive factors affecting the success of intergroup contact, in S. Worchel and W. Austin (eds) *Psychology of Intergroup Relations.* Chicago: Nelson-Hall.

Wilder, D.A. (1993a) Freezing intergroup evaluations: anxiety fosters resistance to counterstereotypic information, in M. Hogg and D. Abrams (eds) *Group Motivation: Social Psychological Perspectives.* New York: Harvester Wheatsheaf.

Wilder, D.A. (1993b) The role of anxiety in facilitating stereotypic judgment of outgroup behavior, in D.M. Mackie and D.L. Hamilton (eds) *Affect, Cognition and Stereotyping.* San Diego, CA: Academic Press.

Wilder, D.A. and Shapiro, P.N. (1984) Role of outgroup cues in determining social identity, *Journal of Personality and Social Psychology,* 47: 342–8.

Wilder, D.A. and Shapiro, P.N. (1989a) Role of competition-induced anxiety in limiting the beneficial impact of positive behavior by an out-group member, *Journal of Personality and Social Psychology,* 56: 60–9.

Wilder, D.A. and Shapiro, P.N. (1989b) Effects of anxiety on impression formation in a group context: an anxiety-assimilation hypothesis, *Journal of Experimental Social Psychology,* 25: 481–99.

Wilder, D.A. and Simon, A.F. (2001) Affect as a cause of intergroup bias, in R. Brown and S. Gaertner (eds) *Blackwell Handbook of Social Psychology: Intergroup Relations.* Oxford: Blackwell.

Wilder, D.A. and Thompson, J.E. (1980) Intergroup contact with independent manipulations of in-group and out-group interaction, *Journal of Personality and Social Psychology,* 38: 589–603.

Wills, T.A. (1981) Downward comparison principles in social psychology, *Psychological Bulletin,* 90: 249–63.

Wilson, L. and Rogers, R.W. (1975) The fire this time: effects of race of target, insult and potential retaliation on black aggression, *Journal of Personality and Social Psychology,* 32: 857–64.

Wilson, W. and Kayatani, M. (1968) Intergroup attitudes and strategies in games between opponents of the same or of a different race, *Journal of Personality and Social Psychology,* 9: 24–30.

Wittenbrink, B., Judd, C.M. and Park, B. (1997) Evidence for racial prejudice at the implicit level and its relationship with questionnaire measures, *Journal of Personality and Social Psychology,* 72: 262–74.

Worchel, S. (1986) The role of cooperation in reducing intergroup conflict, in S. Worchel and W. Austin (eds) *Psychology of Intergroup Relations.* Chicago: Nelson-Hall.

Worchel, S., Andreoli, V. and Folger, R. (1977) Intergroup cooperation and intergroup attraction: the effect of previous interaction and outcome of combined effort, *Journal of Experimental Social Psychology*, 13: 131–40.

Wright, S.C. (2001) Strategic collective action: social psychology and social change, in R. Brown and S. Gaertner (eds) *Blackwell Handbook of Social Psychology: Intergroup Relations*. Oxford: Blackwell.

Wright, S.C., Taylor, D.M. and Moghaddam, F.M. (1990) Responding to membership in a disadvantaged group: from acceptance to collective protest, *Journal of Personality and Social Psychology*, 58: 994–1003.

Zagefka, H. and Brown, R.F. (2002) The relationship between acculturation strategies, relative fit and intergroup relations: immigrant–majority relations in Germany, *European Journal of Social Psychology*, 32: 171–88.

Zanna, M. and Rempel, J.K. (1988) Attitudes: a new look at an old concept, in D. Bar-Tal and A. Kruglanski (eds) *The Social Psychology of Knowledge*. New York: Cambridge University Press.

Zanna, M., Crosby, F. and Loewenstein, G. (1987) Male reference groups and discontent among female professionals, in B. Gutek and L. Larwood (eds) *Women's Career Development*. Newbury Park, CA: Sage.

Zarate, M.A. and Smith, E.R. (1990) Person categorization and stereotyping, *Social Cognition*, 8: 161–85.

INDEX

Aberson, C.L., 53
ability, and effort, 10
Abrams, D., 22, 36, 37, 53, 55
  uncertainty-reduction, 39
accentuation, exaggeration of
    differences in categorization,
    5–6
accessibility, and fit in category
    salience, 6–7
accommodation, speech style, 24
affect
  affective priming, 72–3
  ambivalence-amplification, 76
  anxiety, 75–6
  attitudes and emotions, 83–4
  automatic affect, 74–5
  and cognition, 12–13, 69, 70f, 73
  effect on responses toward outgroup,
    69, 71, 72
  image theory, 119–23
  incidental affect, 72–3
  integral affect, 73–4
  negative emotions, 84–5
  and prejudice, 69–78
  see also aggression
affective priming, definition, 128
affirmative action, 47, 96
  see also positive discrimination
aggression
  and affect, 78–83
  and anonymity, 79, 81
  displaced aggression, 82–3
  negative emotions, 84, 85
  provocation, 80–2

social motives, 17
  see also affect; violence
Albert, S., 13
Alexander, M.G., 86
  image theory, 121
Allen, V.L., 41
allocation matrices, 44
  ingroup bias in, 43–7
  positive–negative asymmetry, 47–8
Allport, G.W., 108
  hostility, 88
  prejudice, 4–5
ally image
  definition, 128
  image theory, 120
altruism, 17
ambivalence-amplification, 76
  definition, 128
ambivalent discrimination, definition,
  128
Amir, Y., 90
Ancok, D., 46
Anderson, B., 112
anger, 84, 85
  see also affect
anonymity, and aggression, 79,
  81
anxiety
  effect of contact, 94
  influence on perception, 71–2
  intergroup anxiety, 75–6
    definition, 130
  terror management theory, 33
  see also affect

appraisal
  appraisal theories of emotion, 12, 84, 122
  definition, 128
  threat and social change, 86
Archer, J., 32
arms race, 114–16
  deterrence beliefs, 117–18
Aronson, Eliot, 95
arousal, *see* affect
Asbach, C., 33
assimilation, 106–7
attention, effect of affect, 69, 71
attitudes
  definition, 83
  group identity, 24–5
  implicit attitudes, 130
  see also beliefs
attraction
  and group identity, 25–6, 27f
  personal attraction and social attraction, 26, 27f
attribution theory, 9–12
  definition, 128
autistic hostility, 88
automatic affect, 74–5
automatic categorization, 7–8
  definition, 128
automatic evaluation, 7
  definition, 128
aversive racism, definition, 128–9
avoidant behaviour
  intergroup settings, 2
  negative emotions, 84, 85
Azzi, A.E., 47

Bagby, J.W., 8
Bangladesh, 94
barbarian image, 120
  definition, 128
Bargh, J., 7
Barnes-Nacoste, R., 96
Baron, R.A., 80
Baron, R.S., 71
Barreto, M., 61
behaviour
  prosocial and antisocial in intergroup research, 3–4
  regulation of and emotions, 12–13
beliefs
  polarization, 24–5
  see also attitudes
Berg, J.H., 2
Berntson, G., 83
Berry, J.W., 107

Betancourt, H., 11
Bettencourt, B.A., 59, 100, 106
bias, *see* discrimination
Biernat, M., 6
Blair, I., 11
Blake, R.R., 94
Blanz, M., 48
Bourhis, R., 24, 58, 61
  power, 57
Bourhis, R.Y., 23, 46, 56
Bower, G.H., 72
Braddock, J.H., 92
Breinlinger, S., 63
Brewer, M.B., 9, 14, 21, 23, 30, 31, 32, 40, 45, 55, 56, 59, 67, 86, 92, 97, 98, 99, 122, 126
  optimal distinctiveness theory, 39, 103
  personalized contact and stereotyping, 100
  role of outgroup in social identity, 41
  universal stereotype, 51
Bronfenbrenner, Urie, 113
Brown, J.D., 53, 54
Brown, R., 52, 58, 59, 100, 102, 104, 108
Brown, R.J., 9, 13, 102, 103, 104
Brown v. Board of Education of Topeka, 89, 92
Bruins, J., 29
Bruner, J.S., 6–7
Burn, S.M., 114
Buss, D.M., 32
Byrne, D., 25
Byrne, J.L., 23

Cacioppo, J., 83
Caddick, B., 58
Campbell, D.T., 5, 48, 59, 73, 97
  universal stereotype, 50–1
Canada, self-esteem and bias experiment, 53–4
Caporael, L.R., 32
Carlson, M., 73
Castro, Fidel, 123–4
categorization
  accentuation, 5–6
  automatic categorization, 7–8
  category accentuation, 128
  category accessibility, 128
  category salience, 6–7
  cognition, 4–5
  and contact, 98–102
  cross-categorization, 8–9, 104–6

decategorization, personalization
    model, 98–100
group polarization, 25f
prejudice, 4–5, 6
recategorization, common ingroup
    identity model, 101
salience, 6–7
self-categorization theory, 36
subcategorization, mutual
    differentiation model, 101–2
see also identity
causal attribution, 9–11
Chammah, A., 29, 30
Chein, Isidor, 89
Cheng, P., 5
Chertkoff, J.M., 46
Cialdini, R.B., 37
    self-esteem and bias, 53
Clark, Kenneth, B., 89
Coates, D., 40
cognition, 1
    and affect, 12–13, 69, 70f, 73
    categorization, 4–5
    social cognition, 9–12
    war, cognitive perspective, 112–23
cognitive psychology, 5
Cohen, E.G., 96, 108
Cohen, S., 93
cohesiveness, groupthink, 124
Cold War, 111, 112
    attributional biases, 114
    emotions and symbolism, 118–19
    mutual distrust and misperception,
        113
    see also USA
Cole, R., 57
collective movements, 61–5, 66f
collective self-esteem, 23
    definition, 128
Collins, M.E., 89
common fate
    definition, 129
    perceived interdependence, 36–7
common ingroup identity model,
    recategorization, 101
comparative fit, 7
    definition, 129
comparison
    social comparison, evaluation, 13–16
    social comparison theory, 34–5
competition
    causes of war, 113
    and conflict, 97
    and cooperation, 16–18, 29–31, 94
    enemy image, 119–20

and positive identity, 98
responding to negative social
    identity, 63
social competition, 52, 132
and trust, ingroups, 50–1
compliance, groupthink, 126
conflict
    biases in attribution, 11–12
    competition, 97
    and contact, 97–8
    mutual distrust, 113
    negative emotions, 84
    realistic group conflict theory, 131
    see also violence; war
Connor, W., 112
contact
    anxiety, effect of contact on, 94
    and categorization, 98–102
    and conflict, 97–8
    contact hypothesis, 88–93, 129
    cooperation in education, 95
    cross-categorization, 104–6
    decategorization, personalization
        model, 98–100
    and desegregation in education,
        88–93
    dual identity model, 103–4
    effectiveness of, 93–6
    importance of cooperative
        environment, 94–5
    recategorization, common ingroup
        identity model, 101
    Robbers Cave experiment, 90–2
    and status, 95–6
    subcategorization, mutual
        differentiation model, 101–2
    theoretical perspectives, 96–108
contact hypothesis
    definition, 129
    desegregation in USA, 88–93
    see also desegregation
contempt, 84, 85
    see also affect
control
    controllability and responsibility, 10
    see also power
Cook, S.W., 89, 90, 92, 93
Cooper, J., 25
    distrust and competition, 113
cooperation
    and competition, 16–18, 29–31, 94
    effect of contact, 94–5
    importance of status, 95–6
    and personalization, 100
    theoretical perspectives, 96–108

Cottam, R., 119
Crano, W.D., 35
creativity, responding to negative
    social identity, 63
crisis
    and decision making, 123–6
    see also war
Crisp, R.J., 106
Crocker, J., 2, 22, 37, 38, 40, 53, 54
Crocker, J.C., 93
Crosby, F., 2, 16, 28, 47, 96
Cross, W.E., 38
cross-categorization, 8–9, 104–6
    definition, 129
culture
    cultural pluralism, 106–7
    image theory, 120

Darley, J.M., 35
Darwin, C., 12
Daubman, K.A., 73
Davis, J.A., 28
decategorization, 98–100
    definition, 129
DeCremer, D., 30
dependence, and race, 85
dependent image, 120–1
    definition, 129
depersonalization, social identities, 22
deprivation
    fraternal deprivation, 16, 28, 129
    and group identity, 26–9
    relative deprivation and justice,
        14–16, 26, 28
Deschamps, J.-C., 8, 9, 102, 104
desegregation, race, USA, 88–93
Desforges, D., 100
Deutsch, M., 89
Devine, P.G., 7, 69, 77
Diehl, M., 45, 51, 52, 57
Diener, E., 83
differentiation
    ingroup and outgroup members, 6–7
    mutual differentiation model, 101–2
    and personalization, 103
    see also salience
Dijker, A.J.M., 75
    emotions and attitudes, 83
Dion, K., 28, 63
Dion, K.L., 30
discontinuity effect, 50
    definition, 129
discrimination
    affirmative action, 47
    collective movements, 61–5, 66f

effects of instability, 57–8
ethnocentrism, 48–50
experiment, intergroup
    discrimination, 43–4
and fairness, 45–7
intentional discrimination, 30
minimal intergroup situation, 45–8
perceived discrimination at personal
    and social levels, 28
positive distinctiveness and self-
    esteem, 52–5
positive-negative asymmetry, 47–8
power, 57
relative trust and relative gain, 50–2
reverse discrimination, 58–61
status differentials, 55–6
types of intergroup discrimination,
    68–9
see also prejudice; race
disgust, 84, 85
    see also affect
displaced aggression, 82–3
    definition, 129
dissonance theory, 90
distinctiveness
    role of social identity, 39–40
    and self-esteem, 52–5
distributive justice, limited by group
    identification, 28
distrust, schema-based, 50–1
    in international relations, 113
Doise, W., 8, 9
Dollard, J., 82
Donnerstein, E., 79
Donnerstein, M., 79
Doosje, B., 38
Dorr, N., 106
Dovidio, J.F., 7, 76, 77, 101
    automatic affect, 74
dual identities
    definition, 129
    dual identity model, 103–4
Dubé-Simard, L., 28
Dutton, D.G., 59
dyadic level, intergroup settings, 2

Eakins, B.W., 75
Eakins, R.G., 75
East Africa, universal stereotype
    experiment, 51
Easterbrook, 69
education
    cooperation and contact, 95
    desegregation in USA, 88–93
Edwards, J., 23

effort, and ability, 10
egalitarianism, 76
egocentrism, and ethnocentrism, 21–2
Eibl-Eibesfeldt, I., 33, 112
Eisenstadt, D., 90
Ellemers, N., 37, 52, 53, 57, 58, 59, 61
Ellsworth, P.C., 12
emotion, see affect
enemy image, 119
   definition, 129
entitlement, psychology of, 63–4
Epstein, J.L., 93
equality
   definition, 129
   social motives, 17
equity, definition, 129
Esses, V.M., 73, 83
ethnicity
   bias, ethnocentric attributions,
      48–50
   ethnic identification in pluralistic
      societies, 107t
   genetic imperative as motivational
      basis for war, 111–12
   human sociobiology on
      ethnocentrism, 32–3
   identification and fraternal
      deprivation, 28
   ingroup and the self, ethnocentrism,
      20–3
   social categories, 5
   universal stereotype, 51
   see also race
ethnocentrism, 20–3
   definition, 129
Eurich-Fulcer, R., 9, 93
evaluation
   automatic evaluation, 7, 128
   self and others, 13–16
evolution, 32
exaggeration, differences in
   categorization, 5–6

failure, see outcomes
fairness, 107
   and intergroup discrimination, 45–7
Farnham, S.D., 21
Fazio, R.H., 7
   automatic affect, 74
   distrust and competition, 113
fear, 12, 84
   see also affect; anxiety; uncertainty
Feinman, S., 74
Festinger, L., 13, 90
   social comparison theory, 34

Fiedler, K., 73
Fischerkeller, M., 119
fit
   comparative fit and normative fit, 7
   normative fit, definition, 131
Ford, T.E., 73
Forgas, J.P., 72, 73
   social identity theory, 41
Frank, Jerome, 111
fraternal deprivation, 16, 28
   definition, 129
Freud, Sigmund, 33
Frey, D., 77
Fridlund, A.J., 12
Funk, C.L., 76

Gaertner , L., 34, 37
Gaertner, S.L., 76, 77, 92, 101, 103,
   104
gain, relative gain in intergroup
   context, 51–2
Gardham, K., 102
Garza, R.T., 96
Gelman, S.A., 5
gender
   deprivation and perceived justice,
      15
   gender identity, 22
   intergroup settings, 3
genetic imperative
   motivational basis for war, 111–12
   see also ethnicity; race
Gerard, H.B., 14, 92
Gibbons, F.X., 40
Giles, H., 23, 24
Gonzalez, A., 95
Gorenflo, D.W., 35
Gouaux, C., 73
Grant, P.R., 46
Greenberg, J., 34
Greenwald, A.G., 7, 23
Griffitt, W.B., 73
group polarization, 24–5
   definition, 130
group schema, 50–2
group status
   definition, 130
   see also status
groupthink
   definition, 130
   war, 123–6
Guimond, S., 28
Gulf War, 113–14
Gurin, P., 37, 40, 65
Gurr, T.R., 112

Hagendoorn, L., 9, 55
Hallmark, W., 118
Hamburger, Y., 100
Hamilton, D.H., 22
Hamilton, D.L., 6
  affect and cognition, 69
Hardie, E.A., 26
Harmon-Jones, E., 34
Haslam, N., 5
Hass, R.G., 76
Heider, F., 9, 119
Helson, H., 14
Henke, R., 9
Henley, N., 2
Herek, G., 125
Herrmann, R.K., 122
  image theory, 119
Hewstone, M., 3, 6, 7, 8, 9, 11, 49, 53,
    54, 93, 100, 102, 103, 106, 108
  intergroup discrimination, 48
hierarchy, 55–8, 85
Hinkle, S., 58
Hirschfield, L., 5
Hirt, E., 37
Hogg, M.A., 22, 35, 36, 37, 41, 53, 104
  attraction, 26, 27f
  status and social identity, 40
  uncertainty-reduction, 39
Holsti, Ole, 123
Holyoak, K., 5
Hornsey, M.J., 104
Horowitz, D., 112, 119
Horowitz, M., 36, 37
hostility
  autistic hostility, 88
  exaggeration of hostile intent,
    113–14
  lack of familiarity, 88
  see also conflict; violence; war
Hough, J.C., Jr, 76, 85
human sociobiology, group identity,
    32–3
Huo, Y., 29, 107
Hymes, D., 23

Ickes, W., 2
identity (group identity/social identity)
  beliefs and attitudes, 24–5
  deprivation and social justice, 26–9
  dual identity model, 103–4
  gender identity, 22
  human sociobiology, 32–3
  interpersonal attraction, 25–6, 27f
  limitations of social psychology
    experiments, 107–8

motivational theories, 36–40
  need for inclusion and
    differentiation, 103
  optimal distinctiveness, 39–40
  outgroups, role of, 41
  personal identity and social identity,
    21–2
  positive identity and competition, 98
  psychodynamic theories, 33–4
  self-categorization theory (SCT), 36
  self-esteem, maintenance of, 37–8
  self-verification, 39
  social comparison theory, 34–5
  social identity theory, 35–6, 53
  speech style, 23–4
  status and distinctiveness, 40
  see also categorization; ingroups
image theory, war, 119–23
imperialist image, 121
  definition, 130
implicit attitudes, 7
  definition, 130
incidental affect, 72
  definition, 130
inclusion, need for, 103
India, deprivation and perceived
    justice, 15, 28
indifference, as source of prejudice, 84
individual
  distinctiveness and social identity,
    39–40
  individual and collective self-esteem,
    23
  internal factors as reason for
    behaviour, 10
  mobility, responding to negative
    social identity, 63
  psychodynamic theories on group
    identity, 33–4
  and self-categorization, 36
  self-esteem and social identity, 37–8
  and social categories, 5
  and social group as reciprocal causal
    system, 18–19
  see also personalization
individuation, and need for inclusion,
    103
ingroup bias
  definition, 130
  see also discrimination
ingroups
  competition and trust, 50–1
  definition, 130
  ethnocentric attributions, 48–50
  favouritism, 130

group schema, 50–2
ingroup favouritism, 26, 130
ingroup members, differentiation
    from outgroup members, 6–7
positive behaviour towards ingroup
    members, 4
role of outgroups in social identity,
    41
and the self, 20–3
see also categorization; identity
injustice, see justice
Insko, C.A., 75
    discontinuity effect, 50
    individual and group behaviour, 31
    relative trust and relative gain in
        intergroup context, 51–2
instability, effect of and
    discrimination, 57–8
integral affect, 72, 73–4
    definition, 130
intentional discrimination, definition,
    130
interdependence, and common fate,
    36–7
intergroup anxiety
    definition, 130
    prejudice, 75–6
intergroup contact, see contact
intergroup discrimination, 43–4, 47–8,
    68
    definition, 130
intergroup emotions
    definition, 130
    see also affect
intergroup power
    definition, 130
    see also power
intergroup settings, definition, 2–3
intergroup social comparison, 36
    definition, 130
international politics, see war
Isen, A.M., 73
Isenberg, D.J., 24
Islam, M.R., 93, 94
isolation, groupthink, 124

Jackson, L.A., 3
Janis, Irving, 123–6
Jaynes, G.D., 76
Jervis, R., 113
    loss aversion in international
        politics, 116–17
Jetten, J., 55
jigsaw, cooperative learning method, 95
John, O.P., 100

Johnson, D.W., 95
Johnson, G.R., 33
Johnson, P., 23, 24
Johnson, R.T., 95
Johnston, L., 100
joint gain
    definition, 130
    joint gain orientation, social
        motives, 16–17
Jones, E.E., 49
Jones, J.M., 57
Jonestown cult suicides, 20
Jussim, L., 3
justice (social justice)
    and affirmative action, 96
    group identity, 26–9
    relative deprivation and perceived
        justice, 14–16

Kahneman, D., 118
    prospect theory, 116
Katz, I., 76
Katz, P.A., 94
Kawakami, K., 7, 28, 63
Kayatami, M., 30
Kelley, H.H., 50, 115
Kelly, C., 63
Kemmelmeier, M., 113–14
Kennedy, John, F., 123–4
Kim, H.-S., 71
Klein, Melanie, 33
Kramer, R.M., 30, 31
    security dilemma, 117
Krueger, J., 6

Lake, R.A., 59
Lamm, H., 24
language, and group identity, 23–4
Larson, R.J., 83
Lazarus, Richard, 12
Leippe, M.R., 90
Lemyre, L., 53
Leonardelli, G.J., 55
Lerner, M.J., 53–4
Lerner, M.L., 46
Levin, S., 59
LeVine, R.A., 48, 51, 97
Liebrand, W.B.G., 16, 18
loss aversion, international politics,
    116–17
loyalty, ingroups, 21
Luhtanen, R., 22, 54

McCallum, D., 31
McCauley, C., 126

McClintock, C.G., 16, 18
McConahay, J.B., 76, 85
MacCrimmon, K.R., 16
Mackie, D., 21
Mackie, D.M., 13, 25, 73, 75
    affect and cognition, 69
    negative emotions, 84
McKirnan, D.J., 65
magnanimity, *see* reverse
    discrimination
Major, B., 2, 38, 40
    psychology of entitlement, 63–4
Manstead, A.S.R., 14, 56
Marcus-Newhall, A., 82
    cross-categorization experiment,
    105–6
markers, human sociobiology, 33
Marks, G., 14
Medin, D., 5
Meertens, R.W., 69
    prejudice and emotions, 84
Meindl, J., 53–4
Mercer, J., 119
Messé, L., 45
Messick, D.M., 16, 21, 30, 45
Middendorf, J., 13
Miller, D.T., 30, 37
Miller, N., 73, 92, 98, 99
    personalized contact and
    stereotyping, 100
Miller, N.E., 82
mindless ingroup favouritism,
    definition, 130
minimal intergroup situation
    definition, 130
    discrimination, 45–8
minority groups
    status and distinctiveness in social
    identity, 40
    see also discrimination; prejudice; race
mirror image, mutual distrust in
    conflict, 113
mobility
    individual mobility, responding to
    negative social identity, 63
    social mobility, 64
Moghaddam, F., 65, 66*f*
mood
    effects on group perceptions, 72–3
mortality, terror management theory,
    33–4
Moskowitz, G.B., 21
motivation, 1
    cooperation or competition, 16–18,
    29–31

motivational theories, social identity,
    36–40
Mouton, J.S., 94
Mullen, B., 40, 45, 55, 59, 106
    status, 56
multiculturalism, 106–7
Mummendey, A., 56, 104
    intergroup discrimination, 48
    reverse discrimination, 61
    types of intergroup discrimination, 68
mutual differentiation
    definition, 132
    mutual differentiation model,
    subcategorization, 101–2
Myers, D., 24

Nacoste, R.B., 47
narcissism, motivational basis for war,
    111
narcissism of minor differences, 33
    definition, 130
nationality, early preferences for own,
    21
natural categories, and social categories
    compared, 5
Nelson, L.J., 34
Newcomb, T.M., 88
Ng, S.H., 25, 46, 57, 61
    bias, 50
normative fit, 7
    definition, 131
Norvell, N., 96

Oakes, P.J., 53
    comparative fit and normative fit, 7
object relations theory, 33
objectivity, social cognition, 9–10
optimal distinctiveness
    definition, 131
    optimal distinctiveness theory
    (ODT), 39–40, 103
Orive, R., 14, 35
Oskamp, S., 30
    attributional biases, 114
Otten, S., 3, 21
    intergroup discrimination, 48
    types of intergroup discrimination, 68
outcomes
    ethnocentric attributions, 48–50
    ingroup attachment following
    success or failure, 38, 38*f*
outgroups
    definition, 131
    differentiation of ingroup members
    from, 6–7

negative behaviour towards, 4
reverse discrimination, 58–61

Pepels, J., 106
perception
    automatic categorization, 8
    see also appraisal
Perdue, C., 7, 74
Perlman, D., 30
permeability
    definition, 131
    group boundaries, 57–8
personalization
    and differentiation, 103
    personalization model,
        decategorization, 98–100
    see also individual
Petta, G., 28
Pettigrew, T.F., 11, 16, 28, 69, 75, 92,
    100
    ethnocentric attributions, 49
    prejudice and emotions, 84
Petty, R.E., 73
Pickett, C.L., 40
Pilisuk, M., 117
    arms race, 115–16
Platow, M., 29, 45, 48, 51, 52
polarization, group polarization, 24–5
positive distinctiveness, 14
    definition, 131
positive-negative asymmetry
    definition, 131
    intergroup discrimination, 47–8
power
    discrimination, 57
    intergroup power, definition, 130
    motivational basis for war, 111
Pratto, F., 33, 55, 111
preference, ingroups, 21
prejudice
    affective priming, 72–3
    ambivalence-amplification, 76
    attitudes and emotions, 83–4
    automatic affect, 74–5
    aversive racism, 76–8
    categorization, 4–5, 6
    definition, 131
    effect of affect, 69–78
    incidental affect, 72–3
    and integral affect, 72, 73–4
    integral affect, 73–4
    intergroup anxiety, 75–6
    see also discrimination; race;
        stereotyping
Prentice, D.A., 26, 30, 37

Prentice-Dunn, S., 76, 81
prisoner's dilemma game, 29–30, 30f,
    31f
    arms race, 115
    definition, 131
    and universal stereotype, 51
promotion, perceived justice, 15
prospect theory, 116
    definition, 131
provocation, and aggression, 80–2
psychodynamic theories, group
    identity, 33–4

Rabbie, Jacob, 36–7
race
    aggression experiment, 79
    ambivalence-amplification model, 76
    automatic affect and stereotyping,
        74–5
    aversive racism, 76–8
    contact as means to reduce
        prejudice, 93–4
    desegregation, 88–93
    dual identity model, 104
    experiment, status and reverse
        discrimination, 60
    intergroup settings, 2–3
    provocation and aggression
        experiments, 80–2
    response of infants to strangers, 74
    threat and social change, 85–6
    see also ethnicity
Rapoport, A., 29, 30
realistic group conflict theory,
    definition, 131
recategorization, 101
    definition, 131
relative deprivation
    definition, 131
    and perceived justice, 14–16, 26, 28
relative gain
    definition, 131
    relative gain orientation, social
        motives, 16
Rempel, J.K., 83
research, prosocial and antisocial
    behaviour, 3–4
responsibility, and controllability, 10
retaliation, see provocation
reverse discrimination, 58–61
    definition, 131
    see also outgroup bias
Reynolds, V., 32
Richardson, D.R., 80
Richardson, K.D., 53

Robbers Cave experiment, 90–2
Roccas, S., 55
Rogers, R.W., 76, 81
Roseman, I.J., 12
Rosenberg, M., 38
Ross, L., 10
Ross, M.H., 112
Rothbart, M., 5, 100
    coercion and conciliation in
        international politics, 118
Rothschild, L., 5
Rubin, M., 53, 54
Runciman, W.C., 16, 28
Rust, M.C., 106
Ryan, E., 23

Sachdev, I., 23, 46, 56, 57, 58, 61
Sagar, H.A., 9, 93
Sande, G., 75, 119
    attributional biases, 114
Santos, S.J., 96
Schachter, S., 34–5
schema-based distrust, 50
    definition, 131
Scherer, K.R., 12
Schermer, V., 33
Schneider, S., 31
Schofield, J.W., 9, 93
Schopler, J.W., 75
    discontinuity effect, 50
Schreiber, H., 61
Schuman, H., 76
Schwartz, I., 38, 53
Schwartz, S.H., 55, 85
Schwarzwald, J., 93
Sears, D.O., 76
segregation, see desegregation; race
self
    and the ingroup, 20–3
    object relations theory, 33
self-categorization theory (SCT), 36
    definition, 132
self-esteem, 37–8
    individual and collective, 22
    positive distinctiveness, 52–4
    role of social identity in
        maintenance of, 37–8
    status in minority/low-status groups,
        40
self-evaluation, 13–14
self-interest, individual and collective, 23
self-stereotyping, definition, 132
self-verification
    definition, 132
    role of social identity in, 39

Shapiro, P.N., 41, 72, 97
    contact and anxiety, 94
Sharan, S., 95
Shaw, R.P., 33, 112
Sherif, Muzafer, 48
    contact and conflict, 97
    deterrence, 117
    intergroup situations, 2
    Robbers Cave experiment, 90–2
Sidanius, J., 33, 58, 61
    hierarchy, 55
    social dominance, 111
Silverstein, B., 113
Simon, A.F., 12, 13
Simon, B., 22, 55, 56, 61
situation
    affect and cognition, 70f
    as reason for behaviour, 10
    and social motives, 18
Slavin, R.E., 95
Smith, A.D., 112
Smith, C.A., 12
Smith, E.R., 7, 13
    negative emotions, 84
Smith, P.M., 24, 53
social attraction, definition, 132
social categories, and natural categories
    compared, 5
social categorization, definition, 132
social change, 85–6
social cognition, 9–12
social comparison
    definition, 132
    social comparison theory, group
        identity, 34–5
social competition, 52
    definition, 132
social creativity, definition, 132
social dilemma, 30
social dilemmas, definition, 132
social dominance, definition, 132
social dominance theory, 111
social identity, definition, 132
social identity theory, 35–6
social mobility, 64
social psychology, 1
social reality, definition, 132
social reality testing, 34
sociobiology, group identity, 32–3
Solomon, S., 33
Spears, R., 14, 56
speech style, group identity, 23–4
sport, and self-esteem, 37
stability, instability and discrimination,
    57–8

Stahelski, A.J., 50, 115
Stangor, C., 73, 83
status
    cooperative work, effect of status,
        95–6
    and discrimination, 55–6
    distinctiveness in minority/low-
        status groups, 40
    and effectiveness of contact, 95–6
    effects of instability of differentials,
        58
    inequality, effects of status on, 97f
    and ingroup bias, 62f
    limitations of social psychology
        experiments, 108
    and reverse discrimination, 58–61
    and social change, 85–6
    and social movements, 61–5
Steele, C.M., 40
Stephan, C.W., 71, 94
    anxiety, 75
Stephan, W.G., 71, 92, 94
    anxiety, 75
stereotyping
    and anxiety, 75–6
    automatic affect, 74–5
    category accentuation, 6
    negative affect, 71–3
    and personalized contact, 100
    self-stereotyping, 22
    universal stereotype, 50–1, 133
    see also prejudice
Stouffer, S., 15
stress, and decision making, 123
Stroessner, S.J., 75
Struch, N., 85
subcategorization, definition, 132
subjectivity, validation of beliefs about
        oneself, 34–5
success, see outcomes
Sumner, W.G., 125
    ingroup and the self, 20
superordinate category identification,
        101
superordinate goals, 91
    definition, 132
Swann, W.B., 39
symbolic representation, intergroup
        relations, 3

Tajfel, Henri, 21, 40, 47, 55
    category accentuation, 5–6
    changing status relationships, 57,
        58
    competition, 98

egocentrism and ethnocentrism,
    21–2
experiment, intergroup
    discrimination, 43–4
generic norm of intergroup
    behaviour, 50
responding to negative social
    identity, 63
social identity theory, 36, 41
Taylor, D.M., 16, 28, 58
    collective behaviour, 65, 66f
Taylor, M., 5
Taylor, S.E., 54
terror management theory, 33–4
    definition, 132
Thompson, J.E., 93
tokenism, maintaining status
    structures, 64
Townsend, A., 37
Trafimow, D., 22, 23
Triandis, Harry C., 23
    private self and collective self, 22
Trolier, T., 6
Tropp, L.R., 92, 100
trust, intergroup schema, 50–1
Turner, John C., 9, 14, 24, 25, 26, 38f,
    41, 45, 52, 53, 55, 59, 98, 125
    changing status relationships, 57, 58
    egocentrism and ethnocentrism,
        21–2
    ingroup preference following defeat,
        38
    responding to negative social
        identity, 63
    self-categorization theory (SCT), 36
    social identity theory, 35–6
    status and social identity, 40
Turner, M., 126
Tversky, A., 118
    prospect theory, 116
Tyler, T.R., 28, 29
    ethnic identification, 107

ultimate attribution error, 11
    definition, 133
uncertainty
    social comparison theory, 34–5
    uncertainty-reduction and social
        identity, 39
universal stereotype, 50–1
    definition, 133
USA
    Bay of Pigs invasion, 123–4
    desegregation, 88–93
    Gulf War, 113–14

perceived justice, 15
see also Cold War

validation, subjective validity, 34–5
Van den Berghe, P.L., 32, 111
Van Knippenberg, A., 7, 52, 53, 56, 57, 58
Van Oers, H., 56
Van Vugt, M., 30
Vanbeselaere, N., 9
Vanneman, R.D., 16, 28
Veitch, R., 73
violence, intergroup behaviour, 3–4
Volkan, V.D., 33

Wagner, U., 41
Wales, Welsh accent, 24
Walker, I., 16, 28
Wallace, M.D., 117–18
Walster, E., 46
war
  arms race, 114–16
  attributional biases, 114
  cognitive perspective, 112–23
  deterrence beliefs, 117–18
  distrust and misattribution, 113–14
  emotions and symbolism, 118–19
  genetic imperative, 111–12
  groupthink, 123–6
  human nature, theories of, 111–12
  image theory, 119–23
  risk and security, 116–17
  see also conflict
Ward, P.I., 41
we-ness, see identity
Weber, J.G., 11
  ethnocentric attributions, 49
Weber, R., 93

Wegener, D.T., 73
Weiner, B., 10
Wellman, H.M., 5
Wentura, D., 21
Wenzel, M., 28, 104
Wetherell, M.S., 25
'white man's burden', image theory, 121
White, Ralph K., 113
  macho pride in Cold War, 111
Wilder, D.A., 6, 12, 13, 41, 72, 76, 93, 97, 99
  contact and anxiety, 94
  intergroup contact, 100
Wilkes, A., 5–6
Williams, R.M., 76
Wills, T.A., 14, 53
Wilson, L., 81
Wilson, S., 25
Wilson, W., 30
Winston, T., 40
Winter, D.G., 113–14
Wittenbrink, B., 74
Wong, Y., 33, 112
Worchel, S., 93, 96, 98
World Trade Center, terrorist attack on, 13, 68
Wright, S.C., 28, 40, 58, 65
  tokenism, 64
Wright-Buckley, C., 2

Zagefka, H., 104
Zalk, S.R., 94
Zanna, M., 15
  attitudes, 83
Zarate, M.A., 7
zero-sum situation, 91
  definition, 133

SOCIAL PSYCHOLOGY AND HEALTH
Second Edition

Wolfgang Stroebe

If you are a student of social or health psychology, or if you are working in one of the health professions, you are likely at some point to address questions such as the following:

- Which behaviour patterns are detrimental to health?
- Why do people engage in such behaviour, even if they know about its negative effects?
- How can people be influenced to change their behaviour?
- What do we mean by stressful life events and how can their impact on health be mediated?

In *Social Psychology and Health* you will find these major health topics discussed from a social psychological perspective. During recent decades there have been significant changes in conceptions of health and illness, with a move towards a broader conception of health to include physical, mental and social well-being. In line with these changes, health psychology has become a dominant force in the health sciences. This relatively new field of psychology is much influenced by social psychological theory and research, and the focus of the book reflects this.

Social Psychology and Health gives an up-to-date perspective on these key health psychology questions. The book argues for an integrative approach that combines psychological, economic and environmental interventions in order to reduce the potential risks to health arising from behaviour or stressful life events.

The second edition of this highly successful textbook has been extensively revised, expanded and updated. Much new material has been added based on research done in the last five years, in particular drawing on the author's own research into obesity and sexual risk behaviour. Many of the epidemiological examples and more than a third of the references have been updated. It is essentially a new book which will make an important contribution to the literature.

Contents
Changing conceptions of health and illness – Determinants of health behaviour: a social psychological analysis – Beyond persuasion: the modification of health behaviour – Behaviour and health: excessive appetites – Behaviour and health: self-protection – Stress and health – Moderators of the stress-health relationship – The role of social psychology in health promotion – Glossary – References – Author index – Subject index.

352pp   0 335 19921 6 (Paperback)   0 335 19922 4 (Hardback)

GROUP PROCESS, GROUP DECISION, GROUP ACTION
Second Edition

Robert S. Baron and Norbert L. Kerr

- How do groups function?
- How are people changed or influenced or affected by the groups they belong to?
- What similarities can we find across groups of different types, in different situations?

Social groups have great influence on our thoughts, decisions and behaviour from our infancy until our deaths. Family groups, work groups, ethnic groups and our friendship networks all shape our perceptions, thoughts and actions, as well as our feelings about ourselves. In this thorough introduction to the social psychological study of group processes, the authors have considerably updated their highly successful first edition.

The new edition develops the existing coverage of topics such as social influence, extreme behaviour in groups, group productivity, social dilemmas, group decision-making and inter-group conflict. It also provides additional chapters examining research and theory regarding social support, and electronic groups. All in all, this authoritative text will familiarize the reader with current theory and the latest findings, exploring the significance and application of group research for our everyday lives.

Contents
Series foreword – Preface – Acknowledgements – Introduction – Social facilitation – Individual vs group process – Task motivation in groups – Social influence and conformity – Extremity in groups – Social combination approaches to group decision making – Social dilemmas – Intergroup conflict and aggression – Stress and social support – Electronic groups – Concluding thoughts – Glossary – References – Index.

c.256pp   0 335 20697 2 (Paperback)   0 335 20698 0 (Hardback)